RUTH

BHB

Baylor Handbook on the Hebrew Bible

General Editor

W. Dennis Tucker Jr.

RUTH
A Handbook on the Hebrew Text

Robert D. Holmstedt

BAYLOR UNIVERSITY PRESS

Cover Design by Pamela Poll
Cover photograph by Bruce and Kenneth Zuckerman, West Semitic Research, in collaboration with the ancient biblical Manuscript Center. Courtesy Russian National Library (Saltykov-Shchedrin).

Library of Congress Cataloging-in-Publication Data

Holmstedt, Robert D.
Ruth : a handbook on the Hebrew text / Robert D. Holmstedt.
p. cm.— (Baylor handbook on the Hebrew Bible)
Includes bibliographical references and index.
ISBN 978-1-932792-91-1 (pbk. : alk. paper)
1. Bible. O.T. Ruth--Criticism, Textual. 2. Bible. O.T. Ruth. Hebrew--Versions. 3. Bible. O.T. Ruth--Language, style. 4. Hebrew language--Grammar. 5. Hebrew language--Discourse analysis. I. Title.
BS1315.52.H65 2009
222>.35066--dc22
2009027671

Printed in the United States of America on acid-free paper with a minimum of 30% pcw recycled content.

TABLE OF CONTENTS

ACKNOWLEDGMENTS

The writing of this commentary proved to be more challenging than I had anticipated. Though I have taught through the book of Ruth in numerous biblical Hebrew courses, when I was forced to comment on the grammar of each verse I realized how many interesting features that even a self-proclaimed grammarian overlooks. It is thus appropriate that I acknowledge my students from the University of Wisconsin at Madison, the University of Wisconsin at Milwaukee, Wheaton College, and the University of Toronto. Without their curiosity and persistence in asking questions, I would not have been as keenly prepared for this project.

I am also indebted to the research assistance provided by Brauna Doidge and Laurel Perkins, both of whom aided me by pouring through commentaries on Ruth, from medieval to modern (many of which did not make it into the text or bibliography) to look for specifically grammatical comments. As they developed as researchers and Hebrew readers, they pushed me to greater clarity in my explanations.

Another pair whose discussions on sundry verses and linguistic issues were invaluable to me is Cynthia L. Miller and John A. Cook. What insight there is in this work would be significantly less had they not answered my many email queries.

Finally, my wife Rachel and our four children deserve credit for putting up with the hours I spent scowling at the text of Ruth. Much of the sensitivity I have gained to the fulness of the story of Ruth, bits of which may come out in the more literary comments, are because I live with an חיל אשת like Ruth, whose loyalty and perseverance constantly affects my view on life.

§1

INTRODUCTION

The book of Ruth is arguably one of the most read books in the Hebrew Bible. The story of loss and redemption resonates with life's troubles and encourages hope for a good outcome. Men and women, young and old, from all walks of life can identify with each of the major characters in the book. Those who suffer loss and blame God know Noʻomi's pain and long for recovery like hers. Those whose way has taken them to strange lands know what it is to live in the confusion by one small step at a time; they can thus empathize with Ruth's perseverance and loyalty to her one remaining pillar. Those who aim to be a knight in shining armor but who also in the journey are tempted to manipulate outcomes for their own benefit, whether large or small, see in Boaz a brother in kind. And we all empathize with the nearer redeemer, the nameless fellow who acts responsibly by protecting his own family's well-being but in doing so comes off as a coward when compared to Boaz. This is a real story, a human story in the fullest sense.

Students of biblical Hebrew (BH) remember the book for an additional reason: Ruth is often the first (or second after the book of Jonah) whole biblical book read with their newly learned language skills. Ruth is commonly used by teachers as a reading objective at the end of the first year of BH, or it is used at the beginning of the second year to review language skills and begin introducing various exegetical methodologies. Read in Hebrew, the book becomes at once more complex linguistically and beautiful in its masterful literary design. Those features that are often completely obscured in translation—

changes in verbs, switches in characters, and use of word order for emphasis—are available to the Hebrew reader. Moreover, the Hebrew student recognizes why it is inappropriate to quote Ruth's statement of loyalty in the context of a traditional wedding! And yet, for all the delight of reading Ruth in Hebrew, the book's language is not as simple as its use in first-year Hebrew courses suggests. The very features lost in translation are not always understood by the most skilled Hebraists.

It is thus with both the intermediate student and the advanced researcher in mind that I have written this commentary. Whether you are still mastering basic verbal forms or a seasoned Hebrew teacher or researcher, I believe that there is something useful for you here. My modus operandi was the careful and informed merging of traditional Hebrew grammatical analysis with insights from the modern linguistic analysis of Hebrew. Thus I frequently refer to the standard English reference grammars for BH while at the same time mention and build upon a select number of recent and linguistically-informed works that have advanced our understanding of the way Hebrew works. Moreover, while I eschew theory-specific terminology, I have also employed a small set of terms that are not common to textbooks or older reference works. In §2 I have summarized my descriptive framework—it will be necessary for most readers to work through this section before moving to the commentary. Finally, in §3 and §4 I take up the issues of dating the book linguistically and the use of langauge to color characters' speech.

As a final note, I ask a favor from readers of this work. Since I continue to use Ruth in my own first and second year courses, I invite you to contact me with questions you may have about the language of Ruth that are not addressed in the commentary. I also welcome alternative explanations for the various grammatical features of the book that have made this project so much fun.

Robert Holmstedt

LINGUISTIC BACKGROUND TO THE GRAMMATICAL COMMENTARY ON RUTH

Since the audience of this commentary and the series as a whole begins with students, I have provided references to the English-based grammar of BH that are commonly used: GKC (Kautzsch 1910), WO (Walke and O'Connor 1990), MNK (van der Merwe, Naudé, and Kroeze 1999), and JM (Joüon and Muraoka 2006).

For questions of phonology, whether background information for comments I make or for issues I do not address, I urge the reader to start with JM and then proceed to the focused studies cited in the footnotes there. If some question has a comparative Semitic component, start with Lipiński 2001. For morphological matters, starting with GKC and JM is wise. Finally, for syntax, semantics, and pragmatics, the current reference works provide an inadequate description of both BH grammar properly speaking and the way that the grammar is manipulated for rhetorical effect. Thus, in the following subsections I briefly outline my approach to Hebrew syntax, semantics, and pragmatics, which is based in my linguistics research and which goes well beyond what readers will find in reference works (excepting the final chapter in MNK, much of which I find lacking, though).

1. Clauses and Their Constituents

Syntax refers to the system of relationships among constituents. **Constituent** is the label used for the individual words or phrases (e.g., nouns/noun phrases, verbs/verb phrases, prepositions/prepositional phrases) that have a syntactic role in a phrase or clause. That is, constituents are the items that relate to each other to form larger, more complex units, from prepositional phrases and noun phrases to clauses.

A **clause** may be simply defined as the combination of at least two constituents, one of which is a **subject** and the other a **predicate**, illustrated in example (1).

(1) A Clause:

וַיָּמָת אֱלִימֶלֶךְ

"Elimelek   died" (Ruth 1:3)

subject   predicate

Subjects are usually nouns, noun phrases (that is, a noun and its modifiers), or some other nominal constituent (such as an adjective used in place of a noun). Predicates are verbal, but the verb may be explicit, or "overt" (such as *qatal*, *yiqtol*, or *wayyiqtol*), as in example (2), or "covert," that is, unseen but nonetheless syntactically and semantically real, as in example (3).

(2) Overt Verbal Clause: *wayyiqtol*

וַיֵּלֶךְ אִישׁ מִבֵּית לֶחֶם יְהוּדָה

"a man from Bethlehem of Judah   went" (Ruth 1:1)

subject   predicate

(3) Covert Verbal Clause: Null-Copula

וְשֵׁם הָאִישׁ אֱלִימֶּלֶךְ

"the name of the man (was)   Elimelek" (Ruth 1:2)

subject   predicate

Covert or "null" verbs are limited to the copula "to be" and form a predicate by linking the subject to non-verbal constituents like participles, nouns, adjectives, and prepositional phrases.

2. Complements and Adjuncts

A challenge in Hebrew syntax is understanding the relationship between a verb and its modifiers. Verbal modifiers fit into two main categories: complements and adjuncts. **Complements** are obligatory constituents modifying the verb in a clause; if such constituents were omitted, the clause would be incomplete. In other words, a verb may require a constituent(s), such as a noun phrase or a prepositional phrase, or both, to fulfill it (i.e., to function as its object or to specify necessary details of location, manner, etc.). The boldfaced constituents in the following examples are complements—their presence is required by the verbs in order for the clauses to be grammatical (i.e., to make sense). Note that different verbs take different types of complements. The most common are **accusative complements** (i.e., direct objects), as in (4).

(4) Accusative Complement: Noun Phrase

וַיִּשְׂאוּ לָהֶם נָשִׁים מֹאֲבִיּוֹת

"they took **Moabite wives** for themselves" (Ruth 1:4)

But also common are non-accusative or **oblique complements**, which are manifested as prepositional phrases in Hebrew, as in (5).

(5) Oblique Complement: Prepositional Phrase

וַתִּשַּׁק לָהֶן

"she kissed **them**" (Ruth 1:9)

Some verbs also allow **infinitives** to function as their complements, as in (6). Since most infinitive phrase complements have the ל preposition, these overlap syntactically with oblique complements.

(6) Infinitive Phrase Complement

וַתֶּחְדַּל לְדַבֵּר אֵלֶיהָ

"she ceased **to speak to her**" (Ruth 1:18)

Finally, words like כִּי and אֲשֶׁר allow a **full clause** to function as a nominal item and thus serve as a verbal complement, illustrated in (7).

(7) Clausal Complement

כִּי שָׁמְעָה בִּשְׂדֵה מוֹאָב כִּי־פָקַד יְהוָה אֶת־עַמּוֹ לָתֵת לָהֶם לָחֶם

"because she heard in the territory of Moab **that Yhwh had seen to his people by giving them bread**" (Ruth 1:6)

The presence and number of complements are generally determined by the valency of the verb, whether it is intransitive (no accusative complements), transitive (one accusative complement), or ditransitive

(two accusative complements). Noun phrases that are accusative complements are sometimes preceded by the accusative marker אֶת (i.e., the
so-called definite direct object maker), but more often than not the אֶת
is missing. Noun phrases that are oblique complements are marked by a
preposition, such as the לְ in (5); alternatively, the oblique complement
may be an adverbial phrase like שָׁם (see וַיֵּשְׁבוּ שָׁם in Ruth 1:4).

In contrast to complements, **adjuncts** are optional constituents
modifying the verb in a clause; such constituents may be omitted
without affecting the basic grammaticality of the clause. The itali-
cized constituents in the following clauses are adjuncts.

(8) Adjunct: Adverb Phrase

וַתִּבְכֶּינָה עוֹד
"they wept *again*" (Ruth 1:14)

(9) Adjunct: Prepositional Phrase

בַּאֲשֶׁר תָּמוּתִי אָמוּת
"I will die *in (the place) that you die*" (Ruth 1:17)

In example (8) the adjunct consists only of the temporal adverb עוֹד.
Clearly, it is not grammatically necessary to specify when or how many
times the women wept; this is simply additional information that the
narrator supplies, presumably to link this statement back to 1:9, where
they wept for the first time. Similarly, the prepositional phrase in (9)
is not obligatory for the grammaticality of the clause: simply stating
אָמוּת is a complete clause in and of itself. In this example, the phrase
בַּאֲשֶׁר תָּמוּתִי serves to specify a place where Ruth indicates that she is
determined to experience death, wherever her mother-in-law dies. This
information is, for the development of Ruth's character as well as her
relationship with No'omi, quite necessary, just not grammatically so.

It is clear that in Hebrew a verb cannot be understood in isolation;
rather, one must consider the combination of a verb and whatever
it requires to introduce its complement, whether it takes accusative complements (with or without אֵת) or some sort of preposition.
Another way to consider the verb-plus-complement package is in
terms of argument structure. An **argument** is a constituent that is a

participant involved in the event or action denoted by the predicate. An analogy might help: we can think of a predicate as the script of a play in which there are a number of roles, which correspond to the constituents. Each and every role must be filled for the play to work. In the same way, each predicate specifies the number of arguments needed to complete its argument structure. "One-place predicates" (e.g., intransitive verbs) take just one argument, an external argument that is the subject, as in (10).

(10) One-place Predicate

וַיָּמָת אֱלִימֶלֶךְ

"Elimelek　　　died"(Ruth 1:3)

external　　　　*predicate*

argument

"Two-place predicates" (e.g., transitive verbs), in contrast, take two arguments, an external one (a subject) and an internal one (e.g., objects, adverbs, prepositional phrases). The example in (11) illustrates a typical two-place predicate.

(11) Two-place Predicate

כִּי־פָקַד יְהוָה אֶת־עַמּוֹ

"that Yhwh　　　cared for　　　　his people" (Ruth 1.6)

external　　　　*predicate*　　　　　*internal*

argument　　　　　　　　　　　　　　*argument*

Some predicates (e.g., ditransitive verbs) may take more than two arguments, such as a subject and two direct objects or a subject, a direct object (e.g., an object), and an oblique object (e.g., a prepositional phrase). The example in (12) is a three-place predicate (the verb נתן "to give" is another common example).

(12) Three-place Predicate

וְהוּא יַגִּיד לָךְ אֵת אֲשֶׁר תַּעֲשִׂין

"he　　　will explain　　to you　　　(the thing) that you will do"

external　*predicate*　　*internal*　　*internal*　　　　　　(Ruth 3:4)

argument　　　　　　*argument*　*argument*

In the commentary I will often identify whether a verb takes complements or not and, if it does, what type of complements fulfill its syntactic and semantic requirements.

3. Verbal Semantics

In this commentary, as in the series as a whole, the terms *qatal*, *yiqtol*, and *wayyiqtol* are used in reference to the primary Hebrew verbs. The advantage of these terms is that they maintain consistency among the commentaries and they are descriptively accurate for the morphology of these verbs. The disadvantage is that they signal nothing about how the semantics of these verbs or how they participate in the verbal system as a whole. Internal and external considerations indicate that the BH verbal system is primarily an aspectual system, not a tense system. (See Cook 2002 for a thorough overview of the history of scholarship on the verbal system as well as a linguistically informed analysis of BH as an aspectual language; see also Dobbs-Allsopp 2004–7 for additional typological support for the aspectual analysis.)

In addition to the primacy of aspect, the system operates with a basic indicative-modal distinction. The coordination of aspect with the indicative-modal divide is illustrated in the summary chart in Table 1.

Note two features of the analysis summarized by this chart. First, the *wayyiqtol* is not aspectual, but is the retention of an older preterite verb (e.g., יַצֵּב in Deut 32:8; Rainey 1990). In BH this has become primarily a verb used in narrative to carry the mainline event and action description; it is in this usage that it has the complex fused form of the *wa-y-yiqtol*. Second, the participle is not included in the chart since it participates only in the margins of the verbal system. Recent study suggests that participles in BH are adjectives that encode an activity or event rather than a quality (Cook 2008a). Thus, when participles are used "verbally," they are actually predicates following a null-copula. The increasing use of the participle as predicates in the Hebrew verbal system in antiquity reflects the transition toward the tense-prominent system of post-biblical Hebrew (e.g., early rabbinic Hebrew).

Table 1
The Semantics of the Biblical Hebrew Verb
(modified from Cook and Holmstedt 2009:88)

Indicative Functions	Suffix	*Qatal*	**Perfect**: perfective (whole view of situation)
	Prefix	*Wayyiqtol*	**Past Narrative (Preterite)**: past event in narrative (or poetry)
		Yiqtol	**Imperfect**: imperfective (partial view of situation)
Modal Functions	Suffix	*(we)Qatal*	**Modal Perfect**: contingent modality/command
	Prefix	*Yiqtol*	**Modal Imperfect**: command or wish (it is negated with לֹא)
		Yiqtol	**Jussive**: command or wish (any person; it is negated with אַל)
		Impv	**Imperative**: command or wish (2nd person only; not negated)

4. Pragmatics

Whereas syntax concerns how constituents relate to each other and semantics concerns how the constituents contain meaning, a third perspective is required to understand BH texts fully: pragmatics. **Pragmatics** concerns how syntactic and semantic options are manipulated, sometimes beyond their strict boundaries of acceptability, to signal meaning beyond the presence and definitions of words. As the arena of language use, from conventions that are easy to formalize to quickly evolving discourse signals such as "like, um, you know," pragmatics is an umbrella category including a broad range of features.

Consider this example. A teenage boy walks into his home and starts up the stairs to his room. His father, sitting in the living room reading the paper, says one word with a rising intonation, "David?" The son stops, goes back down the stairs, and closes the front door before going upstairs again. Clearly the syntax and semantics of the one-word utterance do not provide all the necessary information to understand the fuller meaning. There was a "door-closing" history behind this exchange that allowed the father to use a single word formally unrelated to the result it achieved. This is one end of pragmatics. The more formal end concerns concepts like Topic and Focus, which I will use in the commentary on Ruth and which are summarized in Table 2.

The **Topic** is used either to "orient" the listener to which of three known entities is being provided with additional information or to present scene-setting information (time or place adverbials such as

TABLE 2
Topic and Focus

Topic	Information known in the discourse used to 1) isolate one among multiple discourse entities as the salient agent or patient, or 2) set the scene (e.g., time, place)
Focus	Information contrasted with possible alternatives

"yesterday" or "after a while"). The example in (13) illustrates the agent-shift function.

(13) Subject as a Topic

וּבֹ֫עַז עָלָה הַשַּׁ֫עַר

"and <u>Boaz</u> went up to the gate" (Ruth 4:1)

In this case the verbal subject and agent of the preceding verse was No'omi (3:18) and this clause, in 4:1, shifts the attention to Boaz as the verbal subject and agent.

Focus sets a constituent over against alternatives, whether these alternative exist in the discourse or are assumed from shared knowledge of the world. Focus is often manifested as contrast, illustrated in (14).

(14) Adverb as a Focus

וְרֵיקָם הֱשִׁיבַ֫נִי יְהוָה

"but **empty** Yhwh returned me" (Ruth 1:21ab)

5. Putting All the Pieces Together: Constituent Movement

Finally, it is important for the study of Hebrew syntax to note that constituents "move" around in the clause, for a variety of reasons. Consider the difference between the statement "Ruth left the house" with the question "Did Ruth leave the house?" Although English is predominantly a Subject-Verb (S-V) language, *yes-no* questions like the one just given require a verb, the auxiliary "did," to be in front of the subject. Similarly, contrast the question "Where did Ruth go?" with the statement "Ruth went to the fields." Notice how the open-ended question has both the locative "Where" and the verb "did" in front of the subject..

In English, variation in word order is fairly limited, but not so in Hebrew. For instance, word order in Hebrew changes with the type of verb (indicative versus modal), illustrated by (15) and (16).

(15) S-V (Indicative)

פֶּרֶץ הוֹלִיד אֶת־חֶצְרוֹן

"Perez begat Hezron" (Ruth 4:18b)

(16) V (Modal)-S

יַעַשׂ יְהוָה עִמָּכֶם חֶסֶד כַּאֲשֶׁר עֲשִׂיתֶם עִם־הַמֵּתִים וְעִמָּדִי

"May Yhwh act (Qr) kindly with you just as you have acted with the dead and with me" (Ruth 1:8)

To account for the word order difference between (15) and (16), I use the concept of "triggered" constituent movement, that is, something "triggers" the change in word order. Taking S-V order as basic (see Holmstedt 2002, 2005, 2009a), the V-S order in clauses such as (16) reflects the raising of the verb to a position "higher" in the clause (i.e., toward the front) than the subject. In addition to verbal modality, verb-raising like this is also triggered by initial function words, such as the relative אֲשֶׁר in (17), complement כִּי in (18), the interrogative לָמָה in (19), and the negative לֹא in (20).

(17) אֲשֶׁר-V-S

כְּרָחֵל׀ וּכְלֵאָה אֲשֶׁר בָּנוּ שְׁתֵּיהֶם אֶת־בֵּית יִשְׂרָאֵל

"like Rachel and Leah, who the both of them built the house of Israel" (Ruth 4:11)

(18) כִּי-V-S

שָׁמְעָה בִּשְׂדֵה מוֹאָב כִּי־פָקַד יְהוָה אֶת־עַמּוֹ

"she heard in the territory of Moab that Yhwh had cared for his people" (Ruth 1:6)

(19) Wh-V-S

לָמָּה יְדַבֵּר אֲדֹנִי כַּדְּבָרִים הָאֵלֶּה

"why does my lord speak according to these words?" (Gen 44:7)

(20) NEG-V-S

וְלֹא־יִכָּרֵת שֵׁם־הַמֵּת מֵעִם אֶחָיו וּמִשַּׁעַר מְקוֹמוֹ

"and the name of the dead man will not be cut off from his kins-men or the gate of his place" (Ruth 4.10)

Finally, the *wayyiqtol* reflects triggered raising. The gemination of the first consonant of the verb may represent an assimilated function word, i.e., *wa-X-yiqtol* (where *X* stands for the assimilated function word).

(21) *wa*-(X)-V-S

וַיָּמָת אֱלִימֶלֶךְ

"and Elimelek died" (Ruth 1:3)

The fused, complex nature of the *wayyiqtol* means that no other constituent of the clause can precede this form. Thus, clauses with a *wayyiqtol* are always X-V-S (the X represents the assimilated function word), whereas other verbs allow word order diversity. And this is where Topic and Focus re-enter the picture. There are admittedly few basic word order clauses in Ruth, the simple reason being that narratives are informationally complex. They always contain multiple themes as they develop, and so the only place that can contain a clause without at least a Topic constituent is at the beginning of the narrative as a whole or scenes with new characters. Thus, there is only one example in Ruth of a clause without any triggering mechanism, whether a syntactic one like an initial כִּי or a pragmatic one like Topic or Focus. The single example is at the outset of the genealogy in chapter 4, repeated in (22) from (15) above. (Besides the initiation of narratives or new scenes with new characters, genealogies and proverbs are the only other consistent source of basic S-V clauses.)

(22) S-V-O (No Topic or Focus)

פֶּרֶץ הוֹלִיד אֶת־חֶצְרוֹן

"Perez begat Hezron" (Ruth 4:18b)

The S-V clause in the second half of the verse presents us with one old entity, פרץ, and two new pieces of information, a new verb and object. Critically, we cannot analyze the subject פרץ as a Topic, because there are no other thematic entities from which to choose. פרץ is the only agentive entity available from the preceding clause to serve as the subject of the verb הוליד. Topic does not function redundantly in this way.

In contrast to the single example in (22), the remaining S-V clauses in Ruth present us with either Topic or Focus information. Example (23), repeated from (13) above, is a textbook case of S-V where the subject is a Topic (see the brief discussion after [13]).

(23) S-V-ADV (S=Topic)

וּבֹעַז עָלָה הַשַּׁעַר

"and <u>Boaz</u> went up to the gate" (Ruth 4:1)

Triggered constituent movement is more clearly seen in examples like (24), in which the object has been fronted as a Topic.

(24) O-V-S (O=Topic)

חֶלְקַת הַשָּׂדֶה אֲשֶׁר לְאָחִינוּ לֶאֱלִימֶלֶךְ מָכְרָה נָעֳמִי

"No'omi is about to sell <u>the portion of the field that belongs to our kinsman, Elimelek</u>" (Ruth 4:3)

The object in (24) is fronted, in the mouth of Boaz, in order to orient the other redeemer and the elders to the important Topic at hand: the fact that a plot of land belonging to their extended family is being sold. Certainly this is not a Focus—there is nothing to contrast the field with; no other tracts of land are mentioned or are relevant in the context. Note how the pragmatic fronting of the object-Topic triggers the raising of the verb over the subject, resulting in V-S order.

Focus-fronting results in similar constituent movement, illustrated in (25), which is repeated from (14) above.

(25) ADV-V-S (ADV=Focus)

וְרֵיקָ֖ם הֱשִׁיבַ֥נִי יְהוָֽה

"(and I went away full) but **empty** Yhwh returned me" (Ruth 1:21ab)

The adverb in (25) is Focus-fronted precisely in order to highlight the contrast between the manner in which No'omi left Israel, "full," and in her opinion the manner in which Yhwh has brought her back from Moab, "empty." And, of course, this contrast establishes a dominant motif in the book as a whole.

The combination of syntactically triggered movement and pragmatically triggered movement complicates the word order. Consider example (26).

(26) כִּי-S-V-PP (S=Focus)

כִּי הַמָּ֔וֶת יַפְרִ֖יד בֵּינִ֥י וּבֵינֵֽךְ

"indeed (only) **death** will separate me and you" (Ruth 1:17)

In example (26), the initial function word כִּי should trigger V-S inversion, yet we have S-V order. It seems that Topic and Focus-fronting are movement operations that occur after the syntactic triggering process that produces V-S inversion. The Focus-fronting within the subordinate clause resulted in a second round of constituent movement: the Focus-fronted subject המות has moved (pragmatic-triggering) over the already raised verb (syntactic-triggering), resulting in the כִּי-S-V order.

As with the Topic example above in (23), the constituent movement provoked by syntactic, semantic, and pragmatic concerns are perhaps even clearer when it is not the subject that is Focus-fronted. In (27) the PP is raised as a Focus constituent.

(27) PP-V (PP=Focus)

עִם־הַנְּעָרִים אֲשֶׁר־לִי תִּדְבָּקִין

"you should stick close <u>with the lads that are mine</u>" (Ruth 2:21)

In (27), the verb תדבקין is modal (see comment on 2:8) and would normally appear before any other constituents in the clause. In this case, the PP is raised (pragmatic-triggering) over the modal verb (semantic triggering) in order for Ruth (or Boaz, whom she is quoting) to contrast the extraordinary privileges he gave her with normal (assumed and thus unstated) gleaning privileges.

Finally, there are a few examples in Ruth (and numerous examples in poetic texts) of multiple fronting, as in (28).

(28) S$_{PRO}$-ADV-V (S$_{PRO}$=Topic; ADV=Focus)

אֲנִי מְלֵאָה הָלַכְתִּי

"<u>I</u> went away **full** (but <u>Yhwh</u> returned me **empty**)" (Ruth 1:21a)

The clause in (28) presents us with the first part of No'omi's complaint, the second part of which we discussed above in (25). Not only is the adjective מלאה (used adverbially here) placed before the verb, so too is the personal pronoun אני. The pronoun orients the reader to the desired verbal subject that is already known in the discourse—in the preceding verse, No'omi had just stated "Shaddai has made me very bitter," which means that there were at least two possible subjects from which to select. The fact that No'omi changes from Shaddai to herself as the subject of the next clause is the motivation for use of the subject pronoun as a Topic. The adverbial מלאה is then Focus-fronted and is used to create the contrast between מלאה and ריקם in the next clause in the verse.

What I have just described is the model of syntax, semantics, and pragmatics I have used to discern *how* the narrative in Ruth *means*. The examples above were all taken from clauses with finite verbs, which offer the most complicated structure. But the syntax and pragmatics of null-copula (so-called verbless) clauses, whether the predicate is nominal or participial, differ in one detail only: subject-predicate is the basic word order and it is not affected by syntactic triggers; rather, the only motivation for predicate-subject order is pragmatic (i.e., Topic or Focus). For a fuller explication of the model outlined in this section, see Holmstedt 2005 (on Proverbs) and 2009a (on Ruth and Jonah).

3

THE ROLE OF LINGUISTIC FEATURES
IN DATING THE BOOK

In this section I will present the data most often cited as evidence for dating Ruth. The language of Ruth has been variously dated to the early monarchic period (Campbell 1975:26–28, who suggests Solomon's reign for the basic story, which was finally fixed by writing in the ninth century, "tinged with archaic" features; cf. Wolfenson 1911; Myers 1955; Hubbard 1988:23–35) to the linguistically "transitional" late pre-exilic or early post-exilic periods (Bush 1996:20–30; so also Zevit 2005, who tentatively assigns it to 525–500 B.C.E.), although at least one scholar despairs of identifying the book's date, by linguistic or any other means (Sasson 1979:240–52). The wide range for dating the book's language (as well as Sasson's view that it cannot be dated) indicates just how tricky the use of language as a means of dating is. First, language rarely allows one to determine an absolute date; instead, historical linguistics typically aims for relative dating, that is, situating features with regard to each other on a temporal cline. Second, the type of data adduced is critical:

> The Hebrew of the Bible is sufficiently homogeneous that differences must be tracked on a statistical basis. The sophistication of such study is not in the statistics; advanced statistical methodologies are generally designed to deal with bodies of evidence quite different from what the Bible presents. The sophistication is rather in *the linguistic discrimination of what is counted and in the formulation of ensuing arguments.* (WO §1.4.2f; emphasis added)

Finally, the principles used to determine relative dating are critical. In Hebrew studies, they have been mostly "home-grown," which puts the results at risk of being inaccurate. In fact, the data cited and principles used in the last thirty or so years have become a flash-point for an increasingly vigorous debate about our ability to date biblical texts linguistically.

For nearly two centuries grammarians have discerned in the Hebrew Bible evidence of at least two chronological stages of Hebrew (GKC §2l-w, JM §3b): an early stage from before the exile ("Classical" or "Standard" biblical Hebrew [SBH]) and a later stage from the exilic and post-exilic periods ("Late" biblical Hebrew [LBH]). Moreover, a small number of poetic passages have often been identified as remnants of an even earlier stage, "Archaic" biblical Hebrew. Table 3 summarizes the basic "three-stage model" of BH diachrony, notably excluding Ruth but including reference to epigraphic Hebrew and the Hebrew of the Dead Sea Scrolls and other post-biblical texts (see Sáenz-Badillos 1993 for a good description).

In the last decade this three-stage model has come under strong criticism from a few prolific scholars. The challenges to the model has culminated in the impressive, two-volume work by Young, Rezetko, and Ehrensvärd 2008. While these authors do not challenge the axiom that language changes, they marshal a great deal of lexical data, with some morphological, syntactic, and semantic data, to argue that SBH and LBH are better understood as contemporaneous, closely-related dialects in ancient Israel rather than two chronologically related stages. Over the next few years, if not decades, this bold hypothesis will be tested in the only possible way: by writing up descriptive grammars of each biblical book to be compared against each other. Whether Young, Rezetko, and Ehrensvärd's thesis stands the test of time remains to be seen; however, it does raise three issues relevant to the study of the language of Ruth:

1. What are the grammatical and lexical features that distinguish the language of the book?
2. Is there any evidence of borrowing from Aramaic in the book? If so, how do we account for it?

3. What is the most plausible explanation for the features identified from questions 1–2: dialectal, chronological, or stylistic?

Keeping these questions in mind, below I work through the various data from Ruth that have been used by one scholar or another to date the book.

Orthographic Features

The study of ancient Hebrew spelling and specifically the use of the *matres lectionis* ("mothers of reading"), י, ו, and ה, has led to diachronic conclusions such that the later the text the greater the use of *plene* ("full") spelling. Such a chronological framework seems to make good sense of the Hebrew epigraphs with their generally defective spelling at one end, the Dead Sea Scrolls with their greater use of *matres* at the other, and the Hebrew Bible between. So, for instance, while the book of Ruth contains examples of both full and defective spellings—sometimes with the same words or verbal roots—in general it exhibits a tendency toward defective spelling. For example, there are a few cases of the Qal participle/agentive noun with ו in the first syllable (קוצרים in 2:4-7, 15, יודע in 3:11), but the majority are spelled without the ו (see the forms in 1:1; 2:3, 20; 3:2, 8, 9, 12; 4:1, 3, 4, 6, 8, 14, 16). Also, the three shortened forms of the feminine plural verb (מצאן in 1:9, לכן in 1:12, and קראן in 1:20) are more than balanced by the forms with -נה (see the forms in 1:9-14, 19-21; 4:14, 17).

On the odd form תעבורי, spelled with the ו, as if it were in pause, but vocalized as /û/, see §4 and comment on Ruth 2:8. Two forms in the book not only reflect the consonantal loss of א, which likely happened before the biblical stage of Hebrew, but also the omission of the א in spelling: ותשׁנה (for more common ותשאנה) in 1:14 and צמת (for more common צמאת) in 2:9. Although it might be tempting to use this feature as a linguistic feature for dating the book and, indeed, the elision of the א does happen with greater frequency in Hebrew of the late first millennium, e.g., in the Dead Sea Scrolls, the loss and non-writing of the א also occurs in the Siloam Tunnel inscription

TABLE 3

The Three-Stage Model of Biblical Hebrew in the Context of Extra-biblical Sources

Biblical Texts		Extra-biblical Texts
Archaic Hebrew	10c B.C.E.	Gezer Calendar
Blessing of Jacob (Gen 49)	9c–8c B.C.E.	Sinai bowl
Song of the Sea (Exod 15)		Tell Qasile ostraca
Oracles of Balaam (Num 23–24)		Kuntillet Ajrud votive inscriptions
Song of Moses (Deut 32)		Hazor texts
Blessing of Moses (Deut 33)		Samaria ostraca
Song of Deborah (Judg 5)		Ophel ostraca
some Psalms (e.g., Ps 68)		Nimrud ivories
		Yavneh Yam ostraca
		Khirbet el-Qom funerary inscriptions
		various seals and jar handles
Standard biblical Hebrew	c. 700 B.C.E.	Siloam tunnel
Genesis–Deuteronomy		Silwan tomb inscriptions
Joshua–Kings		Kadesh-Barnea ostraca
Pre-exilic and early exilic Prophets		Gibeon jar handles

most Psalms Job (?) Proverbs (?)	7c B.C.E.	Hinnom Valley silver amulets Wadi Murabbaʿat palimpsest
Late Biblical Hebrew Late exilic and post-exilic Prophets (and Jonah?) Lamentations Chronicles, Ezra–Nehemiah	6c B.C.E.	Lachish ostraca Arad ostraca Khirbet Beit Lei funerary graffiti Azor cemetary jar
Esther Song of Songs Daniel	3c B.C.E.	Dead Sea Scrolls (3c. B.C.E.–1c. C.E.)
Qohelet (Ecclesiastes)	c. 180 B.C.E.	Ben Sira
	132–135 C.E.	Ben Kochba Letters (132–135 C.E.)

from the late 8th century B.C.E. Moreover, the א is written most of the time and we even find it in the name מרא where we expect מרה. Rather than a feature to date the book by, these data seem more likely to be the product of (inadvertent?) scribal changes or the choice of the author to vary the spelling occasionally because "the scribes like it to vary" (Barr 1989:194). This explanation is also likely behind the alternation of שׂדי and שׂדה (cf. Myers 1955:9).

The spelling feature in Ruth that is mentioned more than any other is the name דוד in the genealogy (4:17, 22). This proper name stands out within the Hebrew Bible for the unusual consistency with which it isspelled: it lacks the י in Samuel, Kings (only three plene), Isaiah, Jeremiah, Ezekiel (only one plene), Proverbs, Ruth, Qohelet, and the Psalms (only one plene), but is spelled with the י in Chronicles, Ezra, Nehemiah, and the Minor Prophets. It is thus often asserted that Ruth aligns with the SBH books of the former group, that is, in this feature the book is earlier in its linguistic profile (Bush 1996:23–24). In contrast to this interpretation of the orthographic data stands the thorough study of spelling practices in the Hebrew Bible by James Barr, *The Variable Spellings of the Hebrew Bible* (1989b). After sifting through a great deal of data, Barr concludes that he is "sceptical, then, of all attempts to correlate the spellings and the dates of spellings (if they could be known), with the dates, early or late, when books originated" (1989b:199). Moreover, on the specific issue of דוד versus דויד, Barr rightly notes that

> There is no certain way of telling whether the long spelling was already adopted in the original composition of (say) Chronicles or whether it was made as a systematic change during the later transmission. The very systematic character of it might favour the latter rather than the former. This is supported also by the facts of the Minor Prophets: their fairly consistent use of the long spelling is not likely to go back to the original composition, since the cases in Amos and possibly Hosea may be quite early. (166)

In summary the orthographic profile of the Book of Ruth provides us with no good evidence for its date of composition.

Phonological Features

There are few outstanding phonological features that provide even potential dating evidence. The regular non-assimilation of the נ in מן to noun without an article is sometimes identified as a LBH feature that reflects Aramaic influence (Polzin 1976:66; Sáenz-Badillos 1993:119, 143). In Ruth the נ in מן is always assimilated to nouns without the article, distinguishing it from the observed LBH pattern. However, while it does seem that the נ in מן is less frequently assimilated to nouns without the article in consensus LBH books, it is not a consistent practice. Thus, this feature provides little help in profiling the language of Ruth.

Morphological Features

Three sets of possible dating-related data fall into the category of morphology: the use of the paragogic ("word-extending") נ in 2:8, 9, 21; 3:4, 18; the 2fs *qatal* verb ending in תי- in 3:3, 4; and the מ- pronouns used for feminine antecedents in 1:8, 9, 11, 13, 19, 22; 4:11.

The paragogic נ in Ruth is often called "archaic" (Myers 1955:16–17, followed by many). However, the infrequency of usage in Ruth (i.e., it is limited to just six forms, whereas eleven more lack the נ) as well as the fact that the paragogic נ is scattered throughout all discernible stages in the Hebrew Bible suggests that it cannot be used as dating evidence (so also Sasson 1979:245; see comment on 2:8 for further discussion).

The Ketiv forms of two verbs, ירדתי in 3:3 and שכבתי in 3:4 have unexpected תי- endings. Consonantly, the verbs look like 1cs forms, but the context dictates a 2fs since they follow other regular 2fs verbs and refer to Ruth. It has been noted that the morphology of both forms fits the 2fs we reconstruct for Hebrew before the Bible: the -*ti* ending is the form of the 2fs in Akkadian and Arabic (note the same vowel ending with 2fs -*ki* in Ethiopic) and is often reconstructed for Proto-Semitic (Huehnergard 1995:2130). Thus, many commentators see in these two verbs in Ruth real archaic remnants, suggesting the

old (pre-exilic) age of the composition, or perhaps at least the age
of the oral story (e.g., Myers 1955:11; Sasson 1979:68–69; Hubbard
1988:197, n. 8). Against the archaic remnant view is the inconsistent
use of the forms: why do not all of the 2fs forms in the book have the
the תי- endings? Also, if the majority was updated, through the generations of oral story-telling or through scribal activity, why did these
two go unchanged? It is unlikely that we can identify these forms as
real archaic remnants and thus use them for dating Ruth's language.

   The third morphological set of data that is often invoked in dating discussions is the apparent gender mismatch of the pronouns and
pronominal suffixes (and one *qatal* verb) in 1:8, 9, 11, 13, 19, 22; 4:11.
In each case, the pronoun matches the expected form of the masculine plural even though the obvious antecedents are two women. On
the face of it, the forms appear to represent gender neutralization.
That is, in many gender-inflected languages forms of the less used,
exclusive, and thus "marked" gender (i.e., feminine in Hebrew) tend
to be replaced with the more common, inclusive, and less marked
gender (i.e., masculine in Hebrew), especially in "colloquial speech"
(see Rendsburg 1991:35–67; also JM §149b-c). Alternatively, it has
been suggested that there is no gender mismatch with these forms,
but rather they are rare feminine dual pronouns (Rendsburg 1982,
esp. 77; 2001, esp. 37–38; cf. Bar-Asher 2009). However, it is more
economical (and an option admitted but not chosen in Rendsburg
2001) that the thirty-eight examples Rendsburg lists, including those
in Ruth, are to be taken together with the over one hundred cases of
gender neutralized pronouns as a single phenomenon. In other words,
to propose a feminine dual pronoun is unnecessary. Regardless which
option in chosen, the distribution of the phenomenon in SBH and
LBH texts is not clear and thus should not be used in dating the
language (contra Rendsburg 2001). (Myers' suggestion that the pronouns reflect "a relatively early dialectical peculiarity" [1955:20] is
unsupported.)

   Since none of the three morphological sets of data is clearly date-
able, we are no closer to providing a date for the book of Ruth as a

whole. Thus we turn to the last two grammatical categories: syntax and semantics.

Syntactic and Semantic Features

Since there is only one semantic feature that has figured in the dating of Ruth's language, I will mention it first. This single "semantic" feature concerns the verbal system. It is often claimed that the LBH books (and also Qumran texts) used the so-called *waw*-consecutive (i.e., the *wayyiqtol* and modal *qatal*) verbs less frequently (Sáenz-Badillos 1993: 120, 123–24, 129; JM §119z-zb; Abegg 1998:337–38; but see Smith 1991 for a more cautious statement). In Ruth the *wayyiqtol* is used throughout for the narrative and the modal *qatal* is used frequently (see 1:11, 12; 2:7, 9, 14, 16; 3:3, 4, 9, 13, 18; 4:5, and perhaps 4:15). Even in 4:7, with the narrator's interjection, the two verbs שָׁלַף ... וְנָתַן are modal *qatal* and thus no different from the other cases. However, Ruth also uses non-modal *qatal* clauses (1:14, 22; 4:1, 18-22) in narrative (i.e., non-reported speech) main clauses (there are more in subordinate clauses, but this is typical in all of BH). Admittedly, the non-modal *qatal* main clauses are not used with the frequency that we find in the Qumran texts and this suggests that Ruth falls on the chronological cline between, say, Judges and Ezra-Nehemiah. (With that said, the diachronic studies of verbal syntax and word order have not adequately accounted for the main-vs-subordinate clause distinction as well as the narrative-vs-reported speech distinction, and so an accurate picture of the trends for each biblical and non-biblical text remains a desideratum.)

In contrast to the meager semantic information (at least, as it has been studied), there are at least five syntactic features of Ruth that are often mentioned in discussions of date. First, it has often claimed that both וַיְהִי at the beginning of a clause and וַיְהִי + preposition + infinitive construct are syntactic collocations that decreased in usage in LBH (Sáenz-Badillos 1993:119, 144–45; Polzin 1976:56–58; JM §166q). This construction occurs once in Ruth, in 1:19, and it is cited alongside וַיְהִי בְּשָׁכְבוֹ in 3:4, וַיְהִי בַּחֲצִי הַלַּיְלָה in 3:8, and וְהָיָה

בַּבֹּקֶר in 3:13, as evidence that Ruth patterns with SBH in this regard (Bush 1996:23). And yet neither the use of וַיְהִי as an introductory verb nor the collocation of וַיְהִי + preposition + infinitive construct completely disappeared in LBH books (see, e.g., Esth 2:8; 3:4; 5:2; Dan 8:2, 15; Neh 1:4; 13:3; 2 Chr 12:1; 22:8; 25:14, 16; 26:5). Thus, the three וִיהִי examples and one וְהָיָה example in Ruth do not provide adequate evidence of its linguistic profile vis-à-vis SBH or LBH.

A second syntactic pattern that is often pointed to as an example of change is the use of אֲשֶׁר to introduce complement clauses in LBH instead of the SBH use of כִּי (Sáenz-Badillos 1993:127; Young, Rezetko, and Ehrensvärd 2008:1:258; cf. Polzin 1976:128; JM §157c). In Ruth כִּי presents a verbal complement clause with the שמע in 1:6, ראה in 1:18, ידע in 3:11, 14, and a noun complement with טוב in 2:22 and עדים in 4:9. Thus, Ruth seems to pattern in this case with SBH rather than LBH.

A third syntactic feature that Bush cites in support of categorizing Ruth as SBH is the Predicate-Subject order within the null-copula complement clauses in 1:18 and 3:11, whereas it has been claimed that LBH prefers Subject-Predicate order (Bush 1996:23; Bergey 1983:71–72). This claim rests on an analysis of null-copula clauses that ignores pragmatic (e.g. Topic, Focus) features that influence the order of constituent (see §2, last paragraph, and comments on Ruth 2:6 and 2:10 below). Thus, the distinction made by Bergey is highly questionable and certainly not one by which to date the language of Ruth.

A fourth syntactic collocation used to distinguish Ruth is the use in 1:17 of Y-בֵּין ... X-בֵּין, instead of Y-לְ ... X-בֵּין. Books typically identified as SBH greatly prefer the Y-בֵּין ... X-בֵּין construction, exclusively so in Exodus, Joshua, Judges, and Jeremiah, whereas books typically identified as LBH prefer the Y-לְ ... X-בֵּין construction, exclusively so in Malachi, Daniel, and Nehemiah (Rooker 1994:141–42; JM §103, n. 48). However, it is also so that many SBH texts use both constructions, as do many LBH texts (Young, Rezetko, and Ehrensvärd 2008:1:123–24). Thus, the single occurrence in Ruth should not be taken as determinative.

A fifth syntactic feature that has been used to categorize the language of Ruth is the use of אֵת + suffix versus object suffixes attached directly to the verb. It has been claimed that אֵת + suffix is the preferred choice in SBH whereas LBH shows a marked preference for attaching the suffix directly (Polzin 1976:28–31; Sáenz-Badillos 1993:119, 126, 145). As Young, Rezetko, and Ehrensvärd point out, however, there are generally agreed upon SBH texts, such as Habakkuk and early sections of 1 Kings, that only use the suffix attached to the verb and not אֵת + suffix (2008:261–62). So, while Ruth has only suffixes attached to the verbs and no examples of אֵת + suffix (1:21; 2:4, 13, 15; 3:6, 13 [2x]; 4:15 [2x], 16), how this feature relates to the chronological profile of the book or dating is unclear.

Finally, a syntactic feature that has not been used previously to date Ruth's language but which does help situate it relative to the language of other books is the use of the ה-relative. In his study of the article in BH, James Barr mentions the use of the article as a relative marker (1989a:322–25). He notes that, while grammars often list examples of the type illustrated in (29), they neither provide an accurate grammatical analysis nor recognize the possible diachronic evidence such relatives provide.

(29) Genesis 1:28

וּבְכָל־חַיָּה הָרֹמֶשֶׂת עַל־הָאָרֶץ

"and over every creature <u>that</u> creeps on the ground"

Barr concludes this section of his argument by saying,

> . . . the relative article has a main function other than that of normal determination; it is frequent in some poetic texts in which the usual article is rare; and it may possibly suggest a path which leads from an older state of the language, in which determination by the article was unusual, to the classical state, in which such determination was central. (1989:325)

It is in the potential diachronic information where this issue of the relative article intersects with the language of Ruth. Consider the three examples given in (30)–(32):

(30) Ruth 1:22

וַתָּשָׁב נָעֳמִי וְרוּת הַמּוֹאֲבִיָּה כַלָּתָהּ עִמָּהּ הַשָּׁבָה מִשְּׂדֵי מוֹאָב

"and No'omi returned, Ruth the Moabite, her daughter-in-law, with her, <u>who (also) returned</u> from the territory of Moab"

(31) Ruth 2:6

וַיֹּאמַר נַעֲרָה מוֹאֲבִיָּה הִיא הַשָּׁבָה עִם־נָעֳמִי מִשְּׂדֵה מוֹאָב

"and he said: she is a Moabite girl <u>who returned</u> with No'omi from the territory of Moab"

(32) Ruth 4:3

חֶלְקַת הַשָּׂדֶה אֲשֶׁר לְאָחִינוּ לֶאֱלִימֶלֶךְ מָכְרָה נָעֳמִי הַשָּׁבָה מִשְּׂדֵה מוֹאָב

"the portion of the field that belongs to our kinsman, to Elimelek, No'omi, <u>who returned</u> from the territory of Moab, is now selling"

In each case the underlined verb is accented by the Masoretes as a 3fs *qatal* preceded by the relative article. Most grammars and commentaries suggest reading against the Masoretic accents in these and similar examples. But the Masoretes had no need to indicate the accent on this penultima if the reading tradition had not preserved this placement of the word stress and since, as we will see, this syntactic pattern had long fallen into disuse by the period of the Masoretes, there was every reason for the reading tradition to adjust the word stress to its expected placement. That it did not suggests that the reading tradition preserved a grammatical feature that was much older. Thus, I will consider the word accents in these examples to be historically and linguistically legitimate and use these three examples in Ruth and the larger issue of the development of the relative article to situate Ruth's language.

Recent study of the definite article in both Phoenician and Hebrew suggests that its origin lies in the function of ה as a subordinator, i.e., a relative marker (Gzella 2006:11; contra Pat-El 2009). This accounts for examples like (29) above, in which חיה and הרמשׂת donot exhibit "agreement in definiteness"; it also accounts for the similar construction with adjectives, as in (33):

(33) 2 Samuel 12:4

וַיָּבֹא הֵלֶךְ לְאִישׁ הֶעָשִׁיר

"a traveller came to a man <u>who was rich</u>"

And finally, it accounts for examples such as (34)—cases where the original relativizing function of the ה was extended to finite verbs:

(34) Genesis 21:3

וַיִּקְרָא אַבְרָהָם אֶת־שֶׁם־בְּנוֹ הַנּוֹלַד־לוֹ אֲשֶׁר־יָלְדָה־לּוֹ שָׂרָה יִצְחָק

"and Abraham called the name of his son <u>who was born</u> to him, who Sarah bore for him 'Isaac.'"

Interestingly, for whatever reason this use with finite verbs did not survive; we have only nineteen examples in the Hebrew Bible (and none outside), listed in (35):

(35) ה-relative with finite verb: Gen 18:21; 21:3; 46:27; Josh 10:24; 1 Kgs 11:9; Isa 51:10; 56:3; Ezek 26:17; Job 2:11; Ruth 1:22; 2:6; 4:3; Ezra 8:25; 10:14, 17; 1 Chr 26:28; 29:17; 2 Chr 1:4; 29:36.

A simple study of the verses listed in (35) does not produce an obvious chronological pattern, but further investigation provides the key. When we turn to the examples in which the relative clause with ה modifies a NP not marked with ה, i.e., asymmetric agreement examples like those in (29), (31), and (33), we may reconstruct a change in which Ruth figures prominently. Consider the group of data in (36):

(36) ה-relatives modifying NP head without ה

(a) Finite Verbs: Ruth 2:6; Ezra 10:14, 17; 1 Chr 26:28

(b) Participles: Gen 1:28; 7:21; 49:17; Exod 26:12; 38:26; Lev 11:46; 16:16; Judg 21:19; 1 Sam 25:10; Isa 65:2; Jer 27:3; 32:14; 46:16; 50:16; Ezek 2:3; 21:19; 28:16; 32:22, 24; 47:2; Prov 26:18; Song 4:5; Dan 9:26; Ezra 10:17; 1 Chr 26:28; 2 Chr 31:6.

(c) Adjectives: Gen 41:26; Lev 24:10; Judg 14:3; 16:27; 1 Sam 6:28; 12:23; 16:23; 19:12; 2 Sam 12:4; 1 Kgs 7:8, 12; 2 Kgs 20:4 (Qere); 20:13; 24:4; Isa 7:20; Jer 6:16; 6:20; 17:2; 22:17; 38:14; Ezek 9:2; 21:19; 40:28, 31; 42:9; Zech 4:7; 11:2 (Ketiv); Ps 62:4; 104:18; Eccl 11:5; Neh 9:35; 2 Chr 4:10.

Notice within the first sub-group, Ruth is one of three examples with a finite verb and the other two are from late biblical books. When the participial and adjectival relatives are added, the modest trend is toward a greater use of this construction in texts associated with LBH. Now consider the extra-biblical evidence in (37):

(37) ה-relatives modifying NP head without ה

   (a) Ben Sira: 14.21; 16.7, 9, 10; 36.31a, b; 49.12; 50.9, 26.

   (b) Qumran: 1QS 8:11; 4Q167 f2:3, 252 1:9; 373 f1a+b:4, 394 f1_2ii:8; 11Q19 21:12, 46:5.

   (c) Mishna (only participles; not including over 200 examples with adjective): Shev 2:7, 9; Ter 1:8, 9; Maaser2 1:5; Eruv 8:2; Yoma 7:3; Sheqal 2:1; 4:2; 6:5; Sukk 3:1, 2, 3; 5:4; Meg 1:9; Hagig 3:4; Ketub 8:6; 9:7; Nazir 7:3; Sota 6:3; Qidd 2:9; BabaQ 1:4; 2:5; Shevu 1:7; Ed 6:3; AvodaZ 2:3; 5:9; Avot 1:3; Hor 3:4; Zevah 4:4; 5:2; 8:1; 12:5; 14:1; Menah 9:7; Hul 5:3; Arak 3:1; 4:4; Ker 3:8; Meil 2:3; Mid 1:9; Tamid 1:1; Kelim 2:7; 14:5; Ohol 1:5; 8:2, 5; 18:1, 2; Neg 1:2; 13:7, 9, 12; Para 1:1; 8:3; 11:6; Tohar 4:5; 7:7; Miqw 7:1; Maksh 3:5; 6:7.

To account for the distribution of ה-relatives, I suggest the following reconstruction. The article in Central Semitic was a relatively late innovation in each of the languages. For Northwest Semitic, the lack of clear evidence for an article in Ugaritic suggests that it was an early first millennium innovation. If it began within relative clauses, it was a feature competing with an already established relative particle; in fact, Hebrew already had at least two: אשׁר and the ז-series (if not also שׁ). The biblical examples suggest that the change to include the relative article began by replacing the other relative words slowly at first and in a restricted environment: non-verbal modification in which the head of the relative was also the subject within the relative. Then the change increased—and it expanded to include finite verbs—before finally tapering off with an established but constrained dominance in its original context—non-verbal modification. Notably, the use of the other relative words to introduce participial relatives exhibits a corresponding decrease, so that by the Mishna, הַ-participial relatives are favored 11-to-1 over שַ-participial relatives (שַ replacing אֲשֶׁר by this point), illustrated by the data listed in (38).

(38) אשר/שׁ + participle relative clauses:

(a) Hebrew Bible: Gen 7:8; 39:22; Num 21:34; Deut 1:4; 3:2; 4:46; 1 Kgs 5:13; Isa 11:10; 49:7; Jer 38:16; Ezek 9:2; 13:3; 43:1; Zech 11:5; Pss 115:8; 135:18; Eccl 4:1; 8:12, 14; Esth 8:8; Neh 5:2, 3, 4; 2 Chr 34:10.

(b) Qumran: 1QS 11:6; 4Q274 fli:8; 4Q410 fl:3; 4Q419 fl:9; 4Q504 fl_2Rvi:5.

(c) Ben Sira: 13.2; 38.5.

(d) Mishna: There are over 300 examples of שַ + participle, but many of them are constructions in which הַ either could not be used (since the head is not the subject within the relative, e.g., בִּזְמַן שֶ- "at the time that . . .") or is never used for whatever reason (e.g., -מִי שֶ "whoever . . .").

What I have described here is an example of the 'S'-curve that has been noticed in many linguistic changes. That is, "new forms replac[e] established ones only slowly in the beginning of a change, then accelerat[e] their replacement in the middle stages of a change and finally, as the old forms become rare, slow [. . .] their advance once again" (Kroch 1989:203). If my reconstruction for הַ-relatives is accurate, it places Ruth's use of the relative article in that strong middle surge in which it expanded to include finite verbs, and this middle surge is concentrated in texts often categorized as LBH. Given the support of the 'S'-curve pattern, even if SBH and LBH were slightly different dialects, in this feature they were operating together as a larger dialect and thus we can still legitimately trace linguistic change in the data as a whole. For Ruth, the data thus suggest that the book sits on the relative dating cline between books like Gen-Deut, Josh-Kings on the one side and Ezra-Neh, Chronicles, and Qohelet on the other.

Lexical Features

The final linguistic category by which Ruth (as well as most other biblical books) is dated is its vocabulary. Noting differences in lexical items to distinguish texts had become fundamental to the source criticism of the Pentateuch and Deuteronomistic History (Joshua-Kings) in the nineteenth century, and this method has also become central to the issue of dating texts, particularly in the last thirty years (see Hurvitz 2000, 2006 for summaries of the principles and a good selection of previous research in the sources cited there). For Ruth, ten lexical features (listed in table 4) are often adduced as support for dating the book to one period or another.

Archaic Item

The divine epithet שדי has an interesting distribution in the Hebrew Bible: Genesis (6x), Exodus (1x), Numbers (2x), Isaiah (1x - 13:6), Ezekiel (2x), Joel (1x), Psalms (2x: 68:15, 91:1); Job (31x); Ruth (2x). From this Campbell concludes that שדי "was a current name for God in the patriarchal and amphictyonic [pre-monarchic, tribal] periods, and was revived in the exilic period" (1975:77). The term may thus reflect the story's origin (pre-monarchic or exilic) or a later narrator's

TABLE 4
Lexical Features Often Used in Dating Ruth

Archaic (?) Item
 שדי [name for God] (1:20-21)
Mixed Early and Late Items
 SBH אנכי (2:10, 13; 3:9, 12, 13; 4:4 [2x]) vs. LBH אני (1:21; 4:4)
 SBH [אשה] לקח (4:13) vs. LBH נשא אשה "to take a wife" (1:4)
Aramaic (and hence "Late") Items
 SBH להקים (4:5, 10) vs. Aramaic/LBH לקיּם (4:5, 10)
 שלף נעל "to remove a sandal" (4:7) vs. SBH חלץ נעל or נשל נעל
 שבר "to hope, wait for" (1:13) vs. SBH קוה or יחל
 עגן "to hinder" (1:13)

desire to make the story seem pre-monarchic (but how would the narrator know the word's distributional history?). With such a wide distribution for the the few occurrences, it is difficult to use this word confidently for any dating purposes.

Mixed Early and Late Items

For the 1cs subject pronouns, Polzin asserts that the "sole use of [אני] instead of an alternation between [אני] and [אנכי] is a mark of LBH" (1976:126; see also Sáenz-Badillos 1993:117). In Ruth, both forms are used, although אנכי predominates. The fact that the choice of pronouns in Ruth may reflect the narrator's attention to the social use of language (see comment on 2:10) does not attenuate its role in aligning Ruth with SBH practice. Even though אנכי is found a few times in consensus LBH texts (Dan 10:11; Neh 1:6; 1 Chr 17:1), the predominance of אני in LBH texts suggests that Ruth profiles more closely with SBH practice.

Two idioms for "taking a wife" are used in Ruth, the phrase typical in SBH texts, [אשה] לקח (4:13) as well as the phrase typical in LBH texts, נשא אשה "to take a wife" (1:4). While the phrase נשא אשה appears once in a SBH text (Judg 21:23), it is mostly found in LBH texts (2 Chr 11:21; 13:21; 24:3; Ezra 9:2, 12; 10:44; Neh 13:25). It is also found in Ben Sira 7.23b and the Mishna, to the exclusion of לקח אשה. Thus, the use of נשא אשה in Ruth 1:4 appears to be a clear case of LBH language (see Young, Rezetko, and Ehrensvärd 2008:1:265). Yet, this does not explain the use of the alternate phrase, [אשה] לקח, in 4:13. It is possible that the story-teller simply had at his command (i.e., within his "mental lexicon") two synonymous phrases for expressing "taking a wife." It is possible that Guenther 2005 is correct, that the explanation is a socio-linguistic distinction rather than a diachronic distinction, at least for the book of Ruth. Guenther argues that לקח אשה is the basic phrase for marriage, while נשא אשה implies, among other things, a marriage without a dowry, bride-price, or any other exchange of wealth due to poverty and low status. For Ruth specifically, he says:

In Ruth 1:4 Mahlon and Chilion are described as taking
(נשׂא) Moabite women for themselves after the death of
their father, Elimelech. Elimelech and his family had left
Bethlehem in Judah for Moab because of famine. That they
had mortgaged their land and used up their capital is borne
out by the need for a kinsman to redeem their property when
Naomi returned to Bethlehem. In their poverty, they could
not afford bride-prices for Ruth and 'Orpah. Thus they married poverty-stricken or low status women who brought no
dowry into the marriage. When all three husbands had died,
Naomi, 'Orpah, and Ruth were financially destitute; the
marriages added nothing to the family's ability to survive.
Neither bride-price nor dowry were exchanged in this (נשׂא,
"seizure") marriage. (2005:400)

Although Guenther does not address the use of לקח in 4:13, presumably he would argue that in the case of Boaz the notion of a low-
status marriage was intentionally avoided, even if there was no official
bride-price paid by Boaz. In light of this socio-linguistic and literary
explanation, and the use of both collocations in the book, we should
not place much weight on the use of נשׂא אשׁה in Ruth 1:4 as dating
evidence (contra Bush 1996:26).

In summary, both the use of אני and אנכי, and to a very limited
extent the phrase נשׂא אשׁה, point cautiously toward an SBH classification of Ruth's language.

Aramaic/Late Items

Languages borrow words from other languages for two primary reasons: need and prestige (Campbell 2004:64–65). The word "coffee"
is a good modern example of need-based borrowing: the etymological
entry in the Oxford English Dictionary explains its background and
notes its diffusion as a borrowed word:

Arab. *qahwah*, in Turkish pronounced *kahveh*, the name of
the infusion or beverage; said by Arab lexicographers to have
originally meant "wine" or some kind of wine, and to be a
derivative of a vb.-root *qahiya* "to have no appetite." Some

have conjectured that it is a foreign, perh. African, word disguised, and have thought it connected with the name of Kaffa in the south Abyssinian highlands, where the plant appears to be native. But of this there is no evidence, and the name *qahwah* is not given to the berry or plant, which is called *bunn*, the native name in Shoa being *bn*.

The European langs. generally appear to have got the name from Turkish *kahveh*, about 1600, perh. through It. *caffè*; cf. F., Sp., Pg. *café*, Ger. *kaffee*, Da., Sw. *kaffe*. The Eng. *coffee*, Du. *koffie*, earlier Ger. *coffee, koffee*, Russ. *kophe, kophe*, have *o*, app. representing earlier *au* from *ahw* or *ahv*.

A likely example of need-based borrowing in Hebrew is the word קוֹף "monkey." Since monkeys are not native to ancient Israel, it is understandable that Hebrew had no native word for the animal. However, when the need arose to mention this particular animal (1 Kgs 10:22 // 2 Chr 9:21), the word was borrowed into Hebrew, perhaps via Egyptian (although its origin may be Sanskrit *kapi*; HALOT s.v.).

Prestige-based borrowing reflects a socio-linguistic situation in which a foreign language, whether closely related or not, is associated with higher social or political status or is simply a dominant linguistic cultural influence (e.g., *lingua franca*, as is often the case with the influence of Modern English across the globe). During the Norman French dominance in English (1066–1300) many French words were borrowed into English (e.g., *pork* > Fr. *porc*) even though English already had serviceable terms (e.g., *pig meat*) (Campbell 2004:64). At that time, French was considered more prestigious than English. In Hebrew prestige-borrowing is often invoked to explain the increasing number of Aramaisms (e.g., אִגֶּרֶת "letter") as well as the few Persianisms (e.g., דָּת "law, decree") found in LBH texts. The prestige status for Aramaic came from its role as the administrative language of both the Neo-Babylonian and Persian empires; for Persian the prestige status no doubt derived from the political dominance of the Persians from the 6th to 4th centuries B.C.E.

Whether words are borrowed due to need or prestige, it is important to recognize that the borrowed item is adapted to the borrowing language's phonology and morphology (Campbell 2004:65–69). For instance, the Hebrew אַשָּׁף "conjurer" entered either via Aramaic אָשַׁף or Akkadian *(w)āšipu*, but the Hebrew form is the only one reflecting the gemination of the middle root consonant, which is likely because the word was imported as a *qattāl*-pattern noun, the nominal morphological category used for "nouns of profession" (JM §88Ha and n. 49; also §87d).

A final category of borrowing that relates to Hebrew is loan translations or "calques." In contrast to borrowed words, for which something of the borrowed item's phonetic shape and meaning continue into the borrowing language, loan translations use native words to translate a borrowed concept. Thus, Modern English *gospel* is derived from Old English *gód spel* "good tidings," which was a translation, through Latin *evangelium*, of the Greek εὐαγγέλιον "good tidings." A possible Hebrew example is the use of בְּצֵל in Eccl 7:12 (cf. 6:12; 8:13; see Wise 1990 for the full argument). In these three verses, instead of the normal Hebrew meaning "in the shadow (of)," בְּצֵל may be a loan translation of the cognate Aramaic בטלל, which, unlike the Hebrew phrase, went through a series of semantic shifts: "in the shadow (of)" > "with the help (of)" > "because (of)." Thus, in Ecclesiastes, the Hebrew phrase בְּצֵל has neither the normal denotation of "in the shadow (of)" nor the metaphorical meaning "in the protection (of)," but is a loan translation of what the cognate Aramaic phrase had become, "because."

The question we must ask when considering Ruth's language is whether there is any evidence of borrowed words, and if so, can we use the fact of the borrowing to help date the book's language. Working backwards through the categories, it is first possible to state that there appear to be no loan translations in Ruth. This leaves the possibility of need-based or prestige-based borrowings. In Ruth there are four possible borrowings from Aramaic worth investigating.

The first possible Aramaism is the use of the Piel לְקַיֵּם in 4:7. The more common *binyan* used with קוּם to denote "fulfill (something)" is the Hifil, as in לְהָקִים (4:5, 10). In 4:7, however, we find the Piel, לְקַיֵּם, which is often taken as an Aramaism (HALOT, s.v.; Bush 1996:27; Bergey 1983:40–42; contra Sasson 1979:142, 244; Myers 1955:19). Campbell asserts, however, that middle ו verbs in the *binyanim* that result in the doubling of the ו are "not totally absent from relatively early biblical texts" (1975:148), and he cites the form וַיִּצְטַיָּרוּ (Josh 9:4; mistakenly cited as Judg 9:12 by Campbell), which he takes to be the Hitpael of ציד (so also Myers 155:19). Moreover, he adds that there "is a large number of examples of *Piel* forms of *qwm* in the OT" (148). That is not quite accurate, though: besides the case in Ruth 4:7, there are ten examples (Ezek 13:6; Ps 119:28, 106; Esth 9:21, 27, 29, 31 [3x], 32), all of which belong to exilic or post-exilic texts. But, as Hubbard asserts, there seems to be three different nuances intended by these examples: "to confirm, ratify" (Ps 119:28), "to make happen, make come true" (Ezek 13:6), and "to institute, regulate" (Esth 9:21-32) (1988:249). His point, following Campbell's lead, is that such semantic nuance would have to mean that, even if the Piel לקים was an Aramaism, it would have had to have been incorporated into Hebrew at a reasonably early point. This case is a bit overstated, though, particularly since the passages support only two necessary nuances for the Piel קים: "to fulfill" and "to institute." It seems likely, especially given the distribution, that the use of the Piel לקים aligns with LBH. But whether it is an actual Aramaism is another issue. The question of motivation puts a fine point on it: there is clearly no need to borrow (since the Hifil להקים would suffice) and if Aramaic dominance (a type of prestige) was behind the supposed borrowing, why not use לְקַיֵּם in 4:5 and 4:10 as well? Rather, it seems just as likely, if not more likely, that the use of the Piel in 4:7 reflects an option that was—or, at least, *became* (perhaps by analogy)—available in Hebrew without recourse to borrowing, and the usage in Ruth was an issue of style (i.e., variation on the part of the story-teller).

The second possible Aramaism occurs in the same verse 4:7 (and
also in 4:8): the collocation of שלף with נעל to denote "remove a sandal." Elsewhere the verb שלף is used with חרב to denote "drawing
out a sword" (e.g., Judg 3:22; 1 Sam 31:4 // 1 Chr 10:4) and the verbs
used with "sandal" are חלץ (Deut 24:9, 10; Isa 20:2) or נשל (Exod
3:5; Josh 5:15). This distribution and contrast, along with the regular
practice in the Aramaic Targums using שלף to translate biblical חלץ
and נשל, Bush takes as strong evidence, along with לְקַיֵּם, of the LBH
nature of 4:7 (which he takes to be native to the story and thus not a
later editorial insertion; 1996:28–29). Clearly with two Hebrew verbs
already available this could not have been a need-based borrowing.
This leaves the prestige (or dominance) of Aramaic as a motivation for
the borrowing. Since the verb שלף for "removing a sandal" is well-
known in Aramaic and is not used anywhere else in BH, this example
is a good candidate for an Aramaic borrowing in Ruth, suggesting a
period of increasing Aramaic influence.

A third possible Aramaic borrowing is a rare verb used in 1:13: שבר
"to hope, wait for." The typical verbs throughout the Hebrew Bible
for "hoping, waiting" are קוה and יחל. The verb שבר is also used
outside of Ruth (Isa 38:18; Ps 104:27; 119:116, 166; 145:15; 146:5;
Esth 9:1), but the occurrences lean toward later texts. However, even
if this word had been borrowed from Aramaic, the poetic contexts
of most of the examples, as well as the fact that the verb in Ruth is
used in the mouth of Noʿomi, make it difficult to determine whether
it is an Aramaic word that has become part of the Hebrew standard
lexicon and thus reflects a later (LBH) setting or it is a borrowed word
used for a little literary "spice" (see §4), which could have occurred at
an earlier point (i.e., before the linguistic and cultural dominance of
Aramaic began in the 6th century B.C.E.)

The final item sometimes considered an Aramaic borrowing, and
thus of a later date, is also in 1:13—the Hitpael of the verb עגן "to
hinder (oneself), keep (oneself) from." The closest cognates for this
word come from Mishnaic Hebrew, Jewish Babylonian Aramaic, and
Syriac. Interestingly, Hebrew has other verbs available for the basic

semantics of "withholding oneself"—חשׂך in the Qal and מנע in the Nifal—which suggests that the appearance of עגן likely does not reflect need-based borrowing. It is perhaps an Aramaic word used by the narrator for literary affect (see §4), which would make it a prestige-based borrowing of sorts. However, since this verb is a *hapax legomenon* in the Hebrew Bible, the lack of much evidence at all about this verb prohibits us from making any strong claims about its status as an Aramaism (so Sasson 1979:244).

In summary, there are no clear cases in the book of Ruth of need-based borrowing from Aramaic and only hints of prestige-based borrowing, mostly, it seems, for literary variety. Yet in none of the plausible cases of borrowing is the case strong enough to use for dating the book confidently. However, taken together with the "Early and Late" mixings discussed above, all the relevant data *suggest* (but not strongly) that Ruth was written during a period of Aramaic ascendancy but not dominance and thus it may come from the early Persian period. What makes so many of the items typically used to date the book weak or arguably irrelevant is the greater likelihood that they reflect the author's skill as a story-teller rather than the linguistic setting; that is, while the Aramaic items had to be available in some way *and intelligible to the audience*, their sparse use may primarily reflect an author who went beyond the normal lexical inventory of Hebrew of his day for literary affect.

4

THE USE OF LANGUAGE TO COLOR
CHARACTERS' SPEECH

Skilled story-tellers use a variety of techniques to make their stories flow well and hold their audience's attention. For instance, they
manipulate the pace of the plot, keeping the majority of events flow-
ing at a quick and even pace but achieving climaxes or heightening
tension by pausing to dwell on significant characters or events. They
hop from one place to another in order to give the story a three-
dimensional spatial sense. They choose a few characters to develop
into heroes and villains, tragic sufferers and victorious conquerers,
foreigners and locals, rich and poor, nobility and commoners. And
in all of this, language is their primary medium (as opposed to ges-
tures, etc.). The use of language in the presentation of time, space,
plot structure, and characterization within biblical narrative has been
noted for some time and for good introductions, see Berlin 1983, Bar-
Efrat 1989, and, for a more detailed study, Sternberg 1987.

While this commentary is focused on grammar and not literary
analysis, certain specific uses of language for literary affect must be
highlighted. Specifically, I note in the commentary a number of places
where I have determined the author to be manipulating language for
the purposes of characterization. As WO states, "there are signs that
the speech of men differs from that of women; speech addressed to
young or old may vary from a standard. Speech itself often differs
from narrative prose, and there are traces of dialect variation based on
region in both" (§1.4.1a). A passage from a well-known English play
provides an extreme example of this phenomenon, which is used in
some form by most story-tellers. Consider the following excerpts from
the beginning of George Bernard Shaw's *Pygmalion*.

FREDDY

Oh, very well: I'll go, I'll go. *[He opens his umbrella and dashes off Strandwards, but comes into collision with a flower girl, who is hurrying in for shelter, knocking her basket out of her hands. A blinding flash of lightning, followed instantly by a rattling peal of thunder, orchestrates the incident.]*

THE FLOWER GIRL (Eliza Doolittle)

Nah then, Freddy: look wh' y' gowin, deah.

FREDDY

Sorry *[he rushes off]*.

THE FLOWER GIRL (Eliza Doolittle) *[picking up her scattered flowers and replacing them in the basket]*

There's menners f' yer! Te-oo banches o voylets trod into the mad.

THE MOTHER

How do you know that my son's name is Freddy, pray?

THE FLOWER GIRL (Eliza Doolittle)

Ow, eez ye-ooa san, is e? Wal, fewd dan y' de-ooty bawmz a mather should, eed now bettern to spawl a pore gel's flahrzn than ran awy atbaht pyin. Will yeoo py me f 'them?

THE BYSTANDER

He ain't a tec. He's a blooming busybody: that's what he is. I tell you, look at his boots.

THE NOTE TAKER (Henry Higgins) *[turning on him genially]*

And how are all your people down at Selsey?

THE BYSTANDER [*suspiciously*]

> Who told you my people come from Selsey?

THE NOTE TAKER (Henry Higgins)

> Never you mind. They did. [*To the girl*] How do you come to be up so far east? You were born in Lisson Grove.

THE GENTLEMAN (Colonel Pickering) [*returning to his former place on the note taker's left*]

> How do you do it, if I may ask?

THE NOTE TAKER (Henry Higgins)

> Simply phonetics. The science of speech. That's my profession; also my hobby. Happy is the man who can make a living by his hobby! You can spot an Irishman or a Yorkshireman by his brogue. I can place any man within six miles. I can place him within two miles in London. Sometimes within two streets.

As in Shaw's *Pygmalion*, characters are often distinguished by their speech, not just in plays but also in novels and other types of narrated literature (see, e.g., James Joyce's works). Speech may color the characters as old or young, educated or not, wealthy or poor, respectful or rude, local or foreign. This technique is not a modern invention, either, but is generally identified in biblical narratives and the few other narratives we have from the ancient Near East (see Rendsburg 1996). For instance, the biblical book of Job opens with an immediate "foreign" characterization of the book's protagonist, Job, as a man from "the land of Uz" (1:1). To reinforce the foreignness of both Job and his companions, the speeches are littered with words that are not of a Hebrew origin. Besides the numerous Aramaic words, a likely case of a Phoenician (or pseudo-Phoenician) word appears in (39):

(39) Job 3:8

יִקְּבֻהוּ אֹרְרֵי־יוֹם הָעֲתִידִים עֹרֵר לִוְיָתָן׃

"May those who curse Yamm execrate it, the equipped, who curse Leviathan!"

Although the final word in the first half, יוֹם, looks like the Hebrew word "day," the parallelism with לִוְיָתָן makes no sense. Rather, it has been suggested that with יוֹם the poet has vocalized the word

> . . . according to the neighboring Phoenician pronunciation, whereby stressed *a* had become stressed *o*. By this linguistic sleight of tongue, the poet is able to produce a double entendre. The phrase אֹרְרֵי־יוֹם, whose primary meaning is "those who curse Yamm," comes to convey a second meaning as well. One hears in the phrase אֹרְרֵי־יוֹם the nearly homonymous אוֹר יוֹם, "light of day." The double entendre redoubles the power of the curse: May that night be execrated by the demons whose strength is sufficient to curse the dreaded Yamm/Leviathan; *and* may that night be cursed, eliminated, as all nights are, by the light of day. Our poet adopts a Phoenician vocalization specifically here with the apparent purpose of adding a pagan, Canaanite nuance to the name of the old Canaanite deity Yamm—perhaps the way that ancient Judeans customarily heard the name from the lips of Phoenicians for whom Yamm/Yom(m) was still a deity. (Greenstein 2003:654–55)

Using the characters' speech to accomplish this achieves two related ends for the story-teller. First, it allows the story-teller to stay out of the story, because an intrusive narrator (e.g., "and he said, in a Cockney accent, '. . .'") is cumbersome, disrupts the flow of the story itself, and is mostly reserved for subjective asides or background information (e.g., "he was a nasty sort of fellow" or "and this was the way it was done back then"). Second, it allows a character to be continually distinguished from others with different speech patterns, thus subtly keeping the differences in the audience's mind without being explicit. In fact, in Ruth we see both techniques—the use of speech and the explicit narratorial characterizations: for Boaz and No'omi it is their speech that often sets them apart, both from Ruth and the audience, and for Ruth the story-teller regularly reminds the audience that she is the "Moabite."

In determining whether some element is the author's use of an archaic or dialectal element for reasons of style (e.g., to color characters' speech), we must follow one primary, common-sense principle: the linguistic element cannot be too far removed in time or dialectal geography to be unintelligible to the audience (see also Rendsburg 1996:178–80). Consider, for instance, the prologue in Beowulf:

Beowulf, *Prologue* (c. 1000 C.E.)

Hwæt! Wé Gárdena in géardagum,	Listen! We—of the Spear-Danes in the days of yore
þéodcyninga, þrym gefrnon,	of those clan-kings—heard of their glory,
hú ðá æþelingas ellen fremedon.	how those nobles performed courageous deeds.

Diacritically Marked Text of Beowulf, facing a New Translation *(with explanatory notes), edited and translated by Benjamin Slade (http://www.heorot.dk/beo-intro-rede. html)*

In this selection only the preposition "in" could be used one thousand years later, in a modern novel, for instance, with the expectation that the average reader would understand it. Roughly four centuries later, the language of Chaucer is considerably more intelligible to the modern English reader:

Geoffrey Chaucer, *Cantebury Tales, The Miller's Tale* (14th c. C.E.)

Whilom ther was dwellynge at Oxenford	A while ago there dwelt at Oxford
A riche gnof, that gestes heeld to bord,	a rich churl fellow, who took guests as boarders.
And of his craft he was a carpenter.	He was a carpenter by trade.
With hym ther was dwellynge a poure scoler,	With him dwelt a poor scholar

Hadde lerned art, but al his fantasye	who had studied the liberal arts, but all his delight
Was turned for to lerne astrologye,	was turned to learning astrology,
And koude a certeyn of conclusiouns,	He knew how to work out
To demen by interrogaciouns,	certain problems; for instance,
If that men asked hym, in certein houres	if men asked him at certain celestial hours
Whan that men sholde have droghte or elles shoures,	when there should be drought or rain,
Or if men asked hym what sholde bifalle	or what should happen in any matter;
Of every thyng; I may nat rekene hem alle.	I cannot count every one.

Text and translation from eChaucer (http://www.umm.maine.edu/faculty/necastro/chaucer)

In a culture for which historical linguistic investigation was presumably unknown, the principle of immediate intelligibility holds all the more so. In other words, whereas modern authors may carefully research the history or dialectal variation of modern English in order to use elements that stretch intelligibility (analogous to James Joyce's use of code-switching; see Gordon and Williams 1998), we have no evidence that the ancient Hebrew authors had such data at their disposal. Thus, it is unlikely that the forms available to color a characters' speech—that is, forms that were perceived to be "older," not simply forms that were archaic and still in use—could have been at a greater temporal distance than one or two generations or a greater dialectal distance than the bordering peoples (i.e., Moabite, Edomite, Ammonite, or Phoenician, and Aramaic in the Persian period with its rise as a *lingua franca*).

The implications of this principle for the language of Ruth is that the forms that I suggest below as examples of style-shifting for the purpose of characterizing the speech of Noʻomi, Ruth, or Boaz may be "archaic" from the standpoint of the author and audience, or from a slightly different dialect related to Hebrew, but in neither case could they be too far removed. If we allow the author some linguistic creativity, though, it is also quite possible that the forms are manufactured and have no direct relationship to real historical or dialectal forms. That is, taking the author's and audience's language as the base, the author may have derived a few fictional forms, intelligible but noticeably odd, in order to set apart Boaz' and No'omi's speech. Too many would have been distracting, though, which explains the low frequency of the forms I list below.

Note that the literary use of words from other languages must be distinguished from borrowing (discussed in §3). The switch to another language, whether for single items used for impact (e.g., Job 3:8) or an entire phrase or chapters (e.g., Dan 2:4–7:28), is called "code-switching" or "code-mixing." If the switch is not to another language but to a different register (e.g., literary, formal versus colloquial) or dialect (e.g,. northern vs. southern Hebrew) of the same language, it is called "style-shifting" (Gordon and Williams 1998; Herman 2001). Since the narrator never switches to a different language (or least discernibly so) in Ruth but rather manipulates the grammatical fringes of Hebrew—especially in the speeches of No'omi and Boaz—the examples I discuss below and in the commentary should be considered style-shifting.

Listed below are the seven most likely examples of style-shifting in the book of Ruth (other possible examples are noted in the course of the commentary).

Cases of Style-Shifting in the Book of Ruth

1. Gender "confusion": As I noted in §3, there are a number of pronouns and pronominal suffixes, as well as one *qatal* verb (1:8, 9, 11, 13, 19, 22; 4:11) that are interpretable, but only marginally so, since they do not seem to match the gender of the obvious antecedents. Instead of a dialectal peculiarity or cases of a supposed feminine dual, I suggest that the narrator has used marginal—but understandable—language to give the book a foreign (Moabit-ish?) or perhaps archaic (i.e., "back in those days they talked funny") coloring. It is noteworthy that the majority of instances occur in reported speech (mostly

No'omi's) and all but one are in the first chapter of the book, in which the setting for the entire story is established.

2. The first word in 1:13, הֲלָהֵן, is often included in the list of possible Aramaic borrowings. I have not, though, because I consider it an example of the "gender confusion" noted above in #1. As it stands, it appears to be the combination of the interrogative ה, the preposition ל, and the 3fp suffix. Contextually the 3fp suffix makes no sense since the obvious referent are the potential sons that No'omi could bear. Like most of the items listed in #1, הֲלָהֵן is in the mouth of No'omi and so, I suggest, finds its proper explanation as manipulation of language in order to characterize No'omi's speech as a bit different than the audience's.

3. Although in the great majority of cases it is No'omi's or Boaz' speech that is set apart from the audience's, there are a few cases in which the narrator "reminds" the audience by linguistic cues that Ruth is a foreigner (her Moabite status is also kept in the foreground by the repeated use of the gentilic המאביה). In 2:2 the narrator places a unique collocation in Ruth's mouth: וַאֲלַקֳטָה בַשִׁבֳּלִים. As I discuss in the commentary, this verb elsewhere takes an accusative complement, but here I suggest that the story-teller uses slightly different grammar in the mouth of Ruth as a sign of her slightly different dialect or Moabite understanding of Hebrew.

4. The grammatical mess at the end of 2:7, שִׁבְתָּהּ הַבַּיִת מְעָט, is often emended creatively to produce something translatable. But, following Hurvitz 1982 and Rendsburg 1999, I take the overseer's confused language as a reflection of his nervousness. In other words, the end of the verse is not grammatical Hebrew and intentionally so.

5. In 2:8 the verb תַעֲבוּרִי is given an unexpectedly "long" spelling: the expected form of this verb is תַעֲבְרִי and the /û/ in the penultimate syllable is unusual. Consonantally the verb looks like a pausal form, but the vocalization of pausal forms is with an /o/ in the stressed penultimate syllable. I suggest that the vowel was intentionally odd, although intelligible, to set off Boaz' speech from the audience's. This may also be the explanation behind the collocation of דבק and עם in

2:8, 21—the verb דבק typically takes ב for its oblique complement and only here in Ruth, in Boaz' speech, does דבק עם occur.

6. Five times a *yiqtol* verb is used with the so-called paragogic ן; three times the verb is in the mouth of Boaz (2:8, 9, 21 [as quoted by Ruth]) and twice in the mouth of No'omi (3:4, 18). As with the other examples listed, the use of a known but rare (and possibly no-longer-used) verbal form in the mouths of the two "older" characters is not likely a mistake or coincidence.

7. I have argued against taking the Ketiv forms of two verbs, ירדתי in 3:3 and שכבתי in 3:4, as archaic remnants. Can it be a coincidence that both forms stand at the end of a four-verb sequence within one verse of each other and are both put in the mouth of No'omi? I suggest that the forms are placed in No'omi's mouth to color her speech. As for the archaic appearance of the forms, I find it highly unlikely that the narrator could have had access to knowledge of historical forms no longer in use. Rather, it is simply coincidental that the תי- forms in 3:3, 4 resemble what we reconstruct as their histories (this is also true of תעבורי in 2:8).

These seven features are, in my opinion, best understood as part of the story-teller's creativity and linguistic artistry. And yet they are not simply literary window-dressing. It is no accident that five of the seven features are in the mouths of No'omi and Boaz, while only one is used in Ruth's speech. The narrator sets up a light "linguistic curtain" with the audience on one side and No'omi and Boaz on the other. The implication is that, while the audience is reminded throughout the Ruth is a foreigner, they are also encouraged, by linguistic means, to identify with her. Although No'omi is the story's protagonist and her redemption is an important theological message, Ruth is the heroine of the story, and it is her courage and loyalty that the audience is encouraged to take in the most deeply. No'omi may have been refilled by God, but God has provided for Ruth across cultural and political boundaries—an important reminder for the Israelites at many historical points.

ACT I

The book of Ruth breaks easily into four acts, neatly corresponding to the four chapters. In the first act of the book, chapter 1, we are provided with all the necessary information for us to identify the main characters (with only Boaz left until chapter 2), understand the problem, and empathize with protagonist's plight. The first act itself may be divided into three scenes.

Act I, Scene 1: A Bethlehemite Tragedy in Moab (vv. 1-5)

The first scene consists of vv. 1-5, which establish the historical period internal to the story, introduce us to Elimelek and his family, and move us from Israel to Moab, a move that hints at impending tragedy (movement away from the "promised land" is always a harbinger of bad things in the Hebrew Bible). Appropriately, then, this first scene includes the death of both Elimelek and his two sons, depriving No'omi of her family and means of living. Thus, the central problem of the plot structure is firmly established.

¹When the chieftains ruled there was a famine in the land. So, a certain man from Bethlehem of Judah went to live in the territory of Moab, he, his wife, and his two sons. ²The name of the man was Elimelek and the name of his wife was No'omi and names of his two sons were Mahlon and Kilyon—they were Ephrathites from Bethlehem of Judah. So they entered the territory of Moab and remained there. ³Then Elimelek, the husband of No'omi, died, and she was left alone, she and her two sons. ⁴They took for themselves Moabite wives—the name of the first was 'Orpah and the name of the second was Ruth—and they dwelt there about ten years. ⁵Then the two of them, Mahlon and Kilyon, also died, and the woman was left without her two children and without her husband.

וַיְהִי בִּימֵי שְׁפֹט הַשֹּׁפְטִים וַיְהִי רָעָב בָּאָרֶץ וַיֵּלֶךְ   1:1
אִישׁ מִבֵּית לֶחֶם יְהוּדָה לָגוּר בִּשְׂדֵי מוֹאָב הוּא
וְאִשְׁתּוֹ וּשְׁנֵי בָנָיו:

The initial verse of the book establishes the time-frame and place
in which the events are set, regardless whether the events described
are historical or not. It is likely that the redundancy in "the days of
the judging of the judges," instead of simply "the days of the judges,"
is meant to emphasize that the following story takes place during the
general chaos of the period preceding the establishment of the monar-
chy (Younger 2002:412; Nielsen 1997:40).

וַיְהִי בִּימֵי שְׁפֹט הַשֹּׁפְטִים. *Wayyiqtol* 3ms Qal √היה with
oblique PP complement, בִּימֵי שְׁפֹט הַשֹּׁפְטִים. Although the verb
היה "to be" does not take an accusative complement, it does require
a nominative or oblique complement: it is rarely used in the one-place
predicate sense of Shakespeare's "to be or not to be." The verb היה
often takes either referential subjects, such as NPs like רָעָב in the very
next clause, or proper nouns (e.g, Noah in Gen 5:32); however, it also
can select a null expletive subject, which we translate with the English
expletive "it" or sometimes "there." So, in this first clause in Ruth the
English is "It was in the days of . . . ," whereas the formal subject of
the Hebrew ויהי is a null expletive ∅ (i.e., Hebrew does not require
something like הוא or זה to be present as the expletive subject).

ויהי followed by a temporal phrase (often with an inf constr,
as we have here בִּימֵי שְׁפֹט הַשֹּׁפְטִים) is a typical construction for
establishing the time and/or place of a new narrative section (see Josh
1.1; Judg 1.1; 2 Sam 1.1; Ezek 1.1). Moreover the *wayyiqtol* in general (not just ויהי) begins the books of Leviticus, Numbers, Joshua,
Judges, 1 Samuel, 2 Samuel, 2 Kings, Ezekiel, Jonah, and 2 Chronicles, and many lower level narrative units (e.g., Gen 6:1, 11:1; 14:1;
17:1; 22:1; 26:1; 27:1; 38:1, among many more, at various narrative
levels). Even so, Campbell notes that the sequence of ויהי followed
by the phrase בימי occurs at the beginning of a book only here and in

Esther. Furthermore, he indicates that the phrase ויהי בימי in Esther (and in instances where it does not begin a book, e.g., Gen 14:1; Isa 7:1; Jer 1:3) is followed by the name of an individual; only here, in Ruth, is the phrase בימי ויהי followed by a more general referent, in this case an activity, "the judges' judging" (Campbell 1974:49). Since there is a reasonable chance that any given construction will have one or more unique features, particularly in light of the limited corpus of BH, we should not make too much of the uniqueness of the initial clause in Ruth 1:1. As I have pointed out, using ויהי at a narrative onset, whether at a book's beginning or a lower level of an episodic beginning, is not rare. Additionally, the phrase בימי can be followed by either a proper noun, a common noun (e.g., Ps 37:19; 49:6; Qoh 12:1), or even an activity or event (Gen 30:14; Judg 15:1; 2 Sam 21:9; Chr 26:5). Thus, while the sum of the parts in the first clause in Ruth 1:1 may be unique, there is little that is exceptional about its parts.

While the initial clause in Ruth may not be unique from a grammatical perspective, we must still determine why the *wayyiqtol*, which is often thought to be at least loosely related to temporal sequence (i.e., following a previous action or event), is used to begin any narrative. Two logical options present themselves for understanding the use of this type of verb at the beginning of a book or major narrative section: 1) either each book or unit was written as a continuation of what was perceived to precede it (e.g., Joshua continues from Deuteronomy, Judges from Joshua, 2 Chronicles from 1 Chronicles; see GKC §49b n. 1), or 2) the form ויהי, most often followed by a temporal PP, was associated with establishing scene-setting at narrative onset and is not tightly bound to a sense of temporal succession (for more on this, see comment below on v. 6).

Regarding the former option, it is not transparent what, say, Jonah would "continue," and while it might seem for Christian readers that Ruth naturally follows Judges, in much of Jewish tradition and all extant Hebrew manuscripts, Ruth does not follow Judges but appears in the "Writings," and depending on the specific tradition either follows Song of Songs (most printed Hebrew Bibles before 1937), Proverbs (the Leningrad Codex), or heads up this third part of the Jewish canon (cf. the Talmudic text, Baba Bathra 14b). Thus we are left with the scene-setting use of וַיְהִי, which, as Longacre and Hwang assert, is the type of "presentative formula" that "we might expect at the beginning of books and sections" (1994:341).

וַיְהִי. Note the omission of the *dagesh hazaq* in the prefix of the *wayyiqtol*; this reflects the common omission of the *dagesh hazaq* in sibilants and the consonants וילמנק when a *shewa* is under the consonant; see GKC §20m; JM §18m.

בִּימֵי. Note the *dagesh qal* in the בּ even though it follows a vowel (i.e., the final syllable of וַיְהִי is a CV syllable); the *dagesh qal* is due to the Masoretic assignment of a disjunctive accent (the *revi'i*) to וַיְהִי (GKC §21b; JM §19c).

הַשֹּׁפְטִים. Participle mpl Qal √שפט. The participle/agentive noun שׁוֹפֵט is derived from the verbal root שׁפט, variously glossed "to arbitrate, pass judgment, administer justice, rule, govern" (HALOT s.v.; cf. BDB s.v.). Thus, the nominal form is overwhelmingly rendered as "judge" in ancient (LXX: κριτας; Vul: *iudices*; Pesh: ܕ,) and modern translations (KJV, JPS, NIV, NRSV; cf. TEV). However, a שׁוֹפֵט rarely arbitrates or otherwise acts judicially; instead, the שׁוֹפֵט leads during military crises and otherwise governs generally. Similarly, the gloss "to govern, be in authority" fits a number of uses of the verbal form of שׁפט. So, here in Ruth, and in most other similar cases, a more accurate rendering of the phrase בִּימֵי שְׁפֹט הַשֹּׁפְטִים is "when the chieftains ruled" (see Easterly 1997).

וַיְהִי רָעָב בָּאָרֶץ. *Wayyiqtol* 3ms Qal √היה. This clause follows the initial stage-setting temporal reference with a somewhat blunt introduction of the famine. This statement should be taken simply as the inclusion of a necessary device to set up the sojourn of Elimelek's family; it is possible that it is also meant as an intertextual link back to the patriarchs' experiences with famine (Gen 12:10; 26:1). It does not, though, contain an implicit judgment on the morality or faithfulness of people in Judah at this period because nowhere later does the book bring up this topic.

וַיְהִי רָעָב בָּאָרֶץ. *Wayyiqtol* - Subject NP - oblique PP complement. This is the most common word order in BH narrative (indeed, a slight variation, *wayyiqtol* - Subject NP - PP/inf constr, occurs in the very next clause). As I describe in §2, however, the V-S order itself is derived from a basic S-V order because whatever the gemination in the *wayyiqtol* used to be (it is now unrecoverable), it triggered the S-V-to-V-S inversion.

וַ. The coordination of this clause with the preceding clause illustrates how BH uses parataxis much more often than, say, literary English. Parataxis is the juxtaposition of clauses without any grammatical marker of a formal relationship. Technically, this would exclude coordination, and since the וֹ in Hebrew often serves minimally to mark clause boundaries, we must not assume that it always indicates coordination. In fact, many Hebraists would suggest that the syntactic-semantic relationship between two clauses "joined" by a וֹ must be "interpreted" based on the context; hence, the וֹ does nothing more than mark the beginning of the second of the two clauses. Perhaps Hubbard is correct in asserting about ויהי רעב בארץ that "though a separate sentence in form, it functions (i.e. in its "deep grammar") as the main clause for the preceding temporal clause" (Hubbard, 84, n. 8), thus "When the chieftains ruled, there was a famine in the land," so that the first temporal reference is broader and the second is more specific.

בָּאָרֶץ. This common noun, "earth, country, territory, region," is quite often used to connote the Cisjordan or Israel (see Judg 18:2; 1 Sam 14:29).

וַיֵּלֶךְ אִישׁ מִבֵּית לֶחֶם יְהוּדָה לָגוּר בִּשְׂדֵי מוֹאָב הוּא וְאִשְׁתּוֹ וּשְׁנֵי בָנָיו. This clause contains a significant irony. Due to the famine in Israel, someone from the town named "House of Bread" had to leave to find provision as na alien in a foreign land.

וַיֵּלֶךְ. *Wayyiqtol* 3ms Qal √הלך. The verb הלך does not take complements, but is often followed by an adjunct (mostly PPs) indi-

cating origin or goal. Note the word stress on הָלַךְ. According to the
Masoretic tradition, the word stress of many *wayyiqtol* forms, which
is normally on the final syllable, recedes one syllable. A number of
conditions must be met for this to happen 1) the penultimate syllable
must be open (i.e., a CV structure); 2) the ultimate syllable must be
closed (i.e., a CVC structure); and 3) the vowel in the penultimate
syllable (i.e., under the prefix consonant of the *yiqtol* in the *wayyiqtol*)
must be a *qamets, tsere,* or *hiriq*. There are a number of environments
in which all of these conditions are met but the stress retraction does
not occur; cf. JM §47b-d, 69d, 79m-n.

מִבֵּית לֶחֶם יְהוּדָה. This adjunct PP either modifies the verb
("he walked from Bethlehem") or the man ("a man from Bethlehem").
Although the syntax is formally ambiguous in that there are no explicit
linguistic clues for preferring one option over the other, there is a tendency in Hebrew narrative to introduce a man with reference to his
place of origin, his name, and often with at least one generation of his
ancestry (see 1 Sam 1:1, Job 1:1, and most of the prophetic books; cf.
Hubbard 1988:83, n. 2). This pattern suggests that the PP in Ruth 1:1
should be taken as a nominal modifier, i.e., "a man from Bethlehem"
(so Andersen 1974:90; contra Bush 1996:62–63).

בֵּית לֶחֶם יְהוּדָה. This collocation of two proper nouns (PNs)
represents one of the few exceptions to the general avoidance of PNs
as the first item in a construct phrase (GKC §125a-h; JM §131n-o,
137b). We see this particularly with place names that are referentially
ambiguous (i.e., they are two or more sites with the same name, such
as "Rabbah of the Ammonites" in Deut 3:11; 2 Sam 12:26; 17:27; Jer
49:2; Ezek 21:25). There was more than one town named Bethlehem
(see Josh 19:15 for Bethlehem in the tribal region of Zebulun), and so
the author/narrator specifies this one as "Bethlehem of Judah."

לָגוּר. Inf constr of √גור. The infinitive phrase serves as another
adjunct to the verb הָלַךְ. With monosyllabic hosts, such as the inf
constr of II-ו roots, pronominal suffixes, or nominals like זֶה, the
Masoretes often vocalized the enclitic prepositions (לְ, כְּ, בְּ) as well as

the conjunction וֹ, not with the more common *shewa* (e.g., לְהַקְטִיל)
or *hiriq* (e.g., לִשְׁמֹר), but with a *qamets*, as in לָגוּר. This phenomenon
also sometimes pertains to bisyllabic nouns that have penultimate
word stress, e.g., וָבֹהוּ (Gen 1:2).

בִּשְׂדֵי מוֹאָב. This PP is an adjunct to the inf constr גוּר. The
qatal-pattern noun שָׂדֶה, "field, territory," is apparently based on two
different triconsonantal roots, resulting in two different forms in the
singular (it also has two different forms in the plural, but not for the
same reason). The precise shapes of the singular free ("absolute") form
and the clitic ("construct") form depend on whether a given occurrence of the word is based on √שׂדה or the √שׂדי. With the III-ה
root, the singular free form is שָׂדֶה and the clitic form is שְׂדֵה; with
the III-י root, the singular free form is שָׂדַי (which is the form that
strongly suggests an underlying *qatal* pattern) and the clitic form is
שְׂדֵי. This alternation can be especially confusing when the context
is not clear if the form שְׂדֵי is the singular of the III-י root or simply
the expected masculine plural clitic form of either root (an additional
plural clitic form is שְׂדוֹת). See JM §96Bf for a discussion of this root
and its morphological type.

In the book of Ruth, forms based on both the III-ה and the III-י
roots appear: the III-ה form שָׂדֶה in 1:6; 2:6; 4:3 and the III-י form
in 1:1, 2, 6, 22. Since the form שָׂדֶה, with the final ה, never represents the plural, it would seem that both forms should be taken as the
singular clitic form "in the territory of Moab" for this book, a conclusion that also accords with the LXX translator's rendering of all the
occurrences with the singular ἀγρός (Myers 1955:9; cf. Bush 1996:63;
contra Hubbard 1988:86, n. 15; 97, n. 3).

הוּא. The use of the personal pronoun to "pick up" the initial
subject of the verb and allow the addition of other referents (i.e., "his
wife and two sons") is syntactically complex (see Holmstedt 2009b).
In some cases there is no initial subject NP, making it tempting to take
such conjoined NPs as the syntactic subject of the verb. In the clause
here not only is there already a syntactic subject (אִישׁ), but the 3ms

verb does not agree with the later conjoined subject, which is plural. Both the presence of an explicit subject and the agreement features of the verb suggest that the conjoined NP in this case and perhaps in most other cases are adjuncts to the verb, added at the end of the clause to further specify or clarify the syntactic subject (Naudé 1999, Holmstedt 2009b). In terms of function, the use of a singular constituent (אִישׁ in this verse) for the *syntactic* subject but a conjoined NP (הוּא וְאִשְׁתּוֹ וּשְׁנֵי בָנָיו in this verse) for the *semantic* subject serves both to allow one agent/patient to be at the center of the narrative progression and to include more than one agent/patient in the events (see Revell 1993, de Regt 1996).

וּשְׁנֵי בָנָיו. The numeral bound as a clitic to the count noun technically results in two possibilities: "two of his sons (out of more than two)" and "his two sons (out of two)." The latter interpretation is the contextually determined favorite; for the rare former option, see 1 Sam 10:3-4, where two loaves of bread are given from a total of three.

1:2 וְשֵׁם הָאִישׁ אֱלִימֶ֫לֶךְ וְשֵׁם אִשְׁתּוֹ נָעֳמִי וְשֵׁם שְׁנֵי־בָנָיו מַחְלוֹן וְכִלְיוֹן אֶפְרָתִים מִבֵּית לֶחֶם יְהוּדָה וַיָּבֹאוּ שְׂדֵי־מוֹאָב וַיִּהְיוּ־שָׁם:

Here the Bethlehemites who went to Moab are named. Moreover, the narrator makes a point of mentioning that this was no overnight trip—they went to Moab to live.

וְשֵׁם הָאִישׁ אֱלִימֶ֫לֶךְ וְשֵׁם אִשְׁתּוֹ נָעֳמִי וְשֵׁם שְׁנֵי־בָנָיו מַחְלוֹן וְכִלְיוֹן אֶפְרָתִים מִבֵּית לֶחֶם יְהוּדָה. Departure from the use of the *wayyiqtol*, in this case by the use of a null-copula clause (see §2.1), is a marked linguistic strategy within Hebrew narrative and it may convey any number of discourse signals. In this case, the departure signals the addition of background information: the audience is finally given the names and clan association of the characters

introduced in v. 1. Note that the constituent order is Subject NP
- Predicate NP (so too in each of the two subsequent null-copula
clauses), which is the expected order in pragmatically neutral null-
copula clauses.

אֱלִימֶ֫לֶךְ. Many Hebrew names are compounds consisting of
a theophoric (i.e., divine name) element and a common noun. Quite
often the first element has an י ending, which has been explained as
either a 1cs suffix, e.g., אֱלִימֶ֫לֶךְ "my god is (the) king," or a remnant
of the genitive case from an earlier stage of Hebrew, e.g., מַלְכִּי־צֶ֫דֶק
"king of righteousness." If the י is sometimes a remnant of the case
system in pre-biblical Hebrew, it rarely suggests a genitive nuance in
BH (does אֱלִימֶ֫לֶךְ as a noun make good sense as "god of (the) king"?).
See GKC §90k-l; Bauer-Leander §65; WO §8.2c; JM §93l-m.

נָעֳמִי. When a name, like נָעֳמִי, ends with the י but lacks the
second, often theophoric, element, quite often we are dealing with an
abbreviated form (Fowler 1988:149–69). Thus, it is possible that נָעֳמִי,
derived from the noun נֹ֫עַם "pleasantness, kindness," is an abbreviated
version of נַעֲמִיָּה, "kindness of Yah(weh)" or even "kind (woman) of
Yah(weh)"; alternatively, if the י is a 1cs possessive suffix, then the name
would mean "my pleasant one" (see Hubbard 1988:88–89). Note that,
in contrast to the English pronunciation (inherited through the Greek
tradition) and according to the Masoretic vocalization, the name נָעֳמִי
No'omi has no /a/ vowel; rather, the two *qamets* vowels are both the
/u/-class *qamets hatuf* (also know as *qamets qatan*).

וְשֵׁם שְׁנֵי־בָנָיו מַחְלוֹן וְכִלְיוֹן. The use of the singular שֵׁם
as the subject in the null-copula clause with a compound predicate,
מחלון וכליון, is at first glance grammatically awkward. It is possible
that this lack of Subject-Predicate agreement was deliberately employed
as a rhetorical device, whereby the two sons were presented as a unit.
In other words, neither of the two sons is presented as an individual
character; they serve only as a pair for the sake of allowing their two
wives to enter the narrative.

מַחְלוֹן ... כִּלְיוֹן. The names of the two sons both have an וֹן-suffix, which WO describe as used for adjective, abstract substantives, and diminutives (§5.7b; see JM §88Mf). Thus, מַחְלוֹן, which is apparently from √חלה "to be sick, ill," might be "Sickling" and כִּלְיוֹן, which is apparently from √כלה "to stop, be finished, vanish, fade away," might be "Weakling." (Sasson also suggests that מחלון might be from √מחל, which does not appear in Hebrew but means "sterile" in Arabic [18].) Unless Elimelek and No'omi had a cruel sense of humor, these names appear to have been constructed for the narrative as foreshadowing devices: these boys aren't going to last very long (Younger 2002:415, n. 18; contra Hubbard 1988:90). However, Bush is right in noting that the narrator makes no explicit play on the meaning of names except for No'omi's (1996:63); and yet, this only makes sense since the other characters named in the verse are quickly killed off by the narrator!

אֶפְרָתִים מִבֵּית לֶחֶם יְהוּדָה. It is syntactically possible to take both the plural gentilic noun, אפרתים (singular אֶפְרָתִי; on gentilics see GKC §86h; JM §88Mg; WO §5.7c, 7.2.2), and the PP מבית יהודה לחם as appositional to the just-named characters. Apposition is the juxtaposition of two nouns or noun phrases that have the same referent and the same syntactic function, e.g., subject, complement, adjunct (WO §12.1; JM §131). However, such an analysis would mean that only Mahlon and Kilyon are called Ephrathites, ignoring Elimelek's familial origin. It is more logical to take all three as the antecedents, making this a null subject, null copula clause, "(they) (were) Ephrathites from Bethlehem of Judah." The modifier אפרתים provides the clan, or מִשְׁפָּחָה, of Elimelek's family, which is then followed by the more general town and region references (see Bush 1996:64–65, and sources cited there, for discussion). The language here is quite close to the description of David as וְדָוִד בֶּן־אִישׁ אֶפְרָתִי הַזֶּה מִבֵּית לֶחֶם יְהוּדָה in 1 Sam 17:12; it is reasonable, if not likely, that this was meant to evoke precisely this connection, foreshadowing one of the primary outcomes of the story signaled in the concluding genealogy (see Bush 1996:65).

וַיָּבֹאוּ שְׂדֵי־מוֹאָב‏. *Wayyiqtol* 3mpl Qal √בוא with complement
NP. This clause resumes the narrative from v. 1 and succinctly provides
the conclusion of their trip to Moab: they arrived. The use of a *wayyiqtol*
clause shifts from the narrative background to the narrative foreground
by resuming the narrative progression and plot development. The
NP שדי מואב functions as the complement of the verb ויבאו, which
mostly takes oblique PP complements specifying either the destination
(often with אל or ב) or origin (mostly with מן) of movement. In Ruth
the verb בוא is used with the preposition אל four times: 3:16, 17; 4:11,
13. However, this verb also takes the accusative complement (explicit or
implicit) for the destination of movement thirteen times: Ruth 1:2, 19
(2x), 22; 2:3, 7, 12, 18; 3:4, 7 (2x), 14, 15.

וַיִּהְיוּ־שָׁם‏. *Wayyiqtol* 3mpl Qal √היה. This clause concisely
indicates that once they arrived, they stayed. The most common
meaning of the verb היה is simply "to be, become, happen." One of
the lesser used nuances, though, is "to remain, live" (HALOT, s.v.;
BDB, s.v.; cf. Dan 1:1; Judg 17:12; Exod 34:28). Note that while most
often the locative adverb שם is an adjunct, here it should probably be
analyzed as an oblique (i.e., non-accusative) complement of היה (see
§2.2 and comment on v. 1).

1:3   וַיָּמָת אֱלִימֶלֶךְ אִישׁ נָעֳמִי וַתִּשָּׁאֵר הִיא וּשְׁנֵי בָנֶיהָ:

The individual whose actions initiated the action of the story is
now killed off. His death, of course, sets up the primary complication
of the plot: No'omi is bereft of her primary source of support.

וַיָּמָת אֱלִימֶלֶךְ אִישׁ נָעֳמִי‏. *Wayyiqtol* 3ms Qal √מות. While
it might have been Israelite convention to qualify a woman's name
by her relational status, as in v. 2 where No'omi is referred to as "his
(i.e., Elimelek's) wife" (Bush 1996:68), it is unlikely that males were
typically identified as their wives' husbands, as we have here. The
mention of No'omi here moves the focus of the narrative from the
family patriarch to No'omi, who becomes the central figure in the
narrative from this point on.

וַתִּשָּׁאֵר הִיא וּשְׁנֵי בָנֶיהָ. *Wayyiqtol* 3fs Niph. See v. 5, where the same verb is collocated with מִן. The narrative continues with a *wayyiqtol* clause. In this case, it presents the outcome of Elimelek's death.

הִיא. As I noted on v. 1 a conjoined NP like הִיא וּשְׁנֵי בניה is not the syntactic subject of the singular verb. Rather, the syntactic subject is unexpressed (as is often in the case of Hebrew) and the compound NP הִיא וּשְׁנֵי בניה is an adjunct that was added to specify "who was left." In contrast to the strategy in v. 1, where there is an overt singular syntactic subject (הָאִישׁ), here the absence of an overt syntactic subject followed by the compound NP as an adjunct suggests that the No'omi and her sons were viewed as a semantic unit, i.e., they *all* were left alone (see Naudé 1999, Holmstedt 2009b).

1:4 וַיִּשְׂאוּ לָהֶם נָשִׁים מֹאֲבִיּוֹת שֵׁם הָאַחַת עָרְפָּה וְשֵׁם הַשֵּׁנִית רוּת וַיֵּשְׁבוּ שָׁם כְּעֶשֶׂר שָׁנִים:

We are given no indication of the elapsed time between Elimelek's death and the marriages of his sons. The absence of such temporal indications strongly suggests that that information is irrelevant for the plot or character development within the world of the narrative.

וַיִּשְׂאוּ לָהֶם נָשִׁים מֹאֲבִיּוֹת. *Wayyiqtol* 3mpl Qal √נשׂא (on the adjunct and complement, see notes below). Note the lack of the expected *dagesh* representing the assimilation of the נ to the שׂ; see under ויהי in v. 1. The subject of the verb, the two sons, is implied and easily retrievable from the context. Note also that נשׂא אשה is idiomatic for "taking a wife," and interestingly, this collocation only occurs in Chronicles, Ezra, and Nehehmiah, i.e., post-exilic works. This is one of the linguistic items that is commonly used to date the book to the post-exilic period (Bush 1996:26), but it is not a particularly strong point (Campbell 1975:25; Hubbard 1988:93 n. 9; Zevit 2005:592–93). See §3 concerning the issue of dating BH texts by linguistic means.

לָהֶם. This use of the ל preposition is typically referred to as the "dative of advantage" or some similar term, like "benefactive dative" (WO §11.2.10d; see also GKC §119s; JM §133d). In terms of argument structure, the PP לָהֶם is an adjunct. Note that the adjunct PP is placed closer to the verb than the complement נָשִׁים. This occurs also with phrases using the accusative אֵת with pronominal suffixes (see, e.g., Muraoka 1985:44–45; JM §155t). A likely explanation—and one that is attested cross-linguistically—concerns the phonological "weight" of the phrases: when direct and indirect objects have suffix forms, they are "phonologically light," and they raise with the verb; when the full NP phrases are used they are phonologically "heavy" and they remain in the normal positions further down the clause. Only when these "light" phrases are focused do they remain in the original position toward the end of the clause (see, e.g., Gen 25:31; 29:24; 34:16; Ruth 4:12, 13).

מֹאֲבִיּוֹת. This is the feminine plural gentilic modifier, "Moabite"; here it further defines the common noun נָשִׁים, producing "Moabite wives."

שֵׁם הָאַחַת עָרְפָּה וְשֵׁם הַשֵּׁנִית רוּת. In this verse we are finally introduced to the heroine of the story, Ruth, as well as her foil, Orpah. As with the first set of names provided in v. 2, we have here the departure from the use of a *wayyiqtol* clause by the use of a null-copula clause in order to provide background information.

הָאַחַת. The numeral אֶחָד (m) / אַחַת (f) is used as both the cardinal and ordinal, and in either case the modified noun may be elided, leaving the numeral to function as a substantive (WO §15.2.1b, JM §100a-b, 142b; HALOT s.v., BDB s.v.).

עָרְפָּה ... רוּת. Orpah's name is sometimes connected with עֹרֶף "top of the head, neck" (HALOT, s.v.) and also with biblical phrases referring to "turning one's neck" (i.e., turning back in shame, turning one's back on someone to leave) (Hubbard 1988:94 n. 14). If so, then this wife's name carries an implicit judgment on her decision to leave Noʿomi and return to Moab (v. 14). For the name רוּת the proposed etymological links are fewer and more strained; Hubbard suggests "refreshment, satiation, comfort" from √רוה (Hubbard 1988:94). In both cases the names' possible etymologies may or may not have an intended role in the narrative. If there were an intended role, it cannot have been significant since the author nowhere uses the names explicitly in the characterization of the women.

וַיֵּשְׁבוּ שָׁם כְּעֶשֶׂר שָׁנִים. *Wayyiqtol* 3mpl Qal √ישׁב with oblique complement שָׁם and adjunct PP כעשׂר שׁנים. We are given little explanation for the inclusion of this temporal statement. The verb ישׁב typically takes some sort of complement, whether in the accusative or oblique case (see also 2:14, 23; 4:1a, b, 2a; in 3:18; 4:1c; 4:2b, the complement is assumed from the context). Thus, the locative adverb שָׁם is an oblique complement here (as it was with היה in v. 2) while the PP כעשׂר שׁנים is an adjunct. Note that the preposition כ, which is mostly used for comparison or correspondence, is in a few cases used for the related notion of approximation; thus, "about ten years" (WO §11.2.9b; JM §133g).

כְּעֶשֶׂר שָׁנִים. Following the statement of marriage and the introduction of the two wives, this temporal PP presumably references how long the family group lived in Moab after the two sons were married. However, this assumes that the *wayyiqtol*, וישׁבו, presents the next event after the marriage. It is also possible, though, that it presents a summary of the family's time in Moab since their initial immigration (see Campbell 1975:58; Hubbard 1988:91, n. 2; Sasson 1979:21; Sakenfeld 1999:20; Bush 1996:65; for a brief discussion of the "summary" use of the *wayyiqtol*, see the comment on v. 6, below).

1:5   וַיָּמוּתוּ גַם־שְׁנֵיהֶם מַחְלוֹן וְכִלְיוֹן וַתִּשָּׁאֵר הָאִשָּׁה
מִשְּׁנֵי יְלָדֶיהָ וּמֵאִישָׁהּ:

This verse continues with the removal of the male presence in No'mi's family. Her husband's death is presented in v. 3 and here her sons' deaths are included. In terms of plot development, the problem, No'omi's abandonment, is further complicated.

וַיָּמוּתוּ גַם־שְׁנֵיהֶם מַחְלוֹן וְכִלְיוֹן. *Wayyiqtol* 3mpl Qal √מות.
The syntactic subject of the verb וַיָּמוּתוּ is the first appropriate NP,
שְׁנֵיהֶם. The phrase is in turn modified appositionally by the proper
names of the two referents.

גַם. Syntactically, the גַם is functioning here as a "item adverb"
in that it modifies the NP שְׁנֵיהֶם and not the predicate or the entire
clause (see WO §39.3.1 on these distinctions). Semantically, גַם in this
clause specifies that the subject, שְׁנֵיהֶם, must be added to "something
or someone referred to in the preceding context" (MNK §41.4.5.2);
thus, the fact that "also" both of their sons died is added to what was
stated in v. 3, that the father, Elimelek, died. Pragmatically, the גַם
works here to mark שְׁנֵיהֶם as a Focus constituent. The membership
set established is implicit {both of them, one, the other, none}. The
impact here is to contrast what has happened with what could have
been case and to drive home that No'omi has experienced the worst
possible scenario.

וַתִּשָּׁאֵר הָאִשָּׁה מִשְּׁנֵי יְלָדֶיהָ וּמֵאִישָׁהּ. This clause mirrors
the statement made in v. 3 after the report of Elimelek's death. The
similarity of the two statements serves to reinforce No'omi's isolation
and contributes toward the tension of the unfolding plot.

וַתִּשָּׁאֵר. *Wayyiqtol* 3fs Niph. The collocation of שאר מן is not
common. Occasionally the preposition מִן conveys a privative nuance
(i.e., it marks what is missing or unavailable; see GKC §119w; WO
§11.2.11e[2]; HALOT s.v. √שאר). Thus, the combination of the
Niph verb שאר, "to be remain, be left over," with the privative use of
מן at the head of an adjunct PP results in the sense of "being left without (someone/thing)." To assert, though, that addition of the privative
מן "underscores the extent of Naomi's tragic loss" (Hubbard 96) is
stretching the grammar for the sake of a literary/theological point.

יְלָדֶיהָ. Assuming that the author did not use superfluous variation, it is perhaps significant that this verse refers to Mahlon and
Kilyon as יְלָדִים whereas in v. 3 בָּנִים is used. Given their status as
married men, the relational term בָּנִים would seem more appropriate

than יְלָדִים, which has age and social status connotations that make its application to married men somewhat dissonant. Many commentators suggest that the use of יְלָדִים in v. 5 points to the theme of children in the book and forms an inclusio with הַיֶּלֶד in 4:16 (Campbell 1975:56; Hubbard 1988:96; Bush 1996:66).

Act I, Scene 2: The Return to Judah (vv. 6-19a)

In this scene Noʿomi's journey back to her home in Bethlehem is itself a vehicle for introducing us to Ruth, whom we know only by name from v. 4. While Noʿomi is the protagonist of the story, Ruth is clearly the heroine. And vv. 6-19a establish a baseline for Ruth's character: loyalty, persistence, and kindness. The verbs שׁוּב "return" and הלך "go" are used with great literary artistry and set up the complication this scene adds to the plot: who will "go and return" to her family in Judah and who will "go and return" to her family in Moab? The use of these two verbs is mostly lost in translation but is clear to those working with the Hebrew.

6So she got up, she and her daughters-in-law, and returned from the territory of Moab because she had heard in the territory of Moab that Yhwh had cared for His people by giving food to them. 7Thus, she left the place where she had stayed, and her two daughters-in-law were with her, and they traveled along the road to return to the land of Judah. 8Then Noʿomi said to her two daughters-in-law, "Come now, return, each to the house of her mother. May Yhwh act kindly with you just as you have done with those who are dead and with me. 9May Yhwh give you . . . Find rest, each in the house of her next husband!" Then she kissed them and they lifted their voice and wept. 10But they said to her, "No! With you we will return, to your people!" 11And Noʿomi said, "Return, my daughters. Why would you go with me? Do I still have sons in my womb, that they could become husbands for you? 12Return, my daughters. Go, because I am too old to belong to a man, because even if I thought 'there is hope for me'—even if I both belonged to a man tonight and also bore sons, 13would you wait for them until they grew up? Would you keep yourselves for them by not belonging to another man? No, my daughters, because my bitter-

ness is too much for you, because the hand of Yhwh has come out against me." 14Then they raised their voice and wept again and ʿOrpah kissed her mother-in-law but Ruth clung to her. 15So she said, "Listen here—your sister-in-law has returned to her people and to her gods. Return after your sister-in-law. 16But Ruth said, "Do not press me to abandon you, to turn from going after you. Indeed, wherever you go, I will go, and wherever you lodge, I will lodge. Your people are my people and your god is my god. 17Wherever you die, I will die and there I will be buried. Thus may Yhwh do to me and so much more may He add. Indeed!—Only death will separate between me and you!" 18When she saw that she was determined to walk with her, she ceased speaking to her. 19aThen the both of them traveled until they entered Bethlehem.

1:6   וַתָּ֤קָם הִיא֙ וְכַלֹּתֶ֔יהָ וַתָּ֖שָׁב מִשְּׂדֵ֣י מוֹאָ֑ב כִּ֤י שָֽׁמְעָה֙
בִּשְׂדֵ֣ה מוֹאָ֔ב כִּֽי־פָקַ֤ד יְהוָה֙ אֶת־עַמּ֔וֹ לָתֵ֥ת לָהֶ֖ם
לָֽחֶם׃

This verse as a whole previews the action within the next scene. It leaves the details of the journey for the ensuing narrative but includes the second half of the verse to remind the audience that Yhwh is actively caring for his people. This establishes the framework in which the narrator wants the audience to process Noʿomi's attitude.

וַתָּ֤קָם ... וַתָּ֖שָׁב ... כִּ֤י שָֽׁמְעָה֙. These three clauses in this verse, all with 3fs verbs, mark the first time that Noʿomi is presented as an agent and not a recipient/patient/experiencer of a verbal action or event. With this verse the story-teller makes grammatically explicit what has already been hinted at in vv. 3 and 5: Noʿomi will serve as the central character of the ensuing plot developments.

וַתָּ֤קָם הִיא֙ וְכַלֹּתֶ֔יהָ. *Wayyiqtol* 3ms Qal √קום. Note the singular verb followed by the conjoined phrase consisting of a singular pronoun and a plural noun. Such constructions are often taken as examples of "first-conjunct agreement," in which the verb matches only the features of the nearest subject (see comments above on vv. 1,

3). Note, however, that the very next verb is also singular even *after* the full plural subject (all three women) has been specified. If we consider this type of clause together with the conjoined phrase type we saw above in v. 1, a unified picture begins to emerge. The verb in this clause has a covert syntactic subject, making the conjoined phrase an adjunct not a syntactic subject. The English translation provided above ("she got up, she and her daughters-in-law") illustrates how the syntax of the Hebrew works in a language that does not allow covert subjects in the same way as Hebrew does. The use of a covert subject with a singular verb signals either that a single character remains more prominent than any others who happened to be involved in the events or that the characters are functioning as a group entity. In this case, the former option makes best sense: although the narrator could not very well leave Ruth and Orpah behind, No'omi remains at center stage (see also Bush 1996:85).

וַתָּשָׁב מִשְׂדֵי מוֹאָב. *Wayyiqtol* 3fs Qal √שׁוב with a (locative) PP complement. Though the predominant use of a *wayyiqtol* clause is to carry the narrative forward (i.e., it presents temporally successive actions or events), it may also be used for summary statements, which may preview or review the main features of the episode being summarized (see also ויהיו in 1:2, ויהי in 2:17). More technically, Cook 2002 describes this as the ability to use *wayyiqtol* forms in "temporally overlaid expressions"; in other words, the event that a *wayyiqtol* references may itself include sub-events that are themselves described by *wayyiqtol* forms, occurring either before or after the *wayyiqtol* form that includes them all (see Cook 2002:258–60). With regard to ותשב in this verse, it is clear that this event of "returning" subsumes the events described by ותצא ... ותלכנה in the following verse, v. 7; thus, ותשב in v. 6 previews the next stage of the narrative. This clause brings to completion the event that began the story, the sojourn in Moab.

כִּי שָׁמְעָה בִּשְׂדֵה מוֹאָב כִּי־פָקַד יְהוָה אֶת־עַמּוֹ לָתֵת לָהֶם לָחֶם. *Qatal* 3fs Qal √שׁמע. The first כי clause presents the supporting evidence for the previous assertion (see MNK §40.9.II.2; JM §170da).

שָׁמְעָה ... כִּי. The function word כי has many semantic nuances and at least two primary synactic functions: 1) conjunction ("because, if, when," presenting a clause that is subordinate to a main clause, as we have in the first occurrence in v. 6), and 2) complementizer ("that"). In this second occurrence of כי in v. 6, it is functioning as a complementizer; in other words, it allows a clause to fulfill what is normally a nominal syntactic role, e.g., the accusative complement of a transitive verb.

פָּקַד. *Qatal* 3ms Qal √פקד. A basic meaning of the verbal root פקד is difficult to identify; in many cases it seems to indicate the act of noticing, looking at, or inspecting something, which is the meaning that HALOT (s.v. Qal 2) suggests for this verse. However, the infinitive phrase following the verb makes sense only if Yhwh's act of "looking" is more than a passing glance, but instead a "looking after" in the sense of "caring for."

כִּי־פָקַד יְהוָה אֶת־עַמּוֹ. As I described in §2, the grammar of the book of Ruth has subject-verb (S-V) order as its basic word order, although the S-V order is inverted to V-S order when a trigger is present at the front of the clause, such as the function word כי, as we have in this verse. Thus, without the כי the normal order of the clause would be יהוה פקד את־עמו; but the presence of the trigger produced the inverted V-S order of the clause.

לָתֵת לָהֶם לָחֶם. Inf constr Qal √נתן with ל preposition. On the vocalization of the ל, see above with לָגוּר in v. 1. Syntactically the inf constr is used here as a verbal adjunct, providing further information about the nature of the event or action described by פקד (WO §36.2.3e; JM §124o). In this case the "gerundive" inf constr specifies the manner in which Yhwh cared for his people—by providing food after the period of famine. Within the infinitive phrase the verb נתן is a classic "double object" (ditransitive) verb, similar to English "give": it typically takes two complements, one as the semantic patient in the accusative (often with את), and the other as the goal or recipient (often with ל).

1:7 וַתֵּצֵא מִן־הַמָּקוֹם אֲשֶׁר הָיְתָה־שָּׁמָּה וּשְׁתֵּי כַלֹּתֶיהָ
     עִמָּהּ וַתֵּלַכְנָה בַדֶּרֶךְ לָשׁוּב אֶל־אֶרֶץ יְהוּדָה׃

Although at first glance this verse seems to repeat what was already reported in v. 6, it is in fact the start of the detailed narrative of the return.

וַתֵּצֵא מִן־הַמָּקוֹם אֲשֶׁר הָיְתָה־שָּׁמָּה. *Wayyiqtol* 3fs Qal √יצא with a PP that is either a locative complement or an adjunct; it is not clear whether the verb יצא requires a complement or not. Note that both the main verb and the verb within the relative clause are singular and agree with an implied singular subject, which from context can only be No'omi.

הַמָּקוֹם אֲשֶׁר הָיְתָה־שָּׁמָּה. The locative adverb שמה serves to syntactically and semantically resume the head of the relative clause, המקום. Relative clause resumption serves one of two functions in ancient Hebrew. Either it allows the head of the relative to be focused within the relative clause predication (which is not the case in this verse) or it is required by the verb within the relative (such as when a certain verb requires a specific preposition to be complete). For this verse, it seems that when the head of the relative is a locative noun and the verb היה is used within the relative, the verb requires a locative resumptive constituent, שָׁם or שָׁמָּה (see also Gen 13:3; 2 Sam 15:21; 1 Kgs 5:8; Isa 7:23; the one exception to this is 1 Sam 23:22).

וּשְׁתֵּי כַלֹּתֶיהָ עִמָּהּ. The null-copula clause presents circumstantial information, almost as an afterthought, that No'omi did not travel alone but that her two daughters-in-law were still with her. Thus, the narrator begins the "leaving" part of the episode with the sole survivor of the original family who had moved to Moab. Once, however, the daughters-in-law become agents, the narrative continues with the appropriate plural verbs, as in the next clause.

הָיְתָה. *Qatal* 3fs Qal √היה, "to remain, stay" (see comment above, v. 2).

שָׁ֫מָּה. The use here of שם with the directional ה suffix instead
of שם without the directional ה does not seem to serve a syntactic or
semantic purpose. Not only is it hard to understand what the semantic
nuance of "to remain toward there" would mean, but the comparison
with the combination of היה and שם in v. 2 suggest strongly that the
same force is meant in this verse, simply "she stayed there."

וַתֵּלַ֫כְנָה בַדֶּ֫רֶךְ לָשׁוּב אֶל־אֶ֫רֶץ יְהוּדָה. Note the shift with
ותלכנה to a plural verb instead of the singular, which had been used
up to this point to focus attention on No'omi (and will again be used
in v. 22 for the same affect). Although it is tempting to see the narrator's use of verbs as somewhat erratic, it is nothing if not careful and
consistent: where the focus is on a single character (e.g., No'omi), the
verb is singular even if multiple characters are involved, but where the
narrative involves distinct actions for the multiple characters, as with
the upcoming dialogue among the three women, the verbs are plural
when appropriate (so also Campbell 1975:63).

וַתֵּלַ֫כְנָה. *Wayyiqtol* 3fpl Qal √הלך. The following PP דרב is a
verbal adjunct specifying the means of their travel, "on the road."

לָשׁוּב אֶל־אֶ֫רֶץ יְהוּדָה. Inf constr Qal √שוב; the infinitive
phrase is a second verbal adjunct to תלכנה, but unlike the "gerundive"
(manner) use of the infinitive לתת in v. 6, here the infinitive phrase
provides the purpose of the action in the main verb: they walked *in
order to* return (see WO §36.2.3d; JM §§124l, 168c).

1:8 וַתֹּ֫אמֶר נָעֳמִי לִשְׁתֵּי כַלֹּתֶ֫יהָ לֵ֫כְנָה שֹּ֫בְנָה אִשָּׁה
לְבֵית אִמָּהּ יַ֫עַשׂ יְהוָה עִמָּכֶם חֶ֫סֶד כַּאֲשֶׁר עֲשִׂיתֶם
עִם־הַמֵּתִים וְעִמָּדִי׃

This verse initiates the dialogue between No'omi and her two
daughters-in-law, which dominates this scene and continues through
v. 18. Notice the economy of the narrative: no contextual details of
the dialogue are provided. The audience does not know when or where

the discussion started or how it proceeds (are they standing or sitting?, stopped for lunch or the night?, and so on).

וַתֹּאמֶר נָעֳמִי לִשְׁתֵּי כַלֹּתֶיהָ. *Wayyiqtol* 3fs Qal √אמר. The reported speech is the complement of the verb תאמר and the PP לשתי כלתיה is an adjunct (see comment on 4:1 on the adjunct status of אל and ל PPs with verbs of speaking). No'omi wastes no time in getting to her point: she tells Ruth and 'Orpah to leave her. This would have been the sensible thing for both young women to do, since they would have had a much better chance at provision and care with their own families than by following a widowed mother-in-law to a foreign country.

לֵכְנָה שֹּׁבְנָה. Imperative 2fpl Qal √הלך and √שוב, respectively. The verb הלך does not take a complement, but the verb שוב normally does; here its complement is null although its semantics are in a loose sense satisfied by the following reduced clause. The use of imperatives instead of less forceful jussives reflects either No'omi's social status vis-à-vis the younger women or the importance she assigned to their well-being, or both.

אִשָּׁה לְבֵית אִמָּהּ. This is a reduced distributive clause. In addition to the more common use as a referential noun, אשה (like איש) may be used distributively (WO §15.6a-b; JM §142p, 147d). The ל PP following specifies the range over which the distribution occurs. Note that the third person noun אשה cannot be the syntactic subject of the imperative שבנה, since imperatives are second person only. Instead, אשה לבית אמה as a whole is a reduced clause that itself is an adjunct to the previous verb, שבנה. The null verb within the reduced clause is a semantic copy (i.e., it has been gapped) of שבנה, with the person and number features (3fs) appropriate for its subject אשה. This makes the PP לבית אמה the oblique complement of the null, gapped verb.

בֵּית אִמָּהּ. Although the phrase בית אב "house of (my) father" is much more common (over 140x in the Bible), the בית אם is also mentioned in Gen 24:28 and Songs 3:4, 8:2. It is unclear what the intended nuance is here, if any.

יַעַשׂ יְהוָה עִמָּכֶם֙ חֶסֶד כַּאֲשֶׁר עֲשִׂיתֶם עִם־הַמֵּתִים

וְעִמָּדִי. No'omi's good intentions in instructing her daughters-in-law
to leave her is confirmed in her follow-up statement. It is interesting
that her positive assessment of how Yhwh has treated her is quite different than her assessments in vv. 13 and 20-21 (see comments on
those verses).

יַעַשׂ יְהוָה. The *Qere* is a Jussive 3ms Qal √עשׂה; the *Ketiv* יַעֲשֶׂה
is a (modal) *yiqtol*. Regardless which option is read, the semantics
are identical (or nearly so) in the context of the verse. The *yiqtol* can
be used indicatively or modally, and in the case of the latter, there is
little discernible difference from the jussive. The order of the subject
יהוה and the verb יעשׂה/יעש indicates that a trigger, in this case a
covert semantic trigger (modality), has inverted the normal S-V order
to the V-S order we see. See the comments in §2.5 on the word order
distinction between indicative and modal clauses.

עִמָּכֶם ... עֲשִׂיתֶם. The use of morphologically masculine affixes
when the referents are clearly feminine, Ruth and Orpah, is not typical although it is attested elsewhere (see GKC §135o; JM §149–50).
In Ruth this happens mostly in the mouth of No'omi (see also 1:9,
11, 13), although the narrator and the "people of Bethlehem" both
use the masculine-for-feminine, twice for the narrator (1.19 שְׁתֵּיהֶם
and 1:22 הֵמָּה) and once for the Bethlehemites (4:11 שְׁתֵּיהֶם); in
each case the forms refer to two women. Neither Ruth nor Boaz utter
the gender switch and even the narrator's one switch in 1:19 is followed by multiple cases of 3fpl affixes. Moreover, while No'omi uses a
2mpl *qatal* verb here in v. 8, she uses 2fpl *yiqtol* and imperative verbs
throughout her speech in this section. It is thus difficult to discern
either a grammatical or stylistic reason for the variation. Arguments
that the forms reflect dialectal variation or a vestigial feminine dual
(Campbell 1975:65) do not explain why the expected ן- suffixes for
two females are used elsewhere (1:9, 19 [3x]). It is possible that the
narrator uses marginal language to give the book a foreign or perhaps
archaic coloring. The number of cases could not have been too many,
though, or the language would have interfered with the narrative

rather than contributing to it; this might explain the handful of cases. See also comments at Ruth 2:8 and §4.

עֲשִׂיתֶם. *Qatal* 2mpl Qal √עשׂה.

הַמֵּתִים. Participle mpl Qal √מות. The Participle has long been understood as an "intermediate" form between verbs and nouns, since sometimes it appears verbal, e.g., it takes accusative complements, while other times it appears nominal, e.g., it takes possessive suffixes (GKC §116; see WO §37; JM §121). Recent study, though, indicates that participles in BH are best understood as adjectives that encode an activity or event rather than a quality (Cook 2008a). Thus, when participles are used "verbally," they are actually predicates following a null-copula. Complicating the syntax of המתים is the presence of the definite article ה. Whereas it is typically taught that agreement in definiteness is the hallmark of "attributive" modification, an alternate analysis is required in the face of examples without such agreement (e.g., indefinite noun followed by definite participle; see Gen 49:17; Exod 26:12; Lev 16:16; Judg 21:19; 1 Sam 25:10; Isa 65:2; Jer 27:3; 46:16; 50:16; 51:25; Ezek 2:3; 28:16; 32:22, 24; 41:11; 47:2; Prov 26:18; Song 4:5; Dan 9:26; cf. JM §138b-c). The article in these cases is used to introduce a relative clause in which the participle is part of the predicate (Holmstedt 2002:83–90; see also Barr 1989a; contra WO §19.7). Thus, with המתים in this verse the head of the relative is not explicit and the article is a relative word: "(those) who died" or "(those) who are dead."

עִמָּדִי. This preposition, which is used only with a 1cs suffix, appears to be an alternate form of the more common עַם. According to GKC (§103c) it is likely cognate to Arabic *'inda* "beside, with" and might have had an original form of עַנְדִי (which presumably changed to עַמְדִי by anticipatory dissimilation of alveolar nasal [n] to the bilabial nasal [m] in the context of the alveolar plosive [d]). Others suggest that the preposition is a compound of עַם and יָדִי "at my hand" > "at my side" > "with me" (JM §103, n. 27). Regardless of its etymology, the preposition expresses comitative relations, i.e., "with" (WO §11.2.14a).

יִתֵּן יְהוָה֙ לָכֶ֔ם וּמְצֶ֣אןָ מְנוּחָ֔ה אִשָּׁ֖ה בֵּ֣ית אִישָׁ֑הּ   1:9
וַתִּשַּׁ֣ק לָהֶ֔ן וַתִּשֶּׂ֥אנָה קוֹלָ֖ן וַתִּבְכֶּֽינָה׃

This verse continues No'omi's speech with a second wish. Once
No'omi finishes speaking, the narrative resumes by describing the
women's emotional response.

יִתֵּן יְהוָה֙ לָכֶ֔ם וּמְצֶ֣אןָ מְנוּחָ֔ה אִשָּׁ֖ה בֵּ֣ית אִישָׁ֑הּ. Jussive
3ms Qal √נתן. Note the V-S word order, indicating that this *yiqtol* is
modal. The PP לכם is an oblique complement indicating the recipient. There is no noun to function as the accusative complement for
the verb in this clause, even though נתן requires one. This lack, along
with the following coordinated Imperative וּמְצֶאןָ (it is normal for
a jussive to follow an imperative, but not vice versa), has led to the
suggestion that the imperative clause is the complement for the transitive verb נתן, i.e., "May Yhwh give you (that) you find rest" (JM
§177h; Sasson 1979:22–24), or that the verb is lacking an object and
the imperative expresses a result or purpose (GKC §110i). Campbell
1975:65–66, draws on the Versions and Ruth 2:12 and suggests a lost
object "recompense"), i.e., "May Yhwh give you so that you find rest."
The first and third analyses make little sense for this verse, without
resorting to emendation (although it might be correct for the opposite Jussive-Imperative sequence in 4:11). The second complement
clause analysis is possible, although the force of the Imperative would
thus seem to be completely undermined. The translation given above
reflects a fourth option—that the syntax is interrupted. In classical
terms this is called "anacaluthon" and indicates a clause that is started
one way, paused, and finished a different way. This is a phenomenon
common in everyday speech, though it may also be used for some
effect in literature. Here it may well reflect the emotion of the situation, in which the distraught mother-in-law instructs her daughters-
in-law to abandon her for their own good.

לָכֶ֔ם. On the masculine morphology used for the two feminine
referents, see comment on v. 8.

אִשָּׁה בֵּית אִשָּׁה. On the syntax of this reduced distributive clause, see v. 8 above. The noun בַּית can be taken as a noun used adverbially (the so-called adverbial accusative) or as a short-hand writing of בְּבַית (see GKC §118; WO §10.2.2; JM §126h, 133c). Note that with the phrase בֵּית אִשָּׁה Noʻomi indicates her motivation for sending them away—not just to find comfort with their families but to find another husband to take care of them.

וַתִּשַּׁק לָהֶן. *Wayyiqtol* 3fs Qal √נשׁק. The verb נשׁק typically takes its complement in the oblique with a לְ PP, although it also takes the accusative and one time the oblique with an עַל PP (HALOT s.v.).

וַתִּשֶּׂאנָה קוֹלָן וַתִּבְכֶּינָה. *Wayyiqtol* 3fpl Qal √נשׂא and √בכה. Note the feminine plural verbs, in contrast to עָשִׂיתֶם in v. 8. Admittedly, here the assumed subject is all three women, for which the supposed dual forms would not have been used anyway (see comment above on v. 8). The verb נשׂא typically takes the accusative complement, as it does here, while the verb בכה is intransitive and thus takes no complement.

1:10 וַתֹּאמַרְנָה־לָּהּ כִּי־אִתָּךְ נָשׁוּב לְעַמֵּךְ׃

Presumably after they finished weeping, the two daughters-in-law declare their intentions to ignore Noʻomi's instruction and remain with her. Their statement is strongly put, indicating their resolve.

וַתֹּאמַרְנָה־לָּהּ. *Wayyiqtol* 3fpl Qal √אמר. The PP לה is an adjunct specifying the goal of the verb, the addressee of the speech. The complement of the verb is the reported speech.

כִּי־אִתָּךְ נָשׁוּב לְעַמֵּךְ. The כי is sometimes understood to mark the complement clause, i.e., the so-called כִּי *recitativum*, "They said to her (that) '. . .'" (GKC §157b; JM §157c). Miller, however, argues that the כִּי never introduces reported speech; the כִּי is, rather, inside the reported speech and often has an asseverative or emphatic function (1996:116). For those who include the כִּי as part of the quote, it is often taken as a strong adversative, "no" or "on the contrary" (Hubbard 1988:106; Bush 1996:77; see HALOT s.v. 3). This fits the context well, since the two women go on to assert strongly that they will not do as No'omi wishes but instead stay with her. The strength of the assertion is made clear by the Focus fronting of the adjunct PP אִתָּךְ: the typical position for an adjunct like this would be after the verb, but here it is raised to assert the daughters-in-law's intention over against No'omi's. The strength of their intention is further signaled by the use of the *yiqtol* verb נָשׁוּב ("we will return") rather than the cohortative form נָשׁוּבָה ("let us return"). The PP לְעַמֵּךְ is the oblique complement of the verb שׁוב.

וַתֹּאמֶר נָעֳמִי שֹׁבְנָה בְנֹתַי לָמָּה תֵלַכְנָה עִמִּי הַעוֹד־ 1:11
לִי בָנִים בְּמֵעַי וְהָיוּ לָכֶם לַאֲנָשִׁים:

Apparently No'omi recognized the resolve of the two younger women, because in this verse and the next two verses the narrator has her restate her instructions, with even stronger motive clauses (in the form of rhetorical questions).

וַתֹּאמֶר נָעֳמִי שֹׁבְנָה בְנֹתַי. The subject נעמי is overt, reinvoked due to the shift in speaker; the reported speech is the complement of the verb. Note that there is no PP specifying the addressee (see also comments on 1:8 and 4:1), although this information is easily deducible from the context. Also, while the vocative בנתי provides the addressee within the reported speech, it cannot be the syntactic subject of the imperative, which could take only a second person subject.

שֹׁבְנָה. Imperative 2fpl Qal √שׁוב with a null complement (as in vv. 8, 12; elsewhere the verb שׁוב takes an oblique PP complement; see 1:6, 7, 10, 15, 16, 22; 2:6; 4:3). In the face of Ruth and Orpah's resistance, No'omi's repeated command illustrates the force of her conviction that the younger women would fare better by leaving her (see Hubbard 1988:108). Note that the initial Imperative לכנה is not used here, as it was in v. 8; this may be a literary device to signal No'omi's impatience.

לָמָּה תֵלַכְנָה עִמִּי תֵּלַכְנָה. *Yiqtol* (modal) 3fpl Qal √הלך. The interrogative למה established the modal semantics of the clause. Contextually the question is likely rhetorical in that No'omi does not seek a content answer but simply consent Notice that she does not wait for a response but continues immediately with reasons why the two younger women should not go with her (see Bush 1996:77). The PP עִמִּי is an adjunct, since הלך does not require a complement.

הַעוֹד־לִי בָנִים בְּמֵעָי. Just as with למה in the previous clause, the clitic interrogative ה establishes the modal semantics of both the first null-copula clause and the subsequent *qatal* verbal clause (on the modal use of the *qatal* verb, see §2.3; see also Cook 2008b). The ל is used here to indicate possession (GKC §129; WO §1.2.10f; MNK §39.11.1.3; JM §130b, 133d). The PP במעי is an adjunct to the null-copula, specifying location. The temporal adverb עוֹד qualifies the null copula possessive ל construction: "do I still have sons in my womb?" (WO §39).

בְּמֵעָי. The noun מעה "bowels, inner parts, source of procreation" occurs neither in the singular nor free ("absolute") forms in the Bible. It is impossible to discern whether the clitic ("construct") form מְעֵי or the forms with possessive suffixes, as we have here, are dual or plural.

וְהָיוּ לָכֶם לַאֲנָשִׁים. *Qatal* (used modally) 3cpl Qal √היה. Modal *qatal* clauses are often used to present the consequences of the event or action in a preceding clause (see WO §32.2.4a; JM §119).

לָכֶם. On the seemingly masculine morphology in reference to Ruth and 'Orpah, see the comment on v. 8. The ל in this case does not indicate possession but rather the benefactors of the possible but implausible birth of sons to be husbands for Ruth and 'Orpah. Using a Latin-based grammatical framework, grammarians often refer to this use of the ל as the *dativus commodi* "dative of advantage" or "benefactive dative" (GKC §119q-s; WO §11.2.10d; JM §133d; see also 1:4, 4:6, 8, 10).

לָאֲנָשִׁים. The ל in this PP indicates the new role that the subject of the verb היו (the בנים from the previous clause) will take on, i.e., "they would become your husbands" (GKC §119t; WO §11.2.10, exx. 38–45; MNK §39.11.1.1.c). In this sense, the ל PP is an oblique complement of the verb היה; see comments on vv. 1–2 regarding היה with complements.

1:12 שֹׁבְנָה בְנֹתַי לֵכְןָ כִּי זָקַנְתִּי מִהְיוֹת לְאִישׁ כִּי אָמַרְתִּי יֶשׁ־לִי תִקְוָה גַּם הָיִיתִי הַלַּיְלָה לְאִישׁ וְגַם יָלַדְתִּי בָנִים:

No'omi's rhetoric becomes increasingly sharp, since the improbable event she depicts would have been obviously ludicrous to them all.

שֹׁבְנָה בְנֹתַי לֵכְןָ. The key verbs of this entire scene are once again invoked—No'omi is "returning" to her people, her daughters-in-law want to "return" with her, but No'omi wants them to "return" to their own people. Unlike either v. 8 or v. 11, שבנה is the first verb used with לכן following the vocative בנתי. Starting with the single imperative שבנה is perhaps indicative of No'omi's impatience and frustration. The following imperative, לכן, reinforces No'omi's impatience and exasperation with Ruth and 'Orpah.

כִּי זָקַנְתִּי מִהְיוֹת לְאִישׁ. This כי clause is subordinate to the preceding imperatives and presents the reason that No'omi uses to convince the younger women to leave her (on כי presenting the evidence supporting a preceding assertion, see MNK §40.9.2.2; JM §170da).

זָקַנְתִּי. Qatal 1cs Qal √זקן. This verb in the Qal can be either stative, "to be old," or dynamic, "to grow old." In this clause it is stative.

מִהְיוֹת. Inf constr Qal √היה; the PP is an adjunct to the verb זקנתי. Note that the נ of the preposition מִן does not assimilate to the initial ה of the inf constr; instead the sound is simply lost. The collocation of a stative verb with the comparative use of מִן produces a "comparison of capability" (WO §14.4f; see also GKC §133c; JM §141g). The construction expresses the idea that the quality specified by the stative verb is "too much/too little for" the event or action specified within the inf constr phrase. In this case, No'omi is "too old to belong to a man (i.e., be a wife)."

לְאִישׁ. On the use of the לְ preposition for possession, see the comment on v. 11.

כִּי אָמַרְתִּי יֶשׁ־לִי תִקְוָה גַּם הָיִיתִי הַלַּיְלָה לְאִישׁ וְגַם יָלַדְתִּי בָנִים. *Qatal* 1cs Qal √אמר with the reported speech as its complement. On the lack of an adjunct PP specifying the addressee, see comment on v. 11. This clause provides a second line of evidence supporting No'omi's argument that Ruth and 'Orpah should return to their Moabite families. Moreover, it is clear that the clause contains a irreal conditional (with modal *qatal* verbs). There is only one initial function word, though; the question is, then, whether the כִּי marks the reason or the conditional protasis, since it is used for either function elsewhere (GKC §159; WO §38.2; MNK §40.9; JM §167). When כי is used to introduce a conditional clause, though it is normally used for real conditions, not irreal conditions. This suggests that we should take the כִּי as the subordinating function word for the reason clause and understand the imbedded conditional to be unmarked (or "asyndetic"; see JM §167a).

יֶשׁ־לִי תִקְוָה. The existential predicator יֵשׁ is not needed to indicate possession; the null-copula clauses לִי תקוה or תקוה לִי would have been syntactically acceptable. Here the יֵשׁ functions as a copula in this clause (for an incomplete description of יֵשׁ as a copula, see JM §154k); pragmatically, it is present to help make the focus on the (non)existence of No'omi's hope. In other words, **even if she had** hope (which she does not), then she still would not have any sons to be future husbands for the two women (so also Hubbard 1988:100, n. 25).

גַּם ... וְגַם. The two גם clauses are appositional to the conditional protasis; they further specify the initial condition. גם in these cases is a conjunction (see also 2:8, 15, 16, 22, and 3:12), not an item adverb as it is in 1:5 and 4:10. Marking both clauses with an initial גַם indicates that the two further conditions both build on the initial condition and on each other; this is the "additive" use of גַם. The use of גַם itself indicates that the two additional conditions are possible but extremely unlikely, thus making No'omi's case sure (MNK §41.4.5.2.1c; see also GKC §154a, n. 1; JM §177q).

הָיִיתִי ... יָלַדְתִּי. Modal *Qatal* 1cs Qal √היה and √ילד.

הַלַּיְלָה. The use of the definite article with nouns indicating time, such as יום, לילה, and שׁנה, has a demonstrative force, thus הלילה is "this night, tonight," היום is "this day, today," and השׁנה is "this year" (WO §13.5.2b; JM §137f). Syntactically, such time expressions are adjuncts to the verb within whose scope they lie.

1:13 הֲלָהֵן| תְּשַׂבֵּרְנָה עַד אֲשֶׁר יִגְדָּלוּ הֲלָהֵן תֵּעָגֵנָה לְבִלְתִּי הֱיוֹת לְאִישׁ כִּי־מַר־לִי מְאֹד מִכֶּם כִּי־יָצְאָה בִי יַד־יְהוָה׃

This verse begins with an interrogative clause that is the first apodosis of the conditional protasis in v. 12. As with No'omi's question in v. 11, both this and the next interrogative are rhetorical: No'omi does not expect a substantive reply from Ruth and 'Orpah but for them to agree with her on the negative answer. No'omi finishes off her short speech with a direct negative and a theological statement that must have been intended to put a stop to the entire discussion.

הֲלָהֵן| תְּשַׂבֵּרְנָה עַד אֲשֶׁר יִגְדָּלוּ. *Yiqtol* (modal imperfect or jussive) 2fpl Piel √שׂבר. The verb in the Piel means "to hope for, wait for" and is typically followed by an oblique complement in a אל or ל PP. Here its complement is the PP עַד אֲשֶׁר יִגְדָּלוּ.

הֲלָהֵן. This enigmatic item is one of the interpretive cruces in the book. As it stands, it appears to be the combination of the interrogative ה, the preposition ל, and the 3fpl suffix. Contextually the 3fpl suffix makes no sense since the obvious referents are the potential

sons that No'omi could bear. Commentators have variously suggested
that the 3fpl suffix is a textual error, with the support of the ancient
Versions (Campbell 1975:68; Hubbard 1988:111; Bush 1996:79; Sasson 1979:25), a masculine dual form (to parallel the feminine dual
forms ending in ◻-; see comment on v. 8 and Hubbard 1988:111, n.
31), or a borrowed Aramaic particle הֵן with preposition לְ "therefore"
(GKC §103f, n. 4; HALOT s.v., citing Dan 2.6, 9; 4.24; note that the
HALOT entries seem to suggest that the item was first borrowed into
Aramaic from Hebrew and then, presumably, back into Hebrew!).
This apparent oddity as well as the ◻- forms used for the two young
women (see comment on v. 8)—most of which are in the mouth of
No'omi—may find their proper explanation as the marginal but inter-
pretable use of language in order to characterize No'omi. See §4.

עַד אֲשֶׁר יִגְדָּלוּ. This PP consists of a null (temporal) head relative clause, "until (the time) that they grow up." The morphology of
the *yiqtol* verb does not allow us to determine whether it is an modal
imperfect or jussive; if taken as an imperfect, the modality of the conditional clause indicates that the verb must also be taken as the modal
use of the imperfect.

הֲלָהֵן תֵּעָגֵנָה לְבִלְתִּי הֱיוֹת לְאִישׁ. This clause is the second
apodosis to the conditional protasis in v. 12.

תֵּעָגֵנָה. *Yiqtol* (modal imperfect or jussive) 2fpl Niph √עגה or
√עגן. The form is anomalous in that it does not correspond to the
paradigm form of the Niph for √עגה or √עגן. If the verb is from the
III-heh √עגה, it would have a defective /i/ vowel since the expected
form is *תֵּעָגֶינָה. If the verb is from the √עגן, it is missing the expected
Tiberian indication of the doubled nun as well as the paradigm /a/
vowel, i.e. *תֵּעָגַנָּה. Neither root is attested in BH, although based
on later attestations in rabbinic Hebrew and Aramaic for √עגן as "to
bind, tie, imprison" and used to refer to wives bound to absent husbands (see Jastrow, s.v.), a meaning of "withhold oneself" is typically
proposed for this verse. We may now add two possible attestations
from the Dead Sea Scrolls, both of which refer to "imprisonment"
(4Q203, 4Q206).

לְבִלְתִּי הֱיוֹת לְאִישׁ. Inf constr Qal √היה, preceded by
לבלתי, the typical negator for the infinitive in BH (GKC §114s; WO
§36.2.1g; JM §160l). The infinitive phrase may be used in a variety
of ways to modify the verb of the main clause. Here the context suggests that the infinitive phrase is not a complement of the verb, but an
adjunct. Moreover, it is equally fitting as a negative result of the verb,
i.e., "would you withhold yourself for them with the result of having
no husband?," or a negative gerundive explaining the nature (manner,
means) of the verb, i.e., "would you withhold yourself for them by
having no husband?"

אַל בְּנֹתַי כִּי־מַר־לִי מְאֹד מִכֶּם כִּי־יָצְאָה בִי יַד־יְהוָה.
The negative אַל normally negates Jussives, but may be used without
any verb in a simple exclamative "no" (Gen 19:18; Judg 19:23; 2 Sam
13:16, 25; 2 Kgs 3:13; 4:16; see MacDonald 1975:172–73; HALOT
s.v.; MNK §41.5.3), although it is more common to see לֹא used this
way (see BDB s.v.; GKC §152; JM §160). Simple negations like this
may include an element of emphasis (GKC §152d; JM §160b)—
hence, the classification as a negative "exclamation," although it is
not self-evident that this is always the case with Hebrew אַל and לֹא.
With that said, in this particular verse No'omi's final statement to the
younger women does seem to present the climax of her plea. Syntactically, some argue that there is ellipsis of the verbs in these negative
exclamations, in this case the ellipsis of a Jussive, i.e., "do not withhold yourselves": "The examples in which לֹא is used absolutely as a
negative answer, equivalent to *certainly not! no!* must be regarded as
extremely short verbal-clauses" (GKC §152c; see also GKC §152g; JM
§160j; Bush 1996:80). Similarly, Hubbard suggests that אַל here is an
abbreviation of אל יהי כן (Hubbard 1988:107, n. 9). The best way to
sort through the options is to consider the overall structure of question-answer pairs in Hebrew set in typological relief.

Cross-linguistically, there are three basic types of question-answer
systems (Miller 2005:660–61): 1) yes-no systems (e.g., English), 2)
agreement-disagreement systems (e.g., Japanese), and 3) echoing systems (e.g., Welsh). Biblical Hebrew uses the third type of system:

there is no word for "yes" (as כֵּן develops into in modern Hebrew), but instead a positive answer "echoes" minimally the main predicate of the question (and additional information can be added). A negative answer minimally has the negative that is appropriate to the predicate (which may be unexpressed or may be expressed as well). So if the question has יֵשׁ, the answer will have אֵין. If the implied negative answer is indicative, it will have לֹא (plus or minus the appropriate verb). If the implied negative answer is modal, it will have אַל (plus or minus the appropriate verb). In Ruth 1:13, the use of the אַל instead of לֹא suggests that the implied question is "Would you do X . . .?" and the full implied answer should be understood as "Don't [do X]."

כִּי־מַר־לִי מְאֹד מִכֶּם. The כִּי adjunct clause provides the evidence supporting No'omi's negative assertion (see comment on v. 12; MNK §40.9.2.2; JM §170da). Within the כִּי clause the preposition מִן creates three plausible ways to understand the clause: 1) the מִן creates a comparison between No'omi's and the younger women's suffering, i.e., "because my bitterness is more than yours"; 2) the מִן creates a comparison between No'omi's and the younger women's abilities to cope (the "comparison of capability," WO §14.4f), i.e., "because my bitterness is too much for you (to share)"; and 3) the מִן identifies the cause of No'omi's suffering, i.e., "because my bitterness is on account of you." All three make some sense in the context, although how No'omi's greater bitterness is a good reason for the women to leave her (#1) is unclear and identifying the younger women as the cause of her suffering (#3) is not consistent with her good will toward them expressed both in vv. 8-9 and reflected in v. 14. Option #2, that No'omi sees her suffering as an undue burden for the younger women to bear, makes sense of her obvious warm feelings for Ruth and 'Orpah, and provides a good reason for the women to leave her.

מַר־לִי. A null-copula clause with מר as the subject and the PP לִי as the complement of the null copula (similar to היה taking an oblique complement). On the use of the ל for possession, see comment above on v. 11.

כִּי־יָצְאָה בִי יַד־יְהוָה. Qatal 3fs Qal √יצא. This כִּי clause provides a second, appositional reason for the women to leave, in Noʻomi's opinion. (Appositional causal clauses are not "cumbersome," as Hubbard asserts [1988:107, n. 13], and thus there is no good reason to take this second כִּי in this verse as asseverative.) The reason "that Yhwh is against me" is intended both to explain her extreme bitterness expressed in the preceding clause and to reinforce the necessity of Ruth and ʻOrpah's departure. Note the V-PP-S order within the כִּי clause; this is an example of the triggered raising of the verb over the subject that was discussed in §2.5. Although the natural position of a PP is following the primary constituents (subject, verb, complement), the position of the PP בִי here does not reflect raising for Focus or Topic; instead, "light" PPs, that is, a preposition with a pronominal complement, typically attach to and move with the verb. The verb יצא is most often modified by PP adjuncts with מִן "to come out of/from" or אֶל "to come out toward"; the preposition בְ has the meaning "against" elsewhere (BDB s.v.; HALOT s.v., JM §133c) but not with the verb יצא anywhere else in the Hebrew Bible. Even so, it is not a difficult collocation to make sense of: armies "go out" for battle (Deut 20:1) and here Noʻomi reveals her sense of what has happened to her, God has come out "against" her as the divine warrior and smitten her (so also Hubbard 1988:112–13; Sasson 1979:26).

1:14   וַתִּשֶּׂנָה קוֹלָן וַתִּבְכֶּינָה עוֹד וַתִּשַּׁק עָרְפָּה לַחֲמוֹתָהּ
וְרוּת דָּבְקָה בָּהּ:

This verse, with its three short *wayyiqtol* clauses, shifts from the reported speech in vv. 11-13 back to the narrative framework.

וַתִּשֶּׂנָה קוֹלָן. *Wayyiqtol* 3fpl Qal √נשׂא. The noun קוֹל (note the feminine plural suffix) is the accusative complement of the transitive verb. The assimilation of the root-initial נ in ותשׂנה is expected and the vocalization of א reflects the loss of its consonantal value, i.e., its quiescence. For example, the expected form ותשׂאנה in v. 9 has the א graphemically present but phonetically empty, i.e., it is written to distinguish the verbal root but has no phonetic value. The form וַתִּשֶּׂנָה in this verse, though, shows the complete elision of the א phonologically as well as its absence in spelling (GKC §74k; JM §78e-f). On the usefulness of spelling as a feature for dating the book, see §3.

וַתִּבְכֶּינָה עוֹד. *Wayyiqtol* 3fpl Qal √בכה. Following the verb is the adverb עוֹד "still, again," which in this case is used as a "constituent adverb": "Constituent adverbs modify clauses (and, rarely, individual words) but, in contrast to clausal and item adverbs, they modify the predicate, that is, they specify the time, place, or manner of the predicated situation" (WO §39.3.1d). Adverbs like עוֹד in many languages are important clues to phrase structure. BH has relatively few adverbs and so the evidence from עוֹד is especially important. For instance, עוֹד can come before the verb (e.g., Exod 4:6; 1 Sam 16:11); in these cases, then, the verb remains "lower" in the phrase than the position of the adverb. But in cases like we have in this verse, the verb has taken a position "higher" than the adverb, suggesting that the *wayyiqtol* form involves "verb-raising."

וַתִּשַּׁק עָרְפָּה לַחֲמוֹתָהּ וְרוּת דָּבְקָה בָּהּ. These two clauses continue the narrative. Together they present an important contrast: it becomes clear that ʿOrpah serves as Ruth's foil in the story and from this point on Ruth will become a primary agent while ʿOrpah will recede into the background.

וַתִּשַּׁק עָרְפָּה לַחֲמוֹתָהּ. *Wayyiqtol* 3fs Qal √נשק. On this verb with a לְ PP complement, see comment on v. 9.

וְרוּת דָּבְקָה בָּהּ. *Qatal* 3fs Qal √דבק. The verb דבק takes an oblique complement, typically with a בְּ or לְ PP; here the PP בה completes the verb. The switch from the *wayyiqtol* clause to a *qatal* verbal clause indicates a departure from the primary sequentiality of the narrative framework and suggests that the actions are simultaneous. This non-sequential clause contrasts the actions of Ruth with those of ʿOrpah, i.e., ʿOrpah did X, Ruth did Y. The S-V order of this clause is not basic, but reflects Focus-marking on both the subject and the predicate: Ruth (in contrast to 'Orpah) clung to her mother-in-law (in contrast to leaving her).

1:15 וַתֹּאמֶר הִנֵּה שָׁבָה יְבִמְתֵּךְ אֶל־עַמָּהּ וְאֶל־אֱלֹהֶיהָ
שׁוּבִי אַחֲרֵי יְבִמְתֵּךְ׃

This verse moves us back to dialogue, although this time the cast of characters has been narrowed so that only Ruth and No'omi are in view.

וַתֹּאמֶר הִנֵּה שָׁבָה יְבִמְתֵּךְ אֶל־עַמָּהּ וְאֶל־אֱלֹהֶיהָ. *Wayyiqtol* 3fs Qal √אמר. The reported speech is the complement of the verb. The subject of the 3fs verb is initially ambiguous. The audience must wait until the content of the reported speech clarifies the speaker (No'omi) and the addressee (Ruth).

הִנֵּה שָׁבָה יְבִמְתֵּךְ אֶל־עַמָּהּ וְאֶל־אֱלֹהֶיהָ. *Qatal* 3fs Qal √שוב with a compound oblique complement consisting of two conjoined PPs. According to the Masoretic tradition, which has marked the word stress on the penultimate syllable, this verb is a *qatal*. This is an example in Hebrew where stress is phonemic; if the stress were marked on the final syllable, the form would be a fs participle. Note the return to the thematic verb of this scene, "returning." No'omi has accomplished half of her present goal and now she focuses on the remainder.

The V-S order of the clause is not syntactically triggered (see §2.5), since interjections like הנה, which along with items like vocatives, are not part of the syntax of the clause proper and do not trigger verb-raising. Thus, the fronted verb reflects Focus to contrast the action of the sister-in-law (she returned) with its logical opposite, "staying." One might be tempted to read this clause, at least in English, with contrastive stress, and hence the Focus, on the noun יבמתך, resulting in something like "Your **sister-in-law** has returned so **you** return as well." The problem with this reading of the verse is that for the subjects to be focused like this would require a pronoun את "you" to exist in the second half. The pronoun does not exist in this clause, thus such a reading is not available. Instead, No'omi, the speaker, is contrasting the courses of action that the two daughters-in-law have taken: one returned, one stayed.

אֱלֹהֶיהָ. The morphology of this noun is masculine plural, but as is well known it is often used as a plural of excellence or majesty for God and modified by singular adjectives and verbs (GKC §124g; JM §136d). In this verse either the singular, "her god," or plural, "her gods," makes sense. That is, as we know from the Mesha Stele as well as the Hebrew Bible (e.g., Num 21:29; 1 Kgs 11:33), Kemosh was the national deity of Moab, so the singular could refer to him; but since polytheism was the norm in the ancient Near East, the plural would also be appropriate. There is simply no good evidence suggesting one option over the other (cf. Vrs; Sasson 1979:29–30; Hubbard 1988:114, n. 7, 116; Buth 1996:82).

1:16 וַתֹּאמֶר רוּת אַל־תִּפְגְּעִי־בִי לְעָזְבֵךְ לָשׁוּב מֵאַחֲרָיִךְ
כִּי אֶל־אֲשֶׁר תֵּלְכִי אֵלֵךְ וּבַאֲשֶׁר תָּלִינִי אָלִין עַמֵּךְ
עַמִּי וֵאלֹהַיִךְ אֱלֹהָי:

Ruth's answer to No'omi is consistent with the first response that she and 'Orpah gave in v. 10. Instead of a negative exclamation with a positive assertion of what they will do, "No! We'll return with you," this time Ruth appeals to No'omi to stop pressing her to leave. Expressing one's own intentions for action is a more polite form of interaction than telling another person to do or not to do something, particularly when directed toward a person of greater social standing, such as a mother-in-law. Here, then, we see Ruth lose some patience.

אַל־תִּפְגְּעִי־בִי לְעָזְבֵךְ לָשׁוּב מֵאַחֲרָיִךְ. Jussive 2fs Qal √פגע. The verb פגע "to meet, fall upon, press" usually takes a בּ PP as its oblique complement, as it does here (only occasionally does it take an accusative complement; e.g., Exod 5:3, 20; 23:4). The infinitive phrase לְעָזְבֵךְ could be either an adjunct or a second complement, although it is not clear how a result or gerundive infinitive adjunct would make sense in the context (i.e., "don't press me *with the result of* abandoning you" or "don't press me *by* abandoning you"). The only other use of פגע with both a nominal complement and an infinitive is in Jer 36:25, where the verb is in the Hiphil (although not causative). In that instance, the infinitive phrase is clearly a second complement of the verb and it makes a good parallel to the syntax of this clause.

לְעָזְבֵךְ לָשׁוּב מֵאַחֲרָיִךְ. Inf constr Qal √עזב and √שׁוב. The first infinitive phrase, לְעָזְבֵךְ, is a complement of the previous verb (see comment above), and the second infinitive phrase, לָשׁוּב, is an adjunct of the first infinitive, which along with its own adjunct PP, מאחריך, specifies the means of abandonment.

כִּי אֶל־אֲשֶׁר תֵּלְכִי אֵלֵךְ וּבַאֲשֶׁר תָּלִינִי אָלִין עַמֵּךְ עַמִּי וֵאלֹהַיִךְ אֱלֹהָי. This כי clause provides Ruth's reason that No'omi should stop pressing her to leave: Ruth intends to go with her, even to the grave (as the audience learns from the continuation in the next verse).

אֶל־אֲשֶׁר תֵּלְכִי אֵלֵךְ וּבַאֲשֶׁר תָּלִינִי אָלִין. Both of these clauses have the constituent order PP-V and both PPs include a null-head relative clause, literally, "to (the place) that you go, I will go and in (the place) that you stay I will stay." The PPs in both clauses are adjuncts providing further information about the verbs, but not necessary to complete the verbs. The typical position for PPs is following the verbs and the fronted position of the PPs in these two clauses indicates that they are either Topic or Focus constituents. It is not clear which type of pragmatic function is intended. If they are Topics, it is because the choice that Ruth makes is fronted to orient No'omi to which of the two directions Ruth will comment upon (so Holmstedt 2009a). If they are Focus constituents, the challenge becomes determining precisely what element within the PP carries the Focus. If the subject of the verb within the relative carried Focus, we would expect the overt subject pronoun, i.e., אל אשר אַתְּ תלכי; similarly, if the head of the relative carried the Focus, we would expect an overt head, i.e., אֶל מָקוֹם אֲשֶׁר תֵלְכִי. Since neither is the case here, only the entire PP can carry Focus; thus, "**wherever you go**, I'll go, and **wherever you stay**, I'll stay."

עַמֵּךְ עַמִּי וֵאלֹהַיִךְ אֱלֹהָי. Both null-copula clauses are Subject-Predicate. Based on the context and the tense-aspect of the preceding two verbs as well as the two following verbs, the null-copula in both of these clauses is almost always taken with a future temporal reference: "your people will be my people and your god will be my god." That is, most interpreters understand Ruth to continue stating her intentions, not what has already happened. However, this is not necessary grammatically or contextually. Whereas the traveling and lodging mentioned in the previous clauses or the dying and being buried in the next two have all yet to happen, it is entirely possible that Ruth had already identified with Noʻomi's family, tribe, people, and god when she married Noʻomi's son. In fact, this strengthens Ruth's argument: if these were all still future choices, Noʻomi could continue to argue with her, but if Ruth points out that in her opinion she made her choice years ago by marriage, Noʻomi has a weak case against her.

1:17 בַּאֲשֶׁר תָּמוּתִי אָמוּת וְשָׁם אֶקָּבֵר כֹּה יַעֲשֶׂה יְהוָה
לִי וְכֹה יֹסִיף כִּי הַמָּוֶת יַפְרִיד בֵּינִי וּבֵינֵךְ:

This verse is the continuation of the כִּי clause begun in v. 16.

בַּאֲשֶׁר תָּמוּתִי אָמוּת וְשָׁם אֶקָּבֵר. As with the two V-PP clauses in v. 16, the first clause here has a fronted PP with an imbedded relative clause—the entirety of which carries Focus. This clause ups the ante, so to speak: Noʻomi will not be rid of Ruth until she or both die.

בַּאֲשֶׁר תָּמוּתִי אָמוּת. *Yiqtol* 2fs and 1cs Qal √מות. The null head of the relative clause in this case is formally ambiguous. Null heads for relatives must be interpreted based on context alone and in most cases the context sufficiently narrows the options to one obvious interpretation. For most listeners or readers of this clause within this story, the initial processing would undoubtedly produce a locative interpretation of the null head, "in (the place) that you die, I will die." As Sasson notes (1979:30), however, a manner interpretation of the null head is equally plausible, "in (the way) that you die, I will die." The only piece of evidence that provides direction is in the following clause: שָׁם makes the locative interpretation of the null head of the relative in this context beyond doubt.

וְשָׁם אֶקָּבֵר. *Yiqtol* 1cs Qal √קבר. The basic position for locative adjuncts like the adverb שָׁם is following the verb and any complements. The pre-verbal position in this example indicates that שָׁם has been raised over the verb so that its higher position could signal its Focus-marking. The result is similar to the pragmatics of using "only" in English, "I will be buried **only there**," or, better reflecting the Hebrew word order, "**only there** will I be buried."

כֹּה יַעֲשֶׂה יְהוָה לִי וְכֹה יֹסִיף כִּי הַמָּוֶת יַפְרִיד בֵּינִי וּבֵינֵךְ. Ruth's almost over-the-top climax provides a window on the extent of her determination and stubbornness in this matter. No'omi also recognized this, as the narrator tells us in the next verse.

כֹּה יַעֲשֶׂה יְהוָה לִי וְכֹה יֹסִיף. *Yiqtol* (modal imperfect) 3ms Qal √עשׂה and Hiphil √יסף. These two clauses present the first part of the oath/curse formula. The basic full formula is represented in 1 Sam 3:17: כֹּה יַעֲשֶׂה־לְּךָ אֱלֹהִים וְכֹה יוֹסִיף אִם־תְּכַחֵד מִמֶּנִּי דָּבָר. According to JM,

> There are twelve examples in the books of Samuel and Kings (with the exception of Ru 1.17): 1Sm 3.17; 14.44; 20.13; 25.22; 2Sm 3.9, 35; 19.14; 1Kg 2.23; 2Kg 6.31; with plural verbs: 1Kg 19.2 (Jezebel); 20.10 (Benhadad). It should be noted that the verbal forms are in the indicative, despite the optative sense. In this formula, כה no doubt is the scribe's: the person who pronounced the curse had to name the evils which he was calling down upon himself, e.g., illness, loss of goods, death, as is the case in Jb 31.8ff., 22. It is not inconceivable that an utterance of this formula was accompanied

by some appropriate gesture such as when the speaker omi-
nously passes his hand across his own throat. (§165a, n. 1)

The one clear inaccuracy of this description is in identifying the
verbs as indicative. The irrealis modality of the conditional has scope
over both the protasis and the apodosis, regardless of the order. Thus,
the verbs in the apodosis are modal *yiqtol*. This could not be discerned
syntactically, however. The initial adverb כֹּה "thus, in this way" typically comes in the initial position of the clause, thereby triggering
verb-raising over the subject (S-V > X-V-S). Thus, the position of the
verb higher than the subject would have been triggered by both the
initial adverb and the modality of the clause.

Note that neither verb in the oath/curse apodosis has an explicit
complement. The formula does not specify what God shall do in the
case of the first verb, יַעֲשֶׂה (as I indicated above, כֹּה is an adverb and
so cannot be the complement). In the case of the second verb, יֹסִיף,
the complement is an implied inf constr of the first verb, i.e., יֹסִיף
לַעֲשׂוֹת.

כִּי הַמָּוֶת יַפְרִיד בֵּינִי וּבֵינֵךְ. *Yiqtol* (modal imperfect) 3ms
Hiph √פרד with a compound oblique complement consisting of the
two בֵּין PPs. The כִּי clause stands where the אִם or אִם לֹא protasis of
the oath/curse is expected. Although כִּי can introduce a conditional
clause (WO §38.2d), it does not appear to be so used in oaths or
curses. Instead, it is more likely an asseverative כִּי, "indeed!" or "certainly!" (see JM §165a,e; cf. GKC §149d; WO §40.2.2b). Within the כִּי
clause, which normally contains triggered V-S word order, the subject
has been raised even higher than the verb to signal its Focus-marking
(see §2.5). The subject הַמָּוֶת is Focus-fronted in order to contrast it
not with contextual alternatives, but with logical alternatives—those
established solely from the shared knowledge of the speaker-listener
outside of a particular discourse. So הַמָּוֶת is contrasted with, basi-
cally, anything else that typically might be a reason for a widowed
daughter-in-law to leave her mother-in-law, such as other family or
new marriage. The addition of the English restrictive adverb "only"
captures this particular Focus structure well.

1:18 וַתֵּ֕רֶא כִּי־מִתְאַמֶּ֥צֶת הִ֖יא לָלֶ֣כֶת אִתָּ֑הּ וַתֶּחְדַּ֖ל לְדַבֵּ֥ר
אֵלֶֽיהָ׃

This verse marks the return to narrative from the reported speech of vv. 16-17.

וַתֵּ֕רֶא כִּי־מִתְאַמֶּ֥צֶת הִ֖יא לָלֶ֣כֶת אִתָּ֑הּ. *Wayyiqtol* 3fs Qal √ראה with a כי clause complement. As in v. 15, the last time that No'omi was the agent, the identity of the subject of ותרא is not specified, nor is the referent of the participial subject היא. Both are easily discernible from the context, which likely explains the lack of explicitness.

כִּי־מִתְאַמֶּ֥צֶת הִ֖יא. Participle fs Hith √אמץ. This כי clause is the complement of the transitive verb תרא. The Participle highlights the durative, persistent nature of Ruth's refusal to leave her mother-in-law. Basic word order in participial clauses is subject-participle; the fronting of the participle before the pronominal subject היא indicates that the predicative participle is marked for Focus. In other words, it is not simply that Ruth is determined, nor is it that *Ruth* (as opposed to No'omi) is determined, but that Ruth is *determined*.

לָלֶ֣כֶת אִתָּ֑הּ. Inf constr Qal √הלך. This infinitive phrase is the semantic opposite of לשוב אחריך in v. 16 and thus provides closure to Ruth's speech. Syntactically the infinitive phrase is the complement of the verb מתאמצת. Within the infinitive phrase, the PP אתה is a locative adjunct of the inf constr ללכת.

וַתֶּחְדַּ֖ל לְדַבֵּ֥ר אֵלֶֽיהָ. This clause presents the next action, which may also be taken to be the logical result of the former action. That is, No'omi observed something and then acted based on that observation. This should not be taken as evidence that temporal succession is part of the semantics of the preterite *yiqtol* within the *wayyiqtol* form; instead, it is a pragmatic implicature, i.e., it is a natural interpretation within narrative that the second of two juxtaposed *wayyiqtol* clauses temporally follows the first one unless contextual clues suggest otherwise (see 1:4, 6, 22; 2:17 for a non-sequential *wayyiqtol*).

וַתֶּחְדָּל. *Wayyiqtol* 3fs Qal √חדל. The verb חדל has both intransitive (e.g., Exod 9:29) and transitive manifestations. In this verse it is transitive and the infinitive phrase לְדַבֵּר אֵלֶיהָ is its complement.

לְדַבֵּר. Inf constr Piel √דבר. The verb דבר typically takes an oblique complement with אל or ב as well as PP adjuncts specifying the reason or topic; in contrast to אמר, the verb דבר does not usually take reported speech as its complement (see Miller 1996).

1:19ᵃ וַתֵּלַכְנָה שְׁתֵּיהֶם עַד־בֹּאָנָה בֵּית לָחֶם

The first half of v. 19 concludes Scene 2 of the first Act. It brings them to Bethlehem, the goal of their travels.

וַתֵּלַכְנָה שְׁתֵּיהֶם. *Wayyiqtol* 3fpl Qal √הלך. The verb has the expected feminine plural morphology to match the features of the compound subject No'omi and Ruth, but the following adjective phrase שתיהם has the masculine plural suffixed pronoun (compare to the feminine plural suffixed pronoun in באנה). See comment on v. 8 and §3.

עַד־בֹּאָנָה בֵּית לָחֶם. This PP is a temporal adjunct of the verb תלכנה. Within the PP, the infinitive phrase is the complement of the preposition עד and within the infinitive phrase בית לחם is the complement of the infinitive באנה. While it is more common for the verb בוא to take a PP complement, it may also take an NP complement indicating the locative goal of movement.

בֹּאָנָה. Inf constr Qal √בוא with 3fpl pronominal suffix. The typical 3fpl pronominal suffix is simply ן ָ. JM (§94h) suggests that the addition of the final ה is for assonance, presumably with the preceding verb תלכנה (so also Sasson 1979:31; Hubbard 1988:121, n. 2).

Act I, Scene 3: The Arrival in Bethlehem (vv. 19b-22)

In this final scene of Act I the dialogue between No'omi and her daughters-in-law ceases and the narrator moves No'omi and Ruth on toward Bethlehem. The dialogue that does occur is between No'omi and the women of Bethlehem and is a platform for Noʻomi to air her grievances against Yhwh for what she perceives as injustice in her life. The narrator thus uses Noʻomi's voice to summarize and put a fine point on the plot problem: she believes that Yhwh has "emptied" her life; will it be "refilled"?

¹⁹ᵇAnd when they entered Bethlehem, the whole town was in a stir about them, and they said, "Can this be Noʻomi?" ²⁰She said to them, "Do not call me 'Pleasant' [Noʻomi]! Call me 'Bitter' [Mara] because Shaddai has made me very bitter. ²¹I went away full, but empty Yhwh has returned me. Why should you call me 'Pleasant' when Yhwh has testified against me, indeed, Shaddai has caused calamity to happen to me." ²²So Noʻomi returned—and Ruth, the Moabite, her daughter-in-law, with her, who (also) returned from the territory of Moab—and they entered Bethlehem at the beginning of the barley harvest.

1:19ᵇ וַיְהִ֗י כְּבֹאָ֙נָה֙ בֵּ֣ית לֶ֔חֶם וַתֵּהֹ֤ם כָּל־הָעִיר֙ עֲלֵיהֶ֔ן
וַתֹּאמַ֖רְנָה הֲזֹ֥את נָעֳמִֽי׃

This verse picks up the arrival at and entrance into Bethlehe , which was just mentioned in v. 19a.

וַיְהִ֗י כְּבֹאָ֙נָה֙ בֵּ֣ית לֶ֔חֶם. *Wayyiqtol* 3ms Qal √היה with a PP complement that is itself an infinitive phrase. Semantically, this clause provides the temporal setting for the next main clause. On the verb היה with a temporal PP used to set the scene, see comments on 1:1, 3:4, 8, 13. Both ב and כ prepositions can be attached to an inf constr to create a temporal clause. WO (§32.2.2b) indicate that "ב denotes in general the temporal proximity of one event to another, כ more specifically the more immediately preceding time."

בֵּ֣ית לֶ֔חֶם. This NP is the complement of the verb באנה (see also v. 19a).

וַתֵּהֹ֤ם כָּל־הָעִיר֙ עֲלֵיהֶ֔ן. This is the main clause for which the preceding clause established the temporal setting. The agent has shifted from the two women to "the whole town," which is narrowed

down by the verb in the next clause to the women of the town. As a
group, these characters are nothing but a prop to facilitate the narrative development. They thus remained unspecified and are not
invoked again until the end of chapter 4.

וַתֵּהֹם עֲלֵיהֶן. *Wayyiqtol* 3fs Niph of √המם (GKC §67t) or √הום
(GKC §72v) or Qal of √הום (GKC §72h). The roots המם and הום
may be by-forms in Hebrew or, if etymologically distinct, may have
become conflated. The PP עליהן is an adjunct clarifying the nature
of the activity indicated by תהם.

וַתֹּאמַרְנָה הֲזֹאת נָעֳמִי. The 3fpl *wayyiqtol* indicates that it is
only the women of Bethlehem that the narrator has in view. We are
not given any indication that the men noticed No'omi's return.

הֲזֹאת נָעֳמִי. This interrogative clause could conceivably be
simple and expect a yes/no answer, but the context suggests that the
women of Bethlehem were not seeking an answer to No'omi's identity
but were rather surprised to see her. Thus, with most commentators,
it is best to take this as a rhetorical question used as an exclamation
indicating surprise.

1:20 וַתֹּאמֶר אֲלֵיהֶן אַל־תִּקְרֶאנָה לִי נָעֳמִי קְרֶאןָ לִי מָרָא
כִּי־הֵמַר שַׁדַּי לִי מְאֹד:

No'omi's response is swift and direct and uses a play on names to
make her point. She is no longer pleasant, but bitter, and she gives her
opinion regarding the cause of this change in the next clause.

אַל־תִּקְרֶאנָה לִי נָעֳמִי קְרֶאןָ לִי מָרָא. Jussive 3fpl Qal and
impv fpl Qal √קרא; this verbal root, when it is used in the naming
idiom, takes an accusative complement (the name) and an oblique ל
PP complement (the object named). (For a second form of the naming
idiom, using the noun שֵׁם, see 4:17.) The form of the imperative here,
without the final ה, is also used in 1:9 and 12; see GKC §46f.

מָרָא. No'omi rejects her name "pleasant one" (see comment on v. 2) and takes a name apparently derived from √מרר "to be bitter." The actual form is probably best taken as the adjective מַר "bitter" with a feminine ending. Typically this would produce מָרָה, but the final ה is a *mater lectionis* and the use of the א instead of ה to mark the feminine noun ending, while not common, does occur elsewhere (GKC §80h; JM §89k).

כִּי־הֵמַר שַׁדַּי לִי מְאֹד. This כי clause provides No'omi's reason for her instruction to the women of Bethlehem to call her Bitter. Instead of a simple כי מר לי מאד "because I'm very bitter" (see v. 13), as in v. 13 No'omi fingers the agent she blames for her situation, שַׁדַּי. The V-S word order within the clause reflects verb raising over the subject that was triggered by the initial כי.

הֵמַר. *Qatal* 3ms Hiph √מרר. The Hiph of this root is not used much and elsewhere it appears to take an accusative complement (Job 27:2) or an oblique complement with a ב PP (Exod 23:21, although the verb there is often taken to be from √מרה). Here the ל PP is the oblique complement.

שַׁדַּי. The etymology of this divine epithet is unclear, although it is often suggested that it derived from Akkadian *šadû(m)* "mountain" and the related *šaddû'a* "mountain dweller" and thus originally referred to the "god of the mountain." Regardless of the etymology, within the Bible it is used primarily in texts referring to God's power (e.g., Ezek 1:24; Ps 68:15) or judgment (Isa 13:6; Job 5:17), or in contexts of blessing and cursing (Gen 17:1; Num 24:4). There is also the view expressed in Exod 6:3 that אל שדי was a pre-Mosaic form in which Yhwh appeared to the Patriarchs. Thus, for the author of Ruth, שדי could have both evoked an earlier time (e.g., the time of the Judges) and contextualized No'omi's complaint against the cosmic ruler: "Her fate could have come from no other source—and so also its future reversal" (Hubbard 1988:125). See §3 on the term's use in dating.

אֲנִי מְלֵאָה הָלַכְתִּי וְרֵיקָם הֱשִׁיבַנִי יְהוָה לָמָּה 1:21
תִקְרֶאנָה לִי נָעֳמִי וַיהוָה עָנָה בִי וְשַׁדַּי הֵרַע לִי׃

With the five clauses in this verse No'omi explains her charge
that God embittered her. The meaning of No'omi's imagery is clear:
she had a husband and children when she left Bethlehem and she has
neither on her return.

אֲנִי מְלֵאָה הָלַכְתִּי. The use of the subject pronoun, which is
not syntactically necessary due to the full inflection of Hebrew verbs
(see Holmstedt 2009b), is to present a Topic; in this case the Topic
signals a change in the agent, from God in the previous clause to "I"
(No'omi) in this clause. The adjective מלאה, which is used adverbially here, is also fronted for Focus. The Focus fronted adjective sets up
a contrast with the manner adverb ריקם in the next clause. (On the
pragmatic structure of this and the following clause, see §2.5.)

מְלֵאָה ... רֵיקָם. The feminine singular adjective מלאה does
not modify a nominal item (adjectives can modify pronouns only as
predicates, e.g., "I am full"); rather, it modifies the verb. The masculine singular adjective ריק has a ם- suffix, which is one of the few
adverbial morphemes in Hebrew. However, it is not productive, unlike
the English adverbial suffix -ly (GKC §100; WO §39.3; JM §102);
instead, Hebrew mostly uses non-adverb constituents for adverbial
modification, such as the adjective מלאה.

וְרֵיקָם הֱשִׁיבַנִי יְהוָה. Qatal 3ms Hiph √שוב, with 1cs object
suffix. The fronted adverb ריקם carries Focus and is set in contrast
to the fronted adverbial מלאה in the previous clause. In this manner,
No'omi stresses the extremity of what has happened to her: "I went
away **full**, but **empty** Yhwh returned me (that is why I am bitter)."

לָמָּה תִקְרֶאנָה לִי נָעֳמִי. On the syntax of the naming formula, see above in v. 20. This interrogative clause is, like the one in v.
19b, rhetorical in nature and functions as an exclamation.

וַיהוָה עָנָה בִי וְשַׁדַּי הֵרַע לִי. These two parallel clauses show

S-V order that is not basic but reflects Focus-marked subjects: **Yhwh**
has testified against me, **Shaddai** has caused calamity to happen to
me. The וֹ conjunction on וַיהוה does not itself indicate the semantic
relationship between the previous interrogative clause and the following two. But the context implies that a causal relationship exists, with
the second two clauses providing the evidence that Noʻomi cites for
her refusal to be called by her given name.

עָ֥נָה בִ֖י. *Qatal* 3ms Qal √ענה. The collocation "to testify against"
is legal language; Noʻomi uses this idiom to project the image of herself
in a cosmic court with Yhwh as her accuser. (On the possible intended
ambiguities of phrase, see Moore 1997.) That the verb ענה in the Qal
does not require a complement indicates the PP בִי to be an adjunct for
the verb, specifying the recipient of the speech action. (See Hubbard
126, n. 31 for a brief discussion of the Versional evidence and the proposals of some to repoint the verb to the Piel עִנָּה "to oppress.")

הֵרַ֥ע לִֽי. *Qatal* 3ms Hiph √רעע. This verb in the Hiph, "to
treat someone badly," takes either an accusative complement (e.g.,
Deut 26:6) or an oblique complement with a לֹ PP (e.g., Gen 43:6
and here).

1:22 וַתָּ֣שָׁב נָעֳמִ֗י וְר֤וּת הַמּוֹאֲבִיָּה֙ כַלָּתָהּ֙ עִמָּ֔הּ הַשָּׁ֖בָה
מִשְּׂדֵ֣י מוֹאָ֑ב וְהֵ֗מָּה בָּ֚אוּ בֵּ֣ית לֶ֔חֶם בִּתְחִלַּ֖ת קְצִ֥יר
שְׂעֹרִֽים׃

With this fs verse the narrator brings to a close both this scene as
well as the entirety of Act I. The first clause serves as a summary
by repeating the most salient information of the preceding twenty-
one verses: Noʻomi has returned to Bethlehem and Ruth, one of her
daughters-in-law, has come with her. The second clause sets the audience up for the harvest scene in the second act.

וַתָּ֣שָׁב נָעֳמִ֗י וְר֤וּת הַמּוֹאֲבִיָּה֙ כַלָּתָהּ֙ עִמָּ֔הּ הַשָּׁבָה מִשְּׂדֵי
מוֹאָ֑ב. The 3fs *wayyiqtol* ותשב indicates that once again the narrator

focuses on No'omi as the central character; Ruth is kept in the audience's mind, but only by means of the comitative phrase, not as a second agent. Note also that the narrator keeps Ruth's Moabite origin in the foreground by classifying her as מוֹאֲבִיָה.

וַתָּשָׁב. *Wayyiqtol* 3fs Qal √שׁוב; this verb typically takes an oblique complement indicating either the place of origin or the goal, but here this complement is omitted, perhaps because the phrase הַשָּׁבָה מִשְּׂדֵי מוֹאָב specifies it. *Wayyiqtol* clauses typically present events and actions in sequence; however, this temporal sequencing is the result of a pragmatic implicature arising from the nature of the narrative itself rather than the semantics of the verb (see also the comment above on v. 18). In this case, rather than providing the next event or action, the *wayyiqtol* is used to summarize what has already happened, that is, their return was reported in v. 19 and assumed in vv. 20-21 (GKC §118i; JM §118i). See also 1:4, 6, 18; 2:17.

הַשָּׁבָה מִשְּׂדֵי מוֹאָב. *Qatal* 3fs Qal √שׁוב with the article as a relative word, "who returned." The relative use of the article is well-established (see comment above on v. 8), negating the need to move the Masoretic stress forward on the word so that it is a participle instead of a *qatal* (see also 2:6, 4:3; contra WO §19.7d; JM §145e). The *qatal* verb fits the summary nature of the clause—the return had already happened, whereas a participle would more naturally indicate action in progress. If the relative clause הַשָּׁבָה מִשְּׂדֵי מוֹאָב modifies No'omi, it appears rather superfluous and more than a bit awkward since No'omi's return had just been specified with וַתָּשָׁב. Moreover, relative clauses overwhelmingly modify the nearest appropriate antecedent, which means that Ruth is the head of the relative clause. Many commentators make a great deal out of the fact that Ruth is not technically "returning" to Bethlehem since that is not her place of origin (e.g., Hubbard 1988:129). But from Ruth's perspective, this use of שׁוב is too narrow, since she (and 'Orpah) had earlier pleaded with No'omi to let them "return" with her (v. 10). By including הַשָּׁבָה with Ruth as its subject here, the narrator draws Ruth into the spotlight as a primary agent with Noʻomi. While the verse started with the singular וַתָּשָׁב, highlighting Noʻomi's narrative prominence, the הַשָּׁבָה adds Ruth and the following הֵמָּה בָּאוּ clearly indicates that Ruth will not disappear from the narrative focus as ʻOrpah did.

וְהֵמָּה בָּאוּ בֵּית לֶחֶם בִּתְחִלַּת קְצִיר שְׂעֹרִים. *Qatal* 3cp Qal √בוא, with an NP complement, בֵּית לֶחֶם, and a PP (temporal) adjunct, בִּתְחִלַּת קְצִיר שְׂעֹרִים. On the masculine pronoun for the feminine referents, Noʻomi and Ruth, see comment on v. 8. As in v. 21, the subject pronoun is not necessary with a finite verb and so when it is present it is used to mark pragmatic information such as a shift in Topic or a Focused constituent (see §2.5). Here the pronoun signals a Topic, but it is a subtle usage. The shift in Topic is not from one discourse agent to another, but from one to both. Whereas Noʻomi has been the primary agent in this last scene of Act I, the narrator uses the plural pronoun to signal that from this point onward Noʻomi and Ruth are equally primary in the plot. The narrator's desire to mark the two agents as a single Topic also explains the avoidance of the *wayyiqtol* narrative verb, which would not have allowed the pronoun to reside in a preverbal position of the clause. This is not the first time that both have been equal agents (see v. 19), but since the narrative from the end of v. 19 to the beginning of v. 22 has had only Noʻomi in sight, it is necessary for the narrator to pull Ruth back into the picture in order to close Act I and set the stage for Act II.

Act I followed Noʻomi and her family from Judah to Moab and back to Judah. It established that the family left Judah whole but Noʻomi returned to Bethlehem bereaved, accompanied only by her Moabite daughter-in-law, Ruth. The primary problem of the plot has thus been well established: how will Noʻomi be "refilled" after her complete "emptying," which she has blamed on Yhwh. Act II opens with many questions: what will happen to the two women? How will they find provision? Will either re-marry? Will Noʻomi be reconciled with her god, Yhwh?

ACT II

Act II, Scene 1: Ruth Chances upon the Field
of Noʿomi's Relative (vv. 1-3)

The audience was informed at the very end of Act 1 that Noʿomi and Ruth arrived at Bethlehem at the beginning of the barley harvest; Acts II spans both this harvest (mid-March to mid-April) and the following wheat harvest (mid-April to mid-May). The first scene of Act II sets the stage for a possible plot resolution: Noʿomi has a wealthy relative in whose field Ruth coincidentally finds herself gleaning. It is a tantalizing set-up for a quick solution to the women's material needs.

¹Now Noʿomi had a kinsman of her husband's, a mighty man of position from the clan of Elimelek, and his name was Boaz. ²And Ruth, the Moabite, said to Noʿomi, "Let me go to the fields in order to glean the ears of grain after him in whose eyes I find favor," and she said to her, "Go, my daughter." ³When she went and entered and gleaned in the field after the harvesters, she chanced upon the portion of the field belonging to Boaz who was from the clan of Elimelek.

וּלְנָעֳמִי מֵידָע [מוֹדַע] לְאִישָׁהּ אִישׁ גִּבּוֹר חַיִל   2:1
מִמִּשְׁפַּחַת אֱלִימֶלֶךְ וּשְׁמוֹ בֹּעַז:

Noʿomi has a wealthy relative by virtue of her deceased husband's clan. Might he play the role of the גֹּאֵל, the "kinsman-redeemer"? The audience would surely have caught this hint even though it is not make explicit until v. 20.

וּֽלְנָעֳמִ֞י מידָ֣ע לְאִישָׁ֗הּ אִ֚ישׁ גִּבּ֣וֹר חַ֔יִל מִמִּשְׁפַּ֖חַת אֱלִימֶ֑לֶךְ׃

On the use of null copula clauses in narrative, see the comment on
1:2. Departure from the *wayyiqtol* often accompanies the opening of
a new scene or episode, but this is not an absolute and should not be
taken as a grammatical principle. Here the null copula clause presents background information, that is, information that does not move
the "narrative" time (i.e., the time within the story) forward but does
move the "narrated" time (i.e., the time it takes to tell the story) forward and adds to the information that the audience receives. In this
null copula clause the order is Predicate-Subject. There are multiple
possible reasons for this non-basic order. For example, the predicative
PP לנעמי could be fronted because No'omi is the Topic and thus the
PP serves to provide an anchor for the new information provided by
the following subject NP—מידע. Or, the length of the subject NP—
לאישה איש גבור חיל ממשפחת אלימלך—could have triggered an
automatic switch; this is common in English and is known as "heavy
noun phrase shift" (e.g., instead of *Ruth gave the grain to No'omi*, when
the object is a complex phrase it may be "shifted" to the right of the
indirect object, as in *Ruth gave to No'omi the grain that she had gleaned
in Boaz' field*).

וּֽלְנָעֳמִ֞י מוֹדָ֣ע. The cliticization of a noun (i.e., the "construct"
relationship) is the typical strategy to express the genitive, although a
ל PP may also be used (WO §9.7). In this example, though, the genitive relationship is not modificational (e.g., "a relative of No'omi"),
but is the predicate (e.g., "a relative [belongs] to No'omi") and the ל
PP is the only grammatical strategy for such cases.

מידע. (Kt) and מוֹדָע (Qr). The *Qere-Ketiv* does not alter the
understanding of this clause. The *Ketiv* *מֻידָע appears to be a Pual
ms participle √ידע (attested elsewhere in 2 Kgs 10:11; Ps 31:12; 55:14;
88:9, 19; Job 19:14). Note that the participle cannot be taken as part
of a verbal predicate in this clause since there is no available referent: both choices—"No'omi" and "her husband"—are within PPs
and thus syntactically unavailable to be the subject. The participle

must be taken in its substantive (or better, null-head relative clause) usage: "(one) who was known," that is, "acquaintance, relative." The *Qere* מוֹדַע is a noun from the same root, "relative." This is a rare noun (attested elsewhere only in Prov 7:4) and the Masoretic pointing—using a *patah* instead of a *qamets* in the final syllable—suggests a clitic ("construct") form of the noun. Normally clitics are bound to NPs, but occasionally they may be attached to PPs (WO §9.6), which could be the case with the phrase מוֹדַע לְאִישָׁהּ. With either the *Ketiv* or *Qere*, the syntax of the clause provides the same information: No'omi had a relative.

אִישׁ גִּבּוֹר חַיִל. There are a number of ways to analyze this sequence of words. The first word, אִישׁ, is a noun, and the second word, גִבּוֹר, may function as either an adjective or noun, producing either "a mighty man" or "a man, a warrior" (appositional). The third word, חַיִל, is also a noun "power, wealth, property, character." חַיִל makes no sense in apposition to the previous one or two nouns (i.e., "a man, a warrior, power/property"). It seems best to take the second word, גִבּוֹר, as a clitic bound to חַיִל, and the whole phrase in apposition to the first noun, "a man, a mighty one of wealth/power/character." It is not clear which meaning of חַיִל was intended by the narrator. As the narrative unfolds, Boaz is characterized as all three: he is clearly a wealthy landowner, he has social power, and he is a man of great character. It is likely that the narrator intended all three and thus chose this polyvalent word to foreshadow what the audience will learn and to heighten the anticipation of a quick and happy outcome for No'omi.

וּשְׁמוֹ בֹּעַז. This short verbless clause is the manner by which the character's name is introduced. The Subject-Predicate order is typically used with this "name" formula with the opposite order (e.g., גָּלְיָת שְׁמוֹ 1 Sam 17:4) occurring less than half as often. The placement of the clause after an arguably unnecessarily long description of his qualities and clan-affiliation is likely a delaying tactic in order to increase the tension and audience curiosity ("Who could this wonderful relative *be*?").

2:2   וַתֹּאמֶר֩ ר֨וּת הַמּוֹאֲבִיָּ֜ה אֶֽל־נָעֳמִ֗י אֵֽלְכָה־נָּ֤א הַשָּׂדֶה֙
וַאֲלַקֳטָ֣ה בַשִּׁבֳּלִ֔ים אַחַ֕ר אֲשֶׁ֥ר אֶמְצָא־חֵ֖ן בְּעֵינָ֑יו
וַתֹּ֥אמֶר לָ֖הּ לְכִ֥י בִתִּֽי׃

This verse presents Ruth's solution to the (presumably) impover-
ished state of the two women: she intends to glean in the fields.

אֵֽלְכָה־נָּ֤א הַשָּׂדֶה֙ וַאֲלַקֳטָ֣ה בַשִּׁבֳּלִ֔ים אַחַ֕ר אֲשֶׁ֥ר אֶמְצָא־
חֵ֖ן בְּעֵינָ֑יו. Jussive 1cs Qal √הלך, Piel √לקט, and *yiqtol* Qal √מצא.
The use of the first person jussive (often called the "cohortative") as
well as the politeness particle נא is normal here: a person of lower
social status (e.g., a daughter-in-law) would be expected to use polite,
deferential language to a person of higher social status (e.g., a mother-
in-law) (Shulman 1996:208–12; cf. WO §34.7; MNK §19.4, 45.5; JM
§105c). It is preferable to understand Ruth's statement with the two
jussives—אלכה and אלקטה—to have some petitionary quality even
though some commentators argue differently, that the נא "identifies
the statement as a logical sequence of a previous statement or of the
general situation in which it was spoken. This cohortative and the following one are therefore not petitions for permission but declarations
made after Ruth considered her situation" (Hubbard 1988:136, n. 1;
see also Saakenfeld 1999:39). That Ruth was making a declaration
makes little sense when the response by No'omi is considered; that
is, the fact that the narrator has No'omi give her permission with the
statement לכי בתי suggests strongly the Ruth's statement was, in fact,
seeking such permission.

ר֨וּת הַמּוֹאֲבִיָּ֜ה. Ruth is identified as "the Moabite" here and in
five other places (1:22; 2:6, 21; 4:5, 10). This designation is first used
in 1:4 to describe both wives of No'omi's sons; after the initial use of
the genitilic adjective in 1:4, its continued use feels superfluous if not
awkward. The fact that it continues to be mentioned suggests that the
narrator is intent on keeping Ruth's foreign status highlighted for the
audience.

הַשָּׂדֶה. This NP functions as the complement of וַיָּבֹא; see comment on 1:4. There are three semantic possibilities for understanding the use of the definite article and the noun in this case: 1) The noun is used in reference to the general "arable land"; 2) the noun is a collective, "fields" (so Hubbard 1988:136, n. 2); or 3) the article is used here to point to a generic (that is, specific but unidentified) שׂדה, "a field" (or better "some field" in the sense of "whatever field I find to be adequate"). See WO §13.5.1 on the uses of the article in Hebrew.

וַאֲלַקֳטָה. The absence of the *dagesh* in the ק to mark the gemination characteristic of the Piel is due to a general (but not absolute) rule of degemination when certain consonants (וילמנק and sibilants) have some form of the *shewa*. The *hatef qamets* instead of a simple shewa is due to vowel harmony with following *qamets*.

וַאֲלַקֳטָה בַשִּׁבֳּלִים. This verb elsewhere takes an accusative complement (see Isa 17:5 מְלַקֵּט שִׁבֳּלִים בְּעֵמֶק רְפָאִים). It may also take a spatial adjunct with a PP (see Judg 1:7 הָיוּ ... שִׁבְעִים מְלָכִים מְלַקְּטִים תַּחַת שֻׁלְחָנִי). Thus, here the PP might be a spatial adjunct ("I shall glean *among* the ears of corn"); elsewhere, though, שׁבלים are the object of the action not the location. It may be that the preposition בּ is "partitive" (Hubbard 1988:136, n. 3; cf. WO §11.2.5 #31), i.e., "I shall glean *some of* the ears of corn"; however, the partitive use of בּ is not well-established. A final option is that the language of the book differs from majority usage in that the verb לקט takes an oblique complement marked with the preposition בּ ("I shall glean the ears of corn"); the case that WO cites, Ps 141:4, may be analyzed similarly. It is difficult to determine which of the three options is preferable. The spatial PP option is the least likely since there is no reason to present Ruth as agriculturally ignorant. The partitive PP option has little in its favor either. One argument in support of the third option, that the בּ PP is an oblique complement, is that the story-teller elsewhere exhibits an interest in using small but noticeable differences in the characters' speech patterns to distinguish them (see §4); thus, the slightly different grammar of this clause is, in the mouth of Ruth, a sign of her slightly different dialect or Moabite understanding of Hebrew.

שִׁבֳּלִים. The noun looks mpl but the singular has fs morphology: שִׁבֹּלֶת. The *hatef* vowel under a non-guttural is unusual (cf. JM §9b) and the reduction of a short /u/ to a form of *shewa* in a near open syllable is also unusual (in contrast to short /a/, which nearly always lengthens to /ā/ in near open syllables). The fs form points to a *qittul*-pattern noun, of which few others exist in BH. The word כֻּתֹּנֶת "tunic" is one, and its plural form is instructive: כֻּתֳּנֹת.

אַחַר אֲשֶׁר אֶמְצָא־חֵן בְּעֵינָיו. This is a null-head relative clause preceded by a preposition. As I noted for the null-head relative clauses in 1:13, 16, and 17, the head must be reconstructed based on what is appropriate in the context. Given the 3ms suffix on בעיניו, it is most natural in this verse (contra Sasson 1979:43) to take the implicit head as "the man," "the one," or "him," resulting in a literal translation of "after him who I find favor in his eyes" (for which "after him in whose eyes I find favor" is much smoother English). The addition of this PP is unexpected, given the Torah stipulations that the author has assumed; in other words, she should have had access to the gleanings of any field. The PP has been included as a foreshadowing device setting Boaz up as a man of impeccable character and magnanimity. It may also add to the characterization of Ruth as someone who is not entirely familiar with the traditions of Judah; she is a Moabitess, after all.

וַתֹּאמֶר לָהּ לְכִי בִתִּי. *Wayyiqtol* 3fs Qal √אמר and impv fs Qal √הלך. The verb ותאמר is followed by the adjunct PP לה and the accusative complement, the reported speech לכי בתי. Normal phrasal syntax would have the accusative complement precede the adjunct, but with אמר and other verbs of speaking it is overwhelmingly the case that that the addressee is indicated before the address. The use of the imperative from the socially dominant dialogue partner, the mother-in-law, is not atypical. The fact the Noʻomi's response to Ruth is instructive suggests that Ruth was in fact seeking her permission (see above).

2:3 וַתֵּ֤לֶךְ וַתָּבוֹא֙ וַתְּלַקֵּ֣ט בַּשָּׂדֶ֔ה אַחֲרֵ֖י הַקֹּצְרִ֑ים וַיִּ֣קֶר
מִקְרֶ֔הָ חֶלְקַ֤ת הַשָּׂדֶה֙ לְבֹ֔עַז אֲשֶׁ֖ר מִמִּשְׁפַּ֥חַת
אֱלִימֶֽלֶךְ׃

This clause quickly moves the setting from the unspecified place where Noʿomi and Ruth were staying to the harvest scene in the fields.

וַתֵּ֤לֶךְ וַתָּבוֹא֙ וַתְּלַקֵּ֣ט בַּשָּׂדֶ֔ה אַחֲרֵ֖י הַקֹּצְרִ֑ים. *Wayyiqtol* 3fs Qal √הלך, √בוא, and Piel √לקט. While הלך does not take a complement, בוא typically takes a locative PP complement, which must be assumed in this case (it is easily reconstructable from the PP following the next verb, בשדה). In the case of לקט, the following ב PP clearly presents a spatial adjunct, as does the second PP אחר הקצרים. While there is no complement specified for the verb, לקט should likely not be taken as an intransitive verb; rather, the complement has been elided and should be understood as בשבלים (as in v. 2).

הַקֹּצְרִ֑ים. Participle mpl Qal √קצר. The syntax of the article plus participle can be compositionally analyzed as a null relative head, the relative use of the article, a null-copula, and a participle as an event adjective (see comment on 1:8 and Cook 2008a). For some participles, the adjectival origin is clear in that the participle refers to a person who typically does the event signified by the verbal root. Traditionally called the "substantive use" of the participle, items like שומר "guard," קוצר "harvester," etc., have become agentive nouns.

וַיִּ֣קֶר מִקְרֶ֔הָ חֶלְקַ֤ת הַשָּׂדֶה֙ לְבֹ֔עַז אֲשֶׁ֖ר מִמִּשְׁפַּ֥חַת אֱלִימֶֽלֶךְ. The narrator moves the audience quickly to this narratorial opinion rather than dwelling on how long, which route, etc., Ruth took to get to the fields. The revelation that Ruth just happened to choose a field belonging to Boaz is the mini-climax that vv. 1-2 have been building toward. Grammatically interesting is the use of a *wayyiqtol* clause that does not advance the action or events within the world of the narrative. This clause specifies a feature of Ruth's activities that had already been presented in the narrative by the preceding three verbs. See comment on 1:6 for a discussion of the non-temporal sequence uses of the *wayyiqtol* (see also WO §33.2.2).

וַיִּ֣קֶר מִקְרֶ֔הָ. *Wayyiqtol* 3ms Qal √קרה followed by its cognate subject, lit. "her chance chanced," but idiomatically, "she chanced upon." The Hebrew idiom expresses the idea that Ruth came to Boaz' field by no knowledge of her own. This expression is found elsewhere in the Hebrew Bible only in Qoh 2:14, where the sage comments that he came to understand that מִקְרֶ֨ה אֶחָ֤ד יִקְרֶה֙ אֶת־כֻּלָּ֔ם, "one fate happens to them all (both the wise and the foolish)." This is certainly a loaded statement in the context of Qoheleth; it carries an implied indictment of God's justice. There is no compelling reason (contra Nielsen 1997:55) to suggest a similarly full (in a more positive sense) meaning for the expression in Ruth (i.e., an assertion of God's control).

חֶלְקַ֤ת הַשָּׂדֶה֙ לְבֹ֔עַז. There are two options for understanding the genitive construction here (which is a clitic phrase followed by the genitive use of the ל PP [see also 2:21, 4:3]). The whole phrase could refer to a specific piece of a field that had multiple owners, of which one was Boaz, i.e., "the (specific) portion of the field that belong to Boaz (not some other owner)." Or it could refer to the piece of the arable land ("farm country") that belonged to Boaz, i.e., Boaz' field. The latter option is simpler. Without further information, it is impossible to decide between the two options; however, since the distinction plays no part in the ensuing narrative, the choice matters little for the story.

Act II, Scene 2: Ruth meets Boaz (vv. 4-17)

Scene 2 is the principle scene of Act II. The narrator introduces Boaz to the audience in such a way that emphasizes his character: he is pious, kind, and magnanimous. The scene falls into two primary episodes—conversations between Boaz and his workers (vv. 4-7) and between Boaz and Ruth (vv. 8-16)—with a brief narrative conclusion in v. 17.

4Behold, Boaz came from Bethlehem and said to the harvesters, "Yhwh be with you," *and they said to him,* "May Yhwh bless you." *5Boaz said to his harvester overseer,* "Whose is this maiden?" *6And the harvest overseer answered and said,* "She is a Moabite maiden—the one who returned with No'omi from the territory of Moab. *7And she said,* "Let me glean and gather in sheaves after the harvesters" *and she entered and stood, from then—the morning—until now, this . . . her sitting . . . the house . . . a little." *8Then Boaz said to Ruth,* "Haven't you heard, my daughter? Don't go glean in another field; moreover, don't move from here. You should stick with my servant girls. *9Let your eyes be on the field that they harvest and walk after them. Haven't I commanded the lads not to touch you? So, if you thirst, you should walk to the vessels and drink from whatever the lads draw." *10Then she fell upon her face, prostrated herself to the ground before him, and said,* "Why have I found favor in your eyes so that you have recognized me, though I am a foreigner?" *11Boaz answered her,* "Everything that you have done for your mother-in-law after your husband died has been thoroughly reported to me—that you left your father and your mother and the land of your birth and went to a people whom you did not formerly know. *12May Yhwh repay your deed and may your wage be complete from Yhwh, the God of Israel, whom you have come to take refuge under his wings." *13And she said,* "Why do I find favor in your eyes, my lord, that you have comforted me and have spoken kindly with your maid-servant?—I'm not even one of your own maid-servants." *14Then Boaz said to her,* "At meal-time, come here and eat some of the bread and dip your morsel in the vinegar." *So she sat at the side of the harvesters and he held parched grain out to her. Then she ate and was satiated so that she left some. *15Then she rose to glean and Boaz commanded his servants,* "Let her glean even between the sheaves, and you must not insult her. *16You should even carefully pull out for her some of the bundles and leave them that she may glean them. You must not rebuke her." *17Thus she gleaned in the field until evening. She beat off what she had gleaned and it was about an ephah of barley.*

2:4   וְהִנֵּה־בֹעַז בָּא מִבֵּית לֶחֶם וַיֹּאמֶר לַקּוֹצְרִים יְהוָה
עִמָּכֶם וַיֹּאמְרוּ לוֹ יְבָרֶכְךָ יְהוָה:

In this verse the audience finally meets Boaz, Noʻomi's close relative and the owner of the field that Ruth just happened to choose for gleaning. Nothing is provided about his background; instead, the audience learns that he visits his fields and workers and that the first words out of his mouth reflect his piety.

וְהִנֵּה־בֹעַז בָּא מִבֵּית לֶחֶם. *Qatal* 3ms Qal √בוא with oblique PP complement indicating origin of movement. Instead of a *wayyiqtol* clause the narrator starts with הנה and a *qatal* verbal clause. Since this *qatal* clause continues the temporal sequencing of the narrative, why did the narrator not use a *wayyiqtol*? The presentative exclamation הנה (or any initial particle) cannot be used with a *wayyiqtol*, since the conjunction and verb have been morphologically fused. Thus, the narrator's choice to use הנה determined the type of clause: it could not be a *wayyiqtol*, which leaves the *qatal* as the obvious choice of verb. Note the S-V word order. Since the agent of the preceding clause is Ruth, a good argument can be made that the subject in this clause is also a Topic, marking a shift in the agent to Boaz.

וְהִנֵּה. The function word הנה is a presentative exclamation, "look!" or "see here!" (traditionally, "behold!") and often signals an event that, from the perspective of the addressee (whether a character within the narrative or the audience itself), is unexpected, surprising, or, in this case, highly coincidental (Andersen 1974:94–95; Berlin 1983:91–92; Hubbard 1988:143; cf. MNK §44.3.4). The form differs slightly depending on the context: within reported speech it is simply הנה; within narrative, the conjunction ו is typically prefixed, thus והנה (MacDonald 1975:172; WO §4.2.1).

בָּא. The form of the this verb is ambiguous, it could be a *qatal* 3ms, as I have indicated above, or a participle ms √בוא. In other words, the 3ms perfect and ms participle from II-ו roots are homophonous (they have the same form). In some cases the linguistic context suggests one parsing over the other. Here the evidence relates to the semantics of the perfect versus the participle. The perfect presents an action or event as a whole whereas the participle presents an action or event in process. In this verse, it makes better sense that "Boaz *came*" versus "Boaz *was coming*." It is impossible to tell whether Boaz' arrival occurred very soon after Ruth's (Sasson 1979:46) or after, say, enough time for the harvest overseer to get a good feel for Ruth's character (Campbell 1975:93). We must remember when reading Hebrew narrative that the *narrative* world and the *narrated* world operate differently; thus, regardless how long after Ruth it was that Boaz arrived, the narrator makes it feel like the *very next event* for the audience, thereby adding to the excitement of the story.

וַיֹּאמֶר לַקּוֹצְרִים יְהוָה עִמָּכֶם וַיֹּאמְרוּ לֹו יְבָרֶכְךָ יְהוָה.
This brief exchange provides the narrator the first opportunity to begin revealing information about Boaz' character. Minimally it indicates that he was a Yahwist, although that likely would have been assumed by the audience. Moreso, his greeting and the harvesters' blessing in response suggest that he was a good boss.

יְהוָה עִמָּכֶם. This is a null copula clause, "Yhwh (is) with you." However, the lack of an explicit verb leaves the temporal indication of the null copula dependent on the context. Nothing in the context preceding Boaz' reported speech points in any particular direction; it could be "Yhwh was with you," "Yhwh is with you," or "Yhwh will be with you." If we allow the following context, specifically the harvesters' reported response, to color the semantics, the null copula could have modal semantics (most likely that of the optative, or "wish"), thus, "May Yhwh be with you" (so also Hubbard 1988:144, n. 13).

יְבָרֶכְךָ יְהוָה. Jussive 3ms Piel √ברך with a 2ms suffix. The V-S order of this clause is tied to the modality of the verb: modal verbs raise over the subjects (= V-S), indicative verbs do not (= S-V, without some other "trigger"; see §2.5). Similarly, see 1:8.

2:5   וַיֹּאמֶר בֹּעַז לְנַעֲרוֹ הַנִּצָּב עַל־הַקּוֹצְרִים לְמִי הַנַּעֲרָה
הַזֹּאת:

The story-teller wastes little time in moving toward the meeting
of Ruth and Boaz. The reported speech in this verse is ostensibly the
first thing out of Boaz' mouth following the exchange of greetings
(2:4). In other words, Ruth immediately caught his eye.

נַעֲרוֹ הַנִּצָּב עַל־הַקּוֹצְרִים. The PP עַל הקוצרים does not
modify נער but rather the action indicated by the participle נצב.
Taking the ה as a relative marker (see comments on 1:8 and 2:3), the
adjunct PP resides within the relative clause.

נִצָּב. Participle ms Niph √נצב.

לְמִי הַנַּעֲרָה הַזֹּאת. The order is Predicate-Subject due to the
interrogative phrase למי. As in English, interrogatives are raised into
first position in the clause unless they are left in their original position
for Focus, e.g., *This girl belongs to **whom**?!*

לְמִי. This preposition + interrogative combination occurs twenty
times in the Hebrew Bible. The majority of occurrences signal a genitive ("belonging to whom"), while some indicate benefit when used
with a verb such as "work" (2 Sam 16:19) or "desire" (Esth 6:6). Since
no verb appears with the למי to indicate benefit, which would be
the only other fitting nuance in this verse, the only logical option is
the genitive interpretation, "whose is this maiden?" referring to her
deceased husband or perhaps familial identity.

2:6   וַיַּעַן הַנַּעַר הַנִּצָּב עַל־הַקּוֹצְרִים וַיֹּאמַר נַעֲרָה
מוֹאֲבִיָּה הִיא הַשָּׁבָה עִם־נָעֳמִי מִשְּׂדֵה מוֹאָב:

This verse provides the harvest overseer's response to Boaz (6b-7).
Even though the overseer was introduced in v. 5, he is referred to in the
same way in this verse. It is possible that the phrase הנצב על הקוצרים

is a formal position title and thus cannot be shortened (e.g., to just הַנַּעַר) without becoming vague.

וַיַּעַן הַנַּעַר הַנִּצָּב עַל־הַקּוֹצְרִים וַיֹּאמַר. *Wayyiqtol* 3ms Qal √ענה. Note the use of וַיַּעַן without the content of the actual answer, i.e., the reported speech. The answer is only introduced after וַיֹּאמַר. On the various patterns for introducing direct speech, see Miller 1994, 1996.

נַעֲרָה מוֹאֲבִיָּה הִיא הַשָּׁבָה עִם־נָעֳמִי מִשְּׂדֵה מוֹאָב. A null copula clause followed by a ה-relative clause. The overseer's response identifies Ruth not by name but by her nationality/ethnicity and also by her local connection. The null copula clause exhibits Predicate-Subject order. Predicate-Subject order in null copula clauses is often taken to indicate that the clause is "classifying" the predicate rather than "identifying" it (Andersen 1970; WO §8.4), i.e., it is not the person herself, Ruth, who is being discussed here, but this person's status as a Moabite. Alternatively, the word order in this case might be signaling Focus on the נערה מואביה "it's a *Moabite* girl!" perhaps reflecting the overseer's surprise at a Moabite taking advantage of the Israelite custom of gleaning. The switch to Predicate-Subject order left the relative clause (השבה ... מואב) separated from its head (נערה מואביה); the translation above attempts to reflect both the Focus on the predicate and the distance between the relative head and the relative clause (on the order of null-copula clauses, see also the comment on 2:10). On משדה מואב, see comment on 1:1.

הַשָּׁבָה. *Qatal* 3fs Qal √שוב. The vocalization of this form is identical to the vocalization of a fs Qal participle, but the טעם on the first syllable of the verb indicates that the Masoretes took the word as as *qatal* not as a participle (see 1:22, 4:3). The Masoretic understanding is preferable on semantic grounds: the perfect verb ("she returned") makes better sense in the context than a durative participle ("she is/was returning"). Note that השבה in this verse modifies an indefinite noun, נערה. The lack of definite agreement between נערה and השבה is good evidence that the ה is functioning here as a relative marker. See also §3 and the comments on 1:8, 22.

2:7 וַתֹּאמֶר אֲלַקֳטָה־נָּא֙ וְאָסַפְתִּ֣י בָעֳמָרִ֔ים אַחֲרֵ֖י
הַקּוֹצְרִ֑ים וַתָּב֣וֹא וַֽתַּעֲמ֗וֹד מֵאָ֤ז הַבֹּ֨קֶר֙ וְעַד־עַ֔תָּה זֶ֛ה
שִׁבְתָּ֥הּ הַבַּ֖יִת מְעָֽט׃

This verse continues the reported speech of the harvest overseer. Within his speech he quotes Ruth, making this an example of
reported speech that reports speech. Yet, the speakers are not difficult
to determine, which explains why the narrator wasted no effort in
naming them.

אֲלַקֳטָה־נָּא֙ וְאָסַפְתִּ֣י בָעֳמָרִ֔ים אַחֲרֵ֖י הַקּוֹצְרִ֑ים. According
to the harvest overseer, this is what Ruth requested when she arrived
at the field to glean. He does not indicate his response, although from
her actions (she is still not gleaning when Boaz arrived), it is clear that
she was not given permission.

אֲלַקֳטָה. On this verb, see v. 2. The complement of the verb is
elided, as it was also in v. 3.

וְאָסַפְתִּ֣י בָעֳמָרִ֔ים אַחֲרֵ֖י הַקּוֹצְרִ֑ים. *Qatal* (modal perfect)
1cs Qal √אסף. The complement of the verb may either be elided
(assuming שבלים) or an oblique PP complement, בעמרים. The
objection to the latter option is that this verb takes accusative, not
oblique, complements elsewhere. Thus, it is more likely that the PP
בעמרים is an adjunct specifying the goal or product, "into sheaves,"
or location, "among (the) sheaves" (see Bush 1996:114, and Campbell
1975:94–95, for discussions regarding which PP choice is more likely
given agricultural practices and the custom of gleaning). The second
PP, אחרי הקוצרים, is another adjunct and the preposition אחרי has
both a locational (e.g., positioned "behind" the harvesters) or temporal (e.g., "gleaning 'after' the harvesters are done") meanings (WO
§11.2.1a). Since walking behind logically entails temporal posterior-
ity, both meanings of the preposition apply in this PP.

וַתָּב֣וֹא וַֽתַּעֲמ֗וֹד מֵאָ֤ז הַבֹּ֨קֶר֙ וְעַד־עַ֔תָּה זֶ֛ה שִׁבְתָּ֥הּ הַבַּ֖יִת
מְעָֽט. *Wayyiqtol* 3fs Qal √בוא and √עמד. This sequence of constituents

is the most grammatically difficult in the book. As it stands it reflects contorted syntax; the Versions translated it freely to make sense of it and many commentators suggest emending in a variety of ways (for an overview of the suggestions, see Hubbard 1988:150–51, and Moore 1997). However, Hurvitz's explanation makes the most sense of the text as it stands: the overseer's confused language reflects his nervousness that his "boss" won't be happy with the fact that he let Ruth stay inside the house reserved for Boaz' harvesters (1983:122–23; so also Hubbard 1988:15; Rendsburg 1999:3–4). Thus, the rough, almost stuttering language at the end of the verse, is a literary device intended to convey a character's (the overseer) state of mind and is therefore not meant to reflect smooth syntax; see §4.

מֵאָז הַבֹּקֶר וְעַד־עָתָּה. The PP מאז is a temporal adjunct modifying the preceding verb ותעמוד and the PP is itself further specified by the appositional NP הבקר (contra Hubbard 1988:150, who takes מאז as a preposition "since" and הבקר its complement; see also Campbell 1975:94–95). On the use of the *waw* between the two PPs, מאז and עד־עתה, see WO §39.2; JM §177.

שִׁבְתָּהּ. Inf constr Qal √ישב with a 3fs suffix, lit. "her sitting." This is admittedly awkward and so many suggest reading שָׁבְתָה "she stopped, rested," which is not technically an emendation since only the vowels are changed. The result of such a change is "this one rested (in) the house (only) a little (while)." Grammatically the ms demonstrative זה for Ruth remains a problem and so it has also been suggested that זה should be taken (against the Masoretic טעמים) with the previous word, "until this (time) now." This, too, is grammatically awkward. Rather than grope for grammatical sense or emend the text, it is better to take it all as intentionally broken grammar (see comment above).

2:8 וַיֹּאמֶר בֹּעַז אֶל־רוּת הֲלוֹא שָׁמַעַתְּ בִּתִּי אַל־תֵּלְכִי לִלְקֹט בְּשָׂדֶה אַחֵר וְגַם לֹא תַעֲבוּרִי מִזֶּה וְכֹה תִדְבָּקִין עִם־נַעֲרֹתָי׃

Boaz does not acknowledge the harvest overseer's report but turns immediately to address Ruth. There is no formal greeting, as Boaz had done with his servants; instead Boaz instructs Ruth to stay and glean in his field (this instruction continues through v. 9).

הֲלֹוא שָׁמַעַתְּ בִּתִּי. *Qatal* 2fs Qal √שמע, with a null complement. The initial interrogative could be taken as a rhetorical question, that is, a question that expects agreement not a content answer (GKC §150; WO §18.2g, 40.3). But rhetorical questions assume that the addressee is privy to certain shared information, and it is not at all clear what Ruth could have heard about Boaz. In other words, the narrator has omitted what Boaz assumes Ruth has heard, resulting in a jarring information gap. Instead of a rhetorical question, the interrogative negative in this clause takes on the pragmatic force of a polite or even reproachful instruction: "listen, my daughter" (so Sasson 1979:49; Hubbard 1988:154). Boaz' continuation functions as the complement of the verb שמעת: he first tells Ruth where she should glean—in his field and with his servants (v. 8)—and he then tells her how she should glean (v. 9).

אַל־תֵּלְכִי לִלְקֹט בְּשָׂדֶה אַחֵר. Jussive 2fs Qal √הלך. The infinitive phrase ללקט בשדה אחר is an adjunct indicating the purpose of the action specified by תלכי (indicating the purpose or result is a common use of the inf constr; see WO §36.2.3). Within the infinitive phrase, the PP בשדה אחר is a locative adjunct to the inf constr לקט.

וְגַם לֹא תַעֲבוּרִי מִזֶּה. *Yiqtol* (modal) 2fs Qal √עבר with a PP adjunct, מזה. This clause rephrases and adds to what Boaz said in the preceding clause: "don't go somewhere else; moreover, don't even leave here." The initial גם serves as an item adverb to mark Focus on a specific constituent or conjoins clauses (MNK §4.5). Here it conjoins this clause with the preceding one. The גם may add some emphasis to the second clause, but (contra most commentators; see Hubbard 1988:152, n. 3; Bush 1996:120) its primary function is to add what Boaz considers important qualifying information: not only doesn't he want Ruth to glean in someone else's field, he does not even want her to move. In other words, the second negative instruction is narrower than the first. She might simply leave for the day without gleaning anywhere, which would fulfill the first instruction. Boaz, however, wants her to say and glean in his field, and it is only the combination of all three of his instructions in v. 8 that make his desire explicit.

לֹא. Note the use of לֹא with a (modal) *yiqtol*, instead of אַל with a jussive. It may be that here and in similar negative instructions to his workers in vv. 15 and 16 Boaz is asserting himself more forcefully than אַל with a jussive typically signals. If this is the case, then the previous אַל תלכי expresses his wish while with the next לֹא תעבורי he strengthens his assertion. See Shulman 2000 for an attempt to distinguish the modality of לֹא + modal *yiqtol* versus אַל + jussive.

תַעֲבוּרִי. The expected form of this verb is תַעֲבְרִי and the /û/ in the penultimate syllable is unusual. Consonantally the verb looks like a pausal form, such as תַעֲרוֹצִי in Isa 47:12 (GKC §47e; JM §32d), which are commonly indicated by vowel pointing in the Hebrew Bible (e.g., תַעֲבֹרוּ Gen 18:5) but not with the full spelling using the ו. In contrast, the writing of the *yiqtol* in the "pausal" with the ו predominates in the Dead Sea Scrolls (Qimron 1986:50–53; Abegg 1998:339; Muraoka 2000:341). One could argue, then, that the consonantal form in Ruth 2:8 reflects either the time of its composition (i.e., later in the first millennium, when *plene* spelling increased; cf. Myers 1955:10, 17; but see §3 on orthography and Barr 1989) or a scribal updating at a later time. The /û/ vowel of the form is anomalous, though, and does not reflect the typical pausal forms: GKC (§47g) cites only יִשְׁפּוֹטוּ in Exod 18:26 and תִּשְׁמוּרֶם in Prov 14:3 as parallel examples (and Prov 14:3 is often emended to תִּשְׁמְרֹם for full subject-verb agreement). JM (§44c) suggests that the forms are simply erroneous or, if not the result of scribal error, it may be that "in prepause and in pause a full vowel may have been preferred, and here, with a labial, *u* may have been preferred over *o*." It is also possible that the vowel was intentionally odd, although intelligible, to set off Boaz' speech (see §4 on its function as a stylistic feature).

וְכֹה תִדְבָּקִין עִם־נַעֲרֹתָי תִדְבָּקִין. *Yiqtol* (modal) 2fs Qal √דבק with a so-called paragogic ("word-extending") ן-, which appears more often in biblical texts typically judged to be older (GKC §47m, o; Myers 1955:17–18; WO §31.7; JM §44e, f). Hoftijzer argues that imperfects with a paragogic ן signal "contrastivity," which he describes as "exceptions to normal practice, contradictions, deviations from normal expectation, contrasts within one context, discontinuance of a certain situation, statements (etc.) which are contrary to the wishes, intentions and feelings of other people, or which go against reality in the outside world" (1985:55–56). His explanation for the form and thus the contrastivity here in v. 8 is that "Boaz emphasises this possibility (Ruth staying in his field) to the exclusion of other ones (Ruth not staying there but going to other fields" (1985:18–19). While it is plausible that verbal forms with a final ן reflect an older paradigm, it is difficult if not impossible to distinguish true archaisms from intentional archaizing (that is, later examples used to give a text or speaker a sense of "oldness"). Moreover, any contrastiveness in this verse is due to the adverb כֹה, not the verb: the emphasis in Boaz' statement in v. 8 lies in his insistence about where Ruth should be, not what she should do or with whom she should do it (those concerns come into play in v. 9). Although Hoftijzer claims that the paragogic ן is rarely used on jussive forms, note that the context of this verb as well as the paragogic form in 3:4 strongly suggest modal semantics (the category into which the jussive falls). That is, in both cases Ruth is being told what she "should" do. However the *nun*-forms work in other Northwest Semitic languages (see WO §31.7; JM §44e), the forms as they exist in Ruth cannot be tied to any indicative/modal distinction. Perhaps the paragogic forms in the book reflect an attempt to characterize Boaz' speech (in 2:8, 9, 21) as well as No'omi's (in 3:4, 18) (see §4; cf. Campbell 1975:17, 25; Hubbard 1988:156) and, as is often the case archaizing forms, they do not reflect the original semantic nuance.

כֹה. There are two ways to take the adverb כה in this clause (WO §39.3.4; MNK §41.2.3; JM §102h) and thus two ways to understand the relationship of the clause to the preceding context. As a demonstrative adverb, כה refers back (anaphora) to an action or event or refers forwards (cataphora), as in the common introductory formula in prophetic books כה אמר יהוה. In this clause we see the anaphoric use, that is, this clause indicates the intended result of the previous two instructions Boaz' gives Ruth: if Ruth stays, she will be allowed to stick closely to Boaz' servants. Alternatively, כה is also a locative adverb "here" and so in this clause Boaz may be restating himself the third time for extreme emphatic effect, i.e., "don't go to another field; don't pass from this (field); work here!" (so Campbell 1975:97; Hubbard 1988:155, n. 20; Bush 1996:120; Hoftijzer 1985:19).

תִדְבָּקִין עִם. The verb דבק is used in Ruth in 1:14; 2:8, 21, 23. As noted in the comment on 1:14, דבק typically takes an oblique complement as a ב PP or, less often, as a ל PP. Only here in v. 8 and again in v. 21 is the oblique complement an עם PP. It may be significant that both cases of דבק עם occur in reported speech attributed to Boaz (in contrast to the narrator's use of דבק ב in 1:14 and 2:23). Thus, this pattern may reflect another strategy by which linguistic variation contributes to the characterization of the narrative participants, in this case, Boaz (see also Ruth 3:3 and §4).

2:9 עֵינַיִךְ בַּשָּׂדֶה אֲשֶׁר־יִקְצֹרוּן וְהָלַכְתְּ אַחֲרֵיהֶן הֲלוֹא צִוִּיתִי אֶת־הַנְּעָרִים לְבִלְתִּי נָגְעֵךְ וְצָמִת וְהָלַכְתְּ אֶל־הַכֵּלִים וְשָׁתִית מֵאֲשֶׁר יִשְׁאֲבוּן הַנְּעָרִים:

This verse taken with the last verse create a set of instructions that go well beyond what would have been normal for gleaning. Instead of allowing Ruth to spend time in his field looking for remnant grain in the areas that had already been harvested, he urges her to "stick close to" and "follow right behind" his female harvesters, who would have been bundling the cut grain into sheaves (Bush 1996:121). The implication is that Ruth will get first pick of the remnants since she is being allowed to follow the harvesters so closely. With just this Boaz proves his magnanimity; with the further set of instructions to Ruth in v. 14 and to his harvesters in v. 16 he demonstrates that he views Ruth as a special case and intends to provide for her beyond the call of social duty.

עֵינַיִךְ בַּשָּׂדֶה אֲשֶׁר־יִקְצֹרוּן. This is a null copula clause in which the context suggests that the null copula carries jussive semantics, e.g., "Let your eyes be upon the field that they harvest. . . ." This is attested elsewhere (see JM §163b), but the example commonly cited are from blessings or curses rather than simple wishes like Boaz utters in this verse (so also Hubbard 1988:157, n. 28). Syntactically, the PP בשדה is the locative complement of the null copula, specifying "where" her eyes should "be."

בַּשָּׂדֶה אֲשֶׁר־יִקְצֹרוּן. The preposition ב in בשדה belongs to the matrix clause not the following relative clause since Hebrew does not allow "pied-piping" of the preposition like English (e.g., "the field in which they harvest"). Rather, the head of the relative in this clause is from the accusative object position within the relative, that is, "they harvest a field" is relativized to "the field that they harvest." If the head of the relative clause were a locative adjunct within the relative, Hebrew would require a resumptive PP with the appropriate preposition, i.e., שדה אשר יקצרון בו.

יִקְצֹרוּן. Yiqtol (indicative) 3mpl Qal √קצר with paragogic ן. On the paragogic ending, see comment above in v. 8. Semantically, the imperfective yiqtol functions as a present progressive, "the field that they are harvesting." Contextually the 3mpl verb refers to all the harvesters, men and women, while Boaz is more specific in the next clause with the 3fpl suffix in the reference אחריהן, by which he indicates that Ruth should follow his female servants engaged in the harvest.

וְהָלַכְתְּ אַחֲרֵיהֶן. Qatal (modal) 2fs Qal √הלך. The modal qatal expresses an action that is contingent on the first action, that of the null copula clause. Within this clause, the PP אחריהן is a locative adjunct to the verb of motion הלכת.

הֲלוֹא צִוִּיתִי אֶת־הַנְּעָרִים לְבִלְתִּי נָגְעֵךְ. Qatal 1cs Piel

√צוה with two complements, an accusative NP of the person(s) commanded and an infinitive complement representing the content of the command. This interrogative negative clause is yet another rhetorical question (see also 1:11, 13, 19, 21; 2:8). The obvious answer is "of course I (Boaz) am alerting my servants concerning you (Ruth)." As with many rhetorical questions, there is an implied emphasis on the assumed answer. The tense-aspect of the verb is complicated by the narrative context. From a strict narrative perspective, there has been no opportunity for Boaz to instruct his workers concerning Ruth, which suggests that the perfective *qatal* verb is not situated in the past time frame (so also Hubbard 1988:158; Buth, 121–22; contra Sasson 1979:49). Instead, the sequence of narrative events and dialogue make a performative use of the verb the likeliest interpretation (GKC §106i; WO §30.5.1d; JM §112f). That is, as Boaz addresses Ruth, he is by the act of this statement (which is presumably within hearing of his workers) giving the command. (Note that this requires the negative to be rhetorical, since a non-rhetorical negative is incompatible with a performative utterance: one cannot say "I hereby do not do X.")

נָגְעֵךְ. Inf constr Qal √נגע, with a 2fs object suffix. This verb often takes an oblique complement with a בְ PP; here the object is suffixed and thus accusative. The Qal inf constr of this root is also manifested as גַעַת. While the denotation of the verb is "to touch," in Gen 20:6 and Prov 6:29, it carries sexual connotations. It is thus not clear whether Boaz is concerned for Ruth's general physical safety or specifically concerned with heading off any sexual molestation.

וְצָמִת וְהָלַכְתְּ אֶל־הַכֵּלִים וְשָׁתִית מֵאֲשֶׁר יִשְׁאֲבוּן הַנְּעָרִים. In terms of formal syntax, the first modal *qatal* in this sequence is simply coordinated with the preceding clause. Semantically, however, the context suggests that it is the protasis of a conditional clause which itself is contingent on the preceding situation (see GKC §159e; WO §38.2b; JM §167a–b). In other words, "I have commanded my lads not to touch you so that if you are thirsty. . . ." The apodosis consists of the two following modal *qatal* clauses, "you should go and drink."

וְצָמִת. *Qatal* (modal) 2fs Qal √צמא, an intransitive verb. The elision (sound loss) of syllable-final א is typical in BH and it is sometimes omitted in spelling (see §3; see also ותשׁנה in 1:14; JM §24, 78).

וְהָלַכְתְּ אֶל־הַכֵּלִים. *Qatal* (modal) 2fs Qal √הלך. The PP אל הכלים is a locative adjunct.

וְשָׁתִית מֵאֲשֶׁר יִשְׁאֲבוּן הַנְּעָרִים. *Qatal* (modal) 2fs Qal √שׁתה. The complement of this verb is either implied (e.g., "water") or is fulfilled by the oblique partitive PP, that is, "some of (the water) that the lads draw." The relative clause within the PP has a null head, which can be reconstructed from the context as "water."

יִשְׁאֲבוּן. *Yiqtol* (indicative) 3mpl Qal √שׁאב with a paragogic ן (see comment on v. 8). The complement of this verb has been raised as the (null) head of the relative.

2:10 וַתִּפֹּל עַל־פָּנֶיהָ וַתִּשְׁתַּחוּ אָרְצָה וַתֹּאמֶר אֵלָיו מַדּוּעַ מָצָאתִי חֵן בְּעֵינֶיךָ לְהַכִּירֵנִי וְאָנֹכִי נָכְרִיָּה׃

Boaz' instructions to Ruth have finished and this verse describes her reaction, which reflects deep gratitude and obeisance as well as a bit of wonder.

וַתִּפֹּל עַל־פָּנֶיהָ. *Wayyiqtol* 3fs Qal √נפל, with the assimilation of the initial נ of the root. The PP על פניה is the directional or locative adjunct of the intransitive verb.

וַתִּשְׁתַּחוּ אָרְצָה. *Wayyiqtol* 3fs Hishtafel √חוי. This verb only occurs in the Š-causative-reflexive *binyan*, and only this verb occurs in this *binyan* (see HALOT s.v., JM §59g). Note that the ending וּ makes the verb look plural (the real plural form is יִשְׁתַּחֲווּ), but it is likely due to the loss of the final vowel and consonant in the longer imperfect form יִשְׁתַּחֲוֶה, after which the final ו /w/ became vocalized as וּ /u/ (JM §79t). The אָרְצָה, with the locative ה, is the directional adjunct for the verb.

וַתֹּאמֶר אֵלָיו מַדּוּעַ מָצָאתִי חֵן בְּעֵינֶיךָ לְהַכִּירֵנִי וְאָנֹכִי
נָכְרִיָּה. After prostrating herself before Boaz, Ruth expresses her astonishment at his benevolence by asking why.

מַדּוּעַ מָצָאתִי חֵן בְּעֵינֶיךָ לְהַכִּירֵנִי. The interrogative clause is the reported speech complement of the verb וַתֹּאמֶר. Within this clause, the interrogative itself is a purpose adjunct of the verb מָצָאתִי (*Qatal* 1cs Qal √מצא), the noun חֵן is the complement, the PP בְּעֵינֶיךָ is a locative adjunct, and the infinitive phrase is an adjunct indicating result (WO §36.2.3d).

לְהַכִּירֵנִי. Inf constr Hiph √נכר with assimilation of the initial נ and a 1cs accusative suffix.

וְאָנֹכִי נָכְרִיָּה. This null-copula clause would be labeled as a "classifying" clause in Andersen's 1970 model of null copula clauses that has achieved notable acceptance (see also WO §8.4, where this view is touted). In Andersen's framework, null copula clauses with Subject-Predicate word order are identifying clauses ("Who or what is the subject?"; WO §8.4.1a) while clauses with Predicate-Subject order are classifying clauses ("What is the subject like?"; WO §8.4.2a). Thus, in this scheme, the clause here in Ruth would be an identifying clause indicating who the speaker is, but here Ruth is saying "it's me" but classifying herself as a member of the general semantic class נכריה. Thus, this is a classifying clause that defies Andersen's word order framework. In fact, the general tendency of Subject-Predicate order for identifying clauses and Predicate-Subject order for classifying clauses is not an essential semantic distinction tied to word order but a semantic implication of the pragmatically influenced word order (Buth 1999 contains the most insightful analysis of word order in null copula clauses to date; see also comment above on 2:6). That is, Predicate-Subject order reflects the raising of the Predicate to function either as a Topic or Focus constituent. In our clause here, there is no raising and thus no Topic or Focus; rather, this is simply a basic statement in which Ruth adds information about herself without any syntactic-pragmatic nuances.

The juxtaposition of this null-copula clause with the preceding clause suggests a concessive relationship (JM §171f). That is, Ruth expects the information in this clause "I am a foreign woman" to preclude Boaz' benevolence as expressed in the preceding clause. That her foreign status does not affect Boaz' treatment of her is thus surprising to her. Note Ruth's choice of pronouns: she uses אָנֹכִי instead of אֲנִי. According to Revell 1995, אֲנִי is the default pronoun used by individuals with a perceived social status when speaking to someone of the same or lower status, whereas אָנֹכִי is the default pronoun for those of lower status when speaking to someone of higher status. Usage departing from this default conveys specific social and discourse information. In Ruth's case, it is normal for her to use the non-status אָנֹכִי since she is the foreigner asking to glean and Boaz is the Israelite who owns the field. Ruth also uses אָנֹכִי in 2:13 and 3:9. In contrast, No'omi uses אֲנִי in 1:21 when she addresses her peers and asserts herself with raw emotion (see Revell 1995:205). Interestingly, Boaz uses both pronouns; see comments on 3:12 and 4:4. As for the role that the pronouns have in dating the book, see the §3–§4.

2:11 וַיַּעַן בֹּעַז וַיֹּאמֶר לָהּ הֻגֵּד הֻגַּד לִי כֹּל אֲשֶׁר־עָשִׂית
אֶת־חֲמוֹתֵךְ אַחֲרֵי מוֹת אִישֵׁךְ וַתַּעַזְבִי אָבִיךְ וְאִמֵּךְ
וְאֶרֶץ מוֹלַדְתֵּךְ וַתֵּלְכִי אֶל־עַם אֲשֶׁר לֹא־יָדַעַתְּ תְּמוֹל
שִׁלְשׁוֹם:

Boaz' answer to Ruth summarizes the story up to this point, focusing on what Boaz considers critically revealing about Ruth's character. Undoubtedly, the narrator intends Boaz' perception of Ruth's actions to influence the audience's perception.

וַיַּעַן בֹּעַז וַיֹּאמֶר לָהּ. *Wayyiqtol* 3ms Qal √ענה. It is not certain but likely that the verb ענה is transitive; if so, its complement is not the content of the answer but the person to whom the answer is directed. Here the addressee/complement is not overt but nonetheless obvious: Ruth. When the actual (reported speech) content of the answer is desired, it is added by using the verb אמר. On the collocation of verbs introducing reported speech, see Miller 1994, 1996.

הֻגֵּד הֻגַּד לִי כֹּל אֲשֶׁר־עָשִׂית אֶת־חֲמוֹתֵךְ אַחֲרֵי מוֹת אִישֵׁךְ. Inf abs Hof and *qatal* 3ms Hoph, both from √נגד, with the assimilation of the נ. The inf abs is used here in its most common function: as an open-ended adverb. Since all adverbs "emphasize" the way in which they modify the verb (e.g., place, time, manner), "emphasis" is a useless descriptor for the function of the inf abs. What makes the inf abs unique is its open-ended semantics. It is an adverbial that asks the reader/listener to insert the most contextually appropriate modifier. In the case of this verse, I suggest a manner modification, "it has been thoroughly reported to me," which means, "I know everything relevant about you." However, temporal modification also works well, i.e., "it was just recently reported to me." I will leave it to the reader to come up with other, perhaps equally appropriate, options. Notice the Adv-V-S word order; the use of the inf abs typically triggers the raising of the verb over the subject, as it does here. Syntactically, this clause is the reported speech complement of the preceding verb ויאמר.

כֹּל אֲשֶׁר־עָשִׂית אֶת־חֲמוֹתֵךְ. *Qatal* 2fs Qal √עשׂה. The head of the relative may either be כֹּל used as a substantive or a null head (relegating כל to its more common role as a quantifier); see also 3:5, 11, 16; 4:9. Whereas the verb עשׂה is collocated with the preposition עם in Noʿomi's speech in 1:8 (and is also the narrator's linguistic choice in 2:19), the lexically different but semantically synonymous collocation of עשׂה and את ("with") is placed in Boaz' mouth. This may be yet another subtle cue distinguishing Boaz linguistically; see §4.

וַתַּעַזְבִי אָבִיךְ וְאִמֵּךְ וְאֶרֶץ מוֹלַדְתֵּךְ. *Wayyiqtol* 2fs Qal √עזב with an accusative compound NP complement. This clause does not carry the progression of actions or events within the narrative (in this case, the narrative within the reported speech) forward. Instead, it describes precisely how Ruth dealt so admirably with her mother-in-law. This falls under what WO labels the "epexegetical" use of the

waw (§§33.2.2, 39.2.4), but this is a wrongheaded approach. It is neither the *waw* that has an epexegetical function nor the verbal form
(*wayyiqtol*, modal *qatal*, etc.); rather, in this case and others like it,
we are simply looking at apposition on a clausal level. (Note that this
highlights the inadequacy of the description of apposition by reference grammars, which invariably treat only the apposition of simpler
constituents, such as nouns and noun phrases, but omit clausal apposition; see WO §12; MNK §29; JM §131).

וַתֵּלְכִי אֶל־עַם אֲשֶׁר לֹא־יָדַעַתְּ תְּמוֹל שִׁלְשׁוֹם. *Wayyiqtol*
2fs Qal √הלך, followed by a *qatal* 2fs Qal √ידע within the relative
clause. This clause as a whole follows the preceding clause sequen-
tially. Thus it participates in the apposition to כל אשר עשׂית את
חמותך, but is not itself appositional to the immediately preceding
ותעזבי clause.

תְּמוֹל שִׁלְשׁוֹם. The temporal phrase תמול שלשום modifies
the verb ידעת adverbially. The word תמול may be a noun "yesterday"
as in "we are a yesterday" (Job 8:9), but is nearly always an adverb "yesterday." The word שלשום "three days ago" is always an adverb and
has two possible derivations. It may be שלש "three" with an adverbial
ם-֯ ending, but it is more likely a loanword from Akkadian, *šalšūmi*
"three days," which itself is derived from *ina šalši ūmi* "in/on three
days" often used in the phrase *ina timāli šalši ūmi* "on yesterday (and)
the day before yesterday" (CAD 1989, 17:264, 268; see HALOT s.v.;
JM §102b). Note that "three days ago" for "the day before yesterday"
makes sense only if one counts "today" as the first day and "yesterday"
as "two days ago."

2:12 יְשַׁלֵּם יְהוָה פָּעֳלֵךְ וּתְהִי מַשְׂכֻּרְתֵּךְ שְׁלֵמָה מֵעִם
יְהוָה אֱלֹהֵי יִשְׂרָאֵל אֲשֶׁר־בָּאת לַחֲסוֹת תַּחַת־כְּנָפָיו:

Here Boaz follows his recital of what he has heard about Ruth's
actions with two blessings. The blessings are nearly synonymous,

although the second one is expansive and includes Boaz' assessment of Ruth's new religious loyalty to Yhwh.

יְשַׁלֵּם יְהוָה פָּעֳלֵךְ. *Yiqtol* (jussive) 3ms Piel √שלם. Notice the V-S order of the modal (jussive) clause. The verb שלם with the sense of "repay" typically takes two complements: the object repaid as the accusative complement and the person repaid as an oblique ל PP complement or as a second accusative. Here the person repaid is covert and easily reconstructed from the context, i.e., "to you [Ruth]."

וּתְהִי מַשְׂכֻּרְתֵּךְ שְׁלֵמָה מֵעִם יְהוָה אֱלֹהֵי יִשְׂרָאֵל אֲשֶׁר־בָּאת לַחֲסוֹת תַּחַת־כְּנָפָיו. *Yiqtol* (jussive) 3fs Qal √היה. The long form of the *yiqtol* of היה is תִּהְיֶה and the loss of the final segment (apocopation) results in a form that looks deceptively like the 2fs *yiqtol*, with the final ־ִי, but the 2fs form is תִּהְיִי. As with the previous clause, the V-S order is appropriate for the modal clause.

מֵעִם יְהוָה. With compound prepositions like מעם, one may sometimes discern the semantics of both elements, e.g., "from with," but in many cases, as here, it seems to be simply another way of expressing "from." I recommend restraint from over theologizing such grammatical phenomena, as many commentators tend to do (see, e.g., Hubbard's attempt to identify in the use of מעם the assertion that Yhwh was the source of the wage wished upon Ruth and that "[s]ince it frequently traces momentous turning points in destiny to Yhwh, . . . the preposition gave a nuance of drama to Boaz' pronouncement" [167, n. 78]).

אֲשֶׁר־בָּאת לַחֲסוֹת תַּחַת־כְּנָפָיו. The head of this relative clause is יהוה אלהי ישראל, which is resumed as the pronominal suffix imbedded within the infinitive phrase in the relative. The verb באת requires an oblique complement, which is fulfilled by the infinitive phrase לחסות תחת כנפיו. The dual NP כנפיו "his wings" is a metaphor for Yhwh's protection.

לַחֲסוֹת תַּחַת־כְּנָפָיו. Inf constr Qal √חסה. In 35 out of 37 occurrences in the Hebrew Bible, the verb חסה takes a ב PP to indicate the source of refuge, which suggests that the verb is transitive and takes an oblique complement. Only here and in Psalm 91.4 is the ב PP replaced by the PP תחת כנפיו.

2:13 וַתֹּאמֶר אֶמְצָא־חֵ֫ן בְּעֵינֶיךָ אֲדֹנִי כִּי נִחַמְתָּ֫נִי וְכִי דִבַּ֫רְתָּ עַל־לֵב שִׁפְחָתֶ֫ךָ וְאָנֹכִי לֹא אֶהְיֶ֫ה כְּאַחַת שִׁפְחֹתֶ֫יךָ׃

Apparently, Boaz' explanation for his generosity still leaves Ruth slightly incredulous, and her response, which is intelligible but not smooth, reflects her flustered state of mind.

אֶמְצָא־חֵ֫ן בְּעֵינֶיךָ אֲדֹנִי. *Yiqtol* 1cs Qal √מצא. The semantics of this verb are difficult to nail down. Since III-א verbs do not typically take the suffix ־ה of the 1st person jussive (JM §78h, 114b, n. 2), this verb could be an indicative *yiqtol* or a modal *yiqtol*. If it is an indicative verb, the imperfective *yiqtol* could be taken as a past habitual ("I have been finding"), a past progressive ("I was finding"), a present progressive ("I am finding"), or a general future ("I will find"). None of them make good sense in the context, since Ruth has already found favor in Boaz' eyes. If the verb is modal, it could be specifically jussive, expressing the volitive ("Let me find," "May I find," "Oh that I would find"), a modal *yiqtol* ("I intend to find," "Could I find?," or even "Should I find?"). Again, none of these make good sense: for instance, why would Ruth wish for Boaz' good will when she has already received it? In this bewildering situation, I have identified only one option that does not depart from normal verbal semantics and still makes good sense within the context: the clause is an unmarked interrogative and the verb is an indicative *yiqtol* conveying generic semantics: "(why) do I find favor in your eyes, my lord?" Whether the interrogative is implied, as I suggest here, or the verbal semantics are simply contorted (after all, Ruth is a Moabitess, as the narrator has reminded the audience numerous times), the awkwardness contributes to the "flustered" feel of the verse: Ruth is still confused by the reception that Boaz has given her.

כִּי נִחַמְתָּ֫נִי. *Qatal* 2ms Piel √נחם with 1cs accusative suffix. The verb lacks the characteristic gemination of the second root consonant in the Piel; this is due to the nature of the pharyngeal fricative ח. In this particular verb, the lack of gemination in ח does not produce the lengthening of the preceding vowel (technically, /i/ > /e/ is vowel lowering); the sound segment represented the characteristic gemination is simply lost. Syntactically, this כִּי clause is not causal or emphatic, as it is often understood, but a result clause expressing the outcome (which is unexpected from Ruth's perspective) of Boaz' favor (which is also unexpected): comfort and consolation. On the use of כִּי to introduce a result clause, see WO §38.3b; MNK §40.9; JM §169e.

וְכִי דִבַּ֫רְתָּ עַל־לֵב שִׁפְחָתֶ֫ךָ. *Qatal* 2ms Piel √דבר. This clause is a second result clause modifying the initial clause of the verse. The PP עַל לֵב שפחתך is an adjunct indicating the goal or recipient of the speaking. It is much more common for the verb דבר to take the preposition ל, although WO note that עַל sometimes replaces ל in LBH (§11.2.13g; cf. JM §133f). However, the specific phrase דבר עַל לֵב cannot be taken as "late" given 1) it never occurs with ל instead of עַל, and 2) its distribution in texts generally taken to reflect SBH (Gen 34:3; 50:21; Judg 19:3; 1 Sam 1:13; 2 Sam 19:8; Isa 40:2; Hos 2:16; compare with only two occurrences in "late" texts: 2 Chr 30:22; 32:6.

וְאָנֹכִי לֹא אֶהְיֶה כְּאַחַת שִׁפְחֹתֶ֫יךָ. *Yiqtol* 1cs Qal √היה with oblique PP complement. Again Ruth uses the default pronoun for "non-status" speakers (see comment on v. 10). The verb אהיה is indicative and the *yiqtol* here has a present progressive nuance, which comes out as a simple present ("I am not like . . .") due to the inherent semantics of the existential היה. Ruth's statement here is similar to אנכי נכריה in v. 10 in that she signals her lower social status with אנכי and communicates her bewilderment at Boaz' kindness by commenting on her own marginal status: in v. 10 she mentions her foreign

status, in this verse she asserts that she is not even at the level of Boaz'
servants. The pronouns אנכי is also a Topic constituent and signals
the shift between Boaz as the subject (agent of the verb דברת) in the
preceding clause and Ruth as the subject (patient of the verb אהיה)
(see §2.5).

2:14 וַיֹּאמֶר לָה בֹעַז לְעֵת הָאֹכֶל גֹּשִׁי הֲלֹם וְאָכַלְתְּ מִן־
הַלֶּחֶם וְטָבַלְתְּ פִּתֵּךְ בַּחֹמֶץ וַתֵּשֶׁב מִצַּד הַקּוֹצְרִים
וַיִּצְבָּט־לָה קָלִי וַתֹּאכַל וַתִּשְׂבַּע וַתֹּתַר׃

In this verse Boaz resumes his instructions for Ruth, allowing her
to eat with his workers.

וַיֹּאמֶר לָה בֹעַז לְעֵת הָאֹכֶל גֹּשִׁי הֲלֹם. The lack of a *mappiq*
in the ה is unexpected, and there seems little reason for its absence
although it does happen in a few other places in the Bible (see GKC
§23k; JM §25a). While the spatial deictic הלם clearly modifies the
verb גשי, the PP לעת האכל is ambiguously placed: it may modify
either the verb of speaking or the verb within the reported speech as
a temporal adjunct (i.e., "Boaz said to her at mealtime" or "at meal-
time come here"). The Masoretic טעמים do little to clarify their own
interpretation, since neither the טעם on בעז nor the טעם on האכל
are high level disjunctives: the *revia'* on האֹכל is slightly stronger than
the *geresh* on בֹעז. However, the טעמים mark prosody and not syntax
(see Dresher 1994) and so they are not strong support for any syntactic decision; moreover, note the similar pattern of a *geresh* followed
in a few words by a *revia'* in 2:8, where the *geresh* is on the last word
before the reported speech. Most modern commentators (see Sasson
1979:54; Bush 1996:125; Hubbard 1988:172; WO §34.4.a) take the
PP with the introductory formula. The narrative flow is the primary
evidence cited for the latter decision, since the second half of the verse
describes Ruth as sitting down to eat right after Boaz' instructions,
which admittedly makes for a rough sequence of events. However,
in support of taking the PP with the reported speech, two syntac-

tic observations are relevant: 1) it is common to have a time-setting PP fronted as a Topic (see §2.4–5), and 2) it would have been quite easy for the narrator to situate the PP clearly in the narration framework, e.g., וַיְהִי לְעֵת הָאֹכֶל וַיֹּאמֶר בֹּעַז לָהּ. The "narrative flow" observations of commentators notwithstanding, the combination of the Masoretic טַעֲמִים (which commentators have misunderstood) and the two syntactic observations I provided above nudge me to take the PP as part of the reported speech.

לְעֵת הָאֹכֶל. On the use of ל in temporal phrases, see WO §11.2.10c. Although this particular temporal phrase is not attested elsewhere, the similar phrase לְעֵת (הָ)עֶרֶב occurs five times (Gen 8:11; 24:11; 2 Sam 11:2; Isa 17:14; Zech 14:7).

גֹּשִׁי. Imperative 2fs Qal √נגשׁ. The paradigm form of this verb is גְּשִׁי. The stressed /o/ in the form here, which also occurs three out of five attested times in the mpl imperative גֹּשׁוּ, is anomalous and inexplicable (see GKC §66c). The form, with the vowel and the stress position, appears as if the root were גושׁ (like בוא) rather than נגשׁ (cf. Sasson 1979:55).

וְאָכַלְתְּ מִן־הַלֶּחֶם וְטָבַלְתְּ פִּתֵּךְ בַּחֹמֶץ. Both verbs are modal qatal 2fs Qal, from √אכל and √טבל, respectively. The verb אכלת requires just the single complement, the partitive מן PP "some of the bread." The verb טבלת takes two complements, one accusative פתך and one oblique בחמץ to specify the goal of the motion.

וַתֵּשֶׁב מִצַּד הַקֹּצְרִים. Wayyiqtol 3fs Qal √ישׁב with an oblique PP complement (see comment on 1:4). The narrative resumes with Ruth's actions, which follow immediately upon Boaz' last instruction. She accepts the invitation to eat with the workers and Boaz.

וַיִּצְבָּט־לָהּ קָלִי. Wayyiqtol 3ms Qal √צבט (a hapax legomena whose precise nuance remains unclear); the qamets-qatan is used in place of the paradigm holem because the verb has been prosodically attached to the PP לה, which carries the stress. The resulting closed, unstressed final syllable in the verb requires a "short" /o/ vowel rather than the "long" holem (see GKC §27d, 29b, h; JM §13c). The PP לה is an oblique complement indicating the recipient of the action and the noun קְלִי is the accusative complement. The clause וַיִּצְבָּט לָהּ קָלִי suggests that Boaz has accompanied his kind words with personal action.

וַתֹּאכַל וַתִּשְׂבַּע וַתֹּתַר. *Wayyiqtol* 3fs Qal √אכל, √שׂבע, and Hiph √יתר. The *patah* /a/ in the final syllable of וַתֹּתַר instead of the paradigm *tsere* /e/ is likely due to its pausal status (see JM §32c). The quick succession of verbs suggests the extent of Ruth's hunger while the use of the roots שׂבע and יתר reflect Boaz' generosity (cf. Sasson 1979:56; Bush 1996:126; Hubbard 1988:175); she has, after all, been waiting for some time just to get to the gleaning. The succession also serves to move the narrative promptly to the actual gleaning, which is reported by the very next verb at the start of v. 15.

2:15   וַתָּקָם לְלַקֵּט וַיְצַו בֹּעַז אֶת־נְעָרָיו לֵאמֹר גַּם בֵּין הָעֳמָרִים תְּלַקֵּט וְלֹא תַכְלִימוּהָ׃

The narration of Ruth's actions continues here—she finally begins to glean. Although the most natural reading of this verse is that it immediately follows Ruth's eating in the last verse, the narrator provides no explicit temporal cues. The audience is not supposed to be concerned with the specific chronology of the events but rather with the relative order in which they occur. It is interesting in that light to observe that the narrator quickly interrupts the description of Ruth's gleaning with an aside, which continues through v. 16, to report on one further set of instructions Boaz gives to his workers concerning Ruth. The aside contributes to the character profile of Boaz that the narrator has been building for the entire chapter: this fellow is a true mensch.

וַתָּקָם לְלַקֵּט. *Wayyiqtol* 3fs Qal √קום followed by an inf constr Piel √לקט, which serves as an adjunct of purpose.

וַיְצַו בֹּעַז אֶת־נְעָרָיו לֵאמֹר. *Wayyiqtol* 3ms Piel √צוה. On this verb requiring two complements, see comment above on 2:9.

גַּם בֵּין הָעֳמָרִים תְּלַקֵּט וְלֹא תַכְלִימוּהָ. *Yiqtol* (modal or jussive) 3fs Piel לקט√ and *yiqtol* (modal) 2mpl Hiph כלם√ with a 3fs accusative suffix. The first *yiqtol* carries the nuance of permission, "she is permitted to glean" or "let her glean"; the second *yiqtol* expresses the notion of obligation, "you must not insult [Ruth]") (see comment on לֹא תַעֲבוּרִי in v. 8). The PP בֵּין הָעֳמָרִים is both fronted for Focus and marked with גַּם (see comment on v. 8)—Boaz leaves no doubt that Ruth is to be allowed special gleaning privileges and is not to be treated poorly for it.

2:16 וְגַם שֹׁל־תָּשֹׁלּוּ לָהּ מִן־הַצְּבָתִים וַעֲזַבְתֶּם וְלִקְּטָה
וְלֹא תִגְעֲרוּ־בָהּ:

This verse continues Boaz' final set of instructions to his workers concerning Ruth. The fact that he not only allows Ruth to collect grain by following his harvesters through the field (instead of waiting until the harvest is finished) but also has his harvesters intentionally leave bundles for her goes well beyond the requirements of gleaning as it is described in Lev 19:9-10; 23:22; Deut 24:19-21. Leviticus 19 and 23 indicate that the "corner of the field" is to be left for those who need to glean, while Deuteronomy 24 suggests that forgotten or missed sheaves are to be left for the gleaners. In neither case, though, is the owner or harvesters instructed to intentionally leave behind sheaves from the harvest. Yet, this is precisely what Boaz is doing for Ruth.

וְגַם שֹׁל־תָּשֹׁלּוּ לָהּ מִן־הַצְּבָתִים. Inf abs Qal שלל√ followed by a *yiqtol* (modal) 2mpl Qal of the same root. The root שלל with a meaning "to pull out," which is suggested by the context, only occurs here; elsewhere the root means "to plunder." With the modal *yiqtol* Boaz is obliging his workers to do this. On the adverbial function of the inf abs, see the comment on v. 11. The noun צבתים is a hapax legomena whose meaning can only be contextually derived as something relating to the bundles of grain. The partitive מִן PP is the oblique complement of the verb and the PP לה is an adjunct identifying the recipient (unless this verb requires an indirect object,

which would make the PP לה a second complement). The use of גם
here, as in the previous verse, as well as the adverbial inf abs indicate
that Boaz is placing a great deal of stress on his instructions.

וַעֲזַבְתֶּם וְלִקְּטָה וְלֹא תִגְעֲרוּ־בָהּ. *Qatal* (modal) 2mpl Qal
√עזב and 3fs Piel √לקט, and *yiqtol* (modal) 2mpl Qal √גער. The
first *qatal* continues the deontic modality (obligation) of the previous
clause, and the second modal *qatal*, applying to Ruth, is also deontic
with the nuance of permission. The third verb, like לֹא תַעֲבוּרִי in v. 8
and לֹא תַכְלִימוּהָ in v. 15, appears to be a stronger directive. Syntactically, the verb עזבתם adds to the instruction directed at the workers
while the verb לקטה expresses the desired result from Boaz' perspective. The verb תגערו takes the בה PP as an oblique complement.

2:17 וַתְּלַקֵּט בַּשָּׂדֶה עַד־הָעָרֶב וַתַּחְבֹּט אֵת אֲשֶׁר־לִקֵּטָה וַיְהִי כְּאֵיפָה שְׂעֹרִים:

This verse brings the second scene of Act II to a close by reporting
briefly on Ruth's gleaning activity that fateful day.

וַתְּלַקֵּט בַּשָּׂדֶה עַד־הָעָרֶב. *Wayyiqtol* 3fs Piel √לקט. The word
הערב is in pause (with an *atnah*) and thus has a *qamets* in the stressed
syllable. The PP בשדה is a locative adjunct and the PP עד הערב is
a temporal adjunct for the verb ותלקט. Assuming that Ruth started
gleaning right after the midday meal, the temporal reference here, עד
הערב, suggests that she was able to salvage a good half-day's work
after her initial waiting (v. 7) and conversation with Boaz.

וַתַּחְבֹּט אֵת אֲשֶׁר־לִקֵּטָה. *Wayyiqtol* 3fs Qal √חבט. This rare
verb seemingly refers to the quick and dirty threshing and winnowing
process that Ruth would have had to perform in order to take only the
grain home. The null head of the relative clause אשר לקטה functions as the accusative complement of the verb.

וַיְהִי כְּאֵיפָה שְׂעֹרִים. This is another example of a *wayyiqtol*
clause serving to summarize rather than move the narrative to the
next event or action; see comments on 1:4, 6, 18, 22. The verb has a

null subject "it," referring back to the grain that Ruth beat out and the PP שְׂעָרִים כְּאֵיפָה is a complement of the copular verb indicating the approximate amount. On the use of the preposition כְּ for approximation, see comment on 1:4, WO §11.2.9b, and JM §133g. The noun אֵיפָה is not a clitic or bound form attached to (i.e., "in construct with") שְׂעָרִים, as one might expect, but related only appositionally. That is, the nature of dry measure is specified further by the appositional noun "barley."

Act II, Scene 3: Ruth Returns to No'omi (vv. 18-23)

While Scene 2 presented the dramatic meeting between Ruth and Boaz and suggests a possible plot resolution (i.e., perhaps Boaz will take care of both women and thus solve their immediate problems), Scene 3 describes the aftermath of that fateful day in the fields. After Ruth finishes gleaning, the audience cannot help but wonder if the story will soon end happily. Thus, the narrator has set the audience up for a number of questions and expectations. The scene consists of a narrative statement that moves Ruth from the fields back to No'omi (v. 18), dialogue between Ruth and No'omi (vv. 19-22), and a summary statement concluding both this scene and Act II.

18And she carried it and entered the city and her mother-in-law saw what she had gleaned. She brought it out and gave her what she left over from being satiated. 19Her mother-in-law said to her, "Where did you glean today? Where did you work? May he who blessed you be blessed!" So she related whom she worked with to her mother-in-law and she said, "The name of the man whom I worked with today is Boaz." 20And No'omi said to her daughter-in-law, "He is blessed to the Yhwh who has not abandoned his steadfast love for the living and the dead!" Then No'omi said to her, "The man is near to us! He is one of our kinsmen-redeemers!" 21And Ruth, the Moabite, said, "It is also that he said to me: Stick close to my servants until they have completed the whole of my harvest." 22No'omi said to Ruth, her daughter-in-law, "It is best, my daughter, that you should go out with his maid-servants so others will not molest you in another field." 23Thus she stuck close to Boaz' maid-servants to glean until the barley and wheat harvests were completed. And she lived with her mother-in-law.

וַתִּשָּׂא֙ וַתָּב֣וֹא הָעִ֔יר וַתֵּ֥רֶא חֲמוֹתָ֖הּ אֵ֣ת אֲשֶׁר־ 2:18
לִקֵּ֑טָה וַתּוֹצֵא֙ וַתִּתֶּן־לָ֔הּ אֵ֥ת אֲשֶׁר־הוֹתִ֖רָה מִשָּׂבְעָֽהּ׃

This verse moves Ruth from her gleaning activity back to where
she is staying with No'omi in Bethlehem.

וַתִּשָּׂא֙ וַתָּב֣וֹא הָעִ֔יר. Both verbs are *wayyiqtol* 3fs Qal, from
√נשׂא (with the assimilation of the initial נ) and √בוא, respectively.
The accusative complement of ותשׂא is null and unambiguously
recoverable from the preceding verse: the grain that Ruth had beat
out. The verb בוא typically takes an oblique PP complement to indicate the goal of the movement, but occasionally, as here, it takes an
accusative complement (which is often called an adverbial accusative,
WO §10.2.2; see also MNK §33.2.3; JM §125n).

וַתֵּ֥רֶא חֲמוֹתָ֖הּ אֵ֣ת אֲשֶׁר־לִקֵּ֑טָה. *Wayyiqtol* 3fs Qal √ראה.
The subject of the verb has changed, although, in keeping with the
shift from No'omi to Ruth as the primary narrative agent, No'omi
is not named but referred to as "her mother-in-law." The accusative
complement of the verb is the null head of the relative clause (see v. 17,
where the same phrase is used).

וַתּוֹצֵא֙ וַתִּתֶּן־לָ֔הּ אֵ֥ת אֲשֶׁר־הוֹתִ֖רָה מִשָּׂבְעָֽהּ. The first
two verbs are *wayyiqtol* 3fs Hiph √יצא and Qal √נתן; in the relative
clause the finite verb is a *qatal* 3fs Hiph √יתר and the non-finite verb
is an inf constr Qal √שׂבע with a 3fs genitive suffix. In this clause the
subject switches back to Ruth, although this is not done explicitly and
is discernible simply due to context (only Ruth is likely to have taken
the grain out and given some to the other person and only Ruth had
already been sated with it during her meal in the fields). The accusative complement of ותוצא is null and clearly still "the grain" (reconstructable from the context). The accusative complement of the verb
ותתן is the null head of the relative clause. Within the relative clause,
the accusative complement of the verb הותרה is the raised null head
of the relative and the PP (with imbedded infinitive) משׂבעה is an
adjunct specifying the origin of the leftover grain that Ruth gives to

Noʻomi (i.e., the so-called ablative use of מִן, WO §11.2.11d). Alternatively, if the PP מִשָּׂבְעָה includes not an inf constr but the noun שֹׂבַע
"satisfaction" (so HALOT, s.v.), the PP remains an adjunct but more
likely has a temporal function, "after her satisfaction" (on the temporal function of מִן, see WO §11.2.11c; JM §133e).

2:19 וַתֹּאמֶר֩ לָ֨הּ חֲמוֹתָ֜הּ אֵיפֹ֨ה לִקַּ֤טְתְּ הַיּוֹם֙ וְאָ֣נָה עָשִׂ֔ית
יְהִ֥י מַכִּירֵ֖ךְ בָּר֑וּךְ וַתַּגֵּ֣ד לַחֲמוֹתָ֗הּ אֵ֤ת אֲשֶׁר־עָשְׂתָה֙
עִמּ֔וֹ וַתֹּ֗אמֶר שֵׁ֤ם הָאִישׁ֙ אֲשֶׁ֨ר עָשִׂ֧יתִי עִמּ֛וֹ הַיּ֖וֹם
בֹּֽעַז׃

Noʻomi is still not named, keeping Ruth on center stage. Noʻomi
asks two parallel questions and then utters a blessings on the as-of-
yet (to her) unnamed benefactor. This serves to build excitement for
the connection that is about to be made: Noʻomi knows of her relatives, Ruth knows in whose field she gleaned, and the narrator artfully
delays the connection until the last word of the verse (so also Sasson
1979:58–59).

אֵיפֹ֨ה לִקַּ֤טְתְּ הַיּוֹם֙ וְאָ֣נָה עָשִׂ֔ית. *Qatal* 2fs Piel √לקט and
qatal 2fs Qal √עשׂה. Both clauses are interrogatives headed by locative question words meaning "where." The NP הַיּוֹם, which is used as
an adverbial time adjunct for the verb לקט, also serves as a poetic
hinge between the two parallel clauses. The more common meanings
of √עשׂה is "do" and "make," but it can have the connotation of "per-
forming labor" or "working," which is the notion here.

וְאָ֣נָה. This word reflects the combination of the locative interrogative אָן and the directional suffix ־ה, but, like שָׁם and שָׁמָּה,
often the word as a whole is used without any directional nuance (see
HALOT, s.v.).

יְהִ֥י מַכִּירֵ֖ךְ בָּר֑וּךְ. Jussive 3ms Qal √היה. Note the V-S order of
the modal clause. The ms Qal passive participle בָּרוּךְ is the predicate
of the subject מַכִּירֵךְ (ms Hiph participle √נכר with 2fs accusative

suffix). On the verb היה requiring a non-accusative complement, see the comment on 1:2. Although the more common syntax in blessings and curses is a null-copula clause with the Predicate (e.g., ברוך or ארור)–Subject order (see v. 2 below and WO §8.4.2e), when the copula is overt, the order we see in this clause is more common (Jer 20:14; 1 Kgs 10:9; Psa 113:2; Job 1:21; Prov 5:18; Ruth 2:19; 2 Chr 9:8; compare to only two cases in which the predicative pariciple precedes the subject, Gen 27:33; Deut 7:14). It is thus inaccurate to take the order in this clause to reflect any particular "emphasis" (so also Buth 1996:134; contra Campbell 1975:105–6; Hubbard 1988:183–84).

וַתַּגֵּד לַחֲמוֹתָהּ אֵת אֲשֶׁר־עָשְׂתָה עִמּוֹ. *Wayyiqtol* 3fs Hiph √נגד and *qatal* 3fs Qal √עשׂה. Once again there is an unspecified but contextually clear shift in verbal subjects, from No'omi to Ruth. The oblique complement (indirect object) precedes the accusative complement—this is common particularly when the oblique complement is a "light" phrase and the accusative complement is a "heavy" phrase, as in this case (although descriptively inadequate, see JM §155o). The null head of the relative clause is ambiguous and two natural options present themselves: it may be identified as the place where Ruth worked or the person that Ruth worked with. The former, locative option answers No'omi's question directly, since she asks "where?" but leaves the referent of the 3ms suffix in the PP within the relative unidentified and syntactically ungoverned—who is this "him" and how can an anaphoric pronoun refer back to an unspecified referent? (Such a clause is commonly considered a syntactic failure in linguistic analysis.) The latter, personal option at least provides a referent to which the pronoun may refer, even if the referent is null. In this case, though, the "who is the him?" question that arises from the lack of specificity is answered in the very next clause, which suggests that the second, personal option is preferred. The awkward grammar of this clause is very likely due to the narrator's interest in delaying the mini-climax. Ruth's answer of No'omi's "where" with a "who" effectively identifies the real intent of No'omi's query (similarly Hubbard 1988:184–85; Bush 1996:134).

וַתֹּ֗אמֶר שֵׁ֤ם הָאִישׁ֙ אֲשֶׁ֣ר עָשִׂ֤יתִי עִמּוֹ֙ הַיּ֔וֹם בֹּ֑עַז. Ruth
continues her narration, overlapping the previous clause with some
repetition. However, critical elements are added, such as the head of
the relative clause, שֵׁם הָאִישׁ, and predicate of the null-copula clause,
the proper noun בֹעַז.

2:20 וַתֹּ֨אמֶר נָעֳמִ֜י לְכַלָּתָ֗הּ בָּר֥וּךְ הוּא֙ לַיהוָ֔ה אֲשֶׁר֙
לֹא־עָזַ֣ב חַסְדּ֔וֹ אֶת־הַחַיִּ֖ים וְאֶת־הַמֵּתִ֑ים וַתֹּ֧אמֶר לָ֣הּ
נָעֳמִ֗י קָר֥וֹב לָ֙נוּ֙ הָאִ֔ישׁ מִגֹּאֲלֵ֖נוּ הֽוּא׃

No'omi is finally named in this scene, and Ruth is pushed back
on stage just a bit. The reason is that when No'omi learns the identity
of their new benefactor, she bursts forth in blessing. No'omi as the
main character of the whole story is again in focus and is perhaps on
the verge of significant shift from the bitterness at the end of chapter
1. However, the blessing contains some ambiguity (see below)—does
she make a statement about Boaz' or Yhwh's faithfulness? Thus, the
audience is left with only the hint of resolution.

בָּר֥וּךְ הוּא֙ לַיהוָ֔ה אֲשֶׁר֙ לֹא־עָזַ֣ב חַסְדּ֔וֹ אֶת־הַחַיִּ֖ים וְאֶת־
הַמֵּתִֽים. This long clause is a blessing with an important addendum.
As I noted for v. 19, when the blessing lacks an overt copula, it typically starts with the predicate (here a ms Qal passive participle √ברך).
The subject is the 3ms pronoun הוּא, and the ל PP adjunct, which is
the host for the long addendum, specifies the goal (WO §11.2.10d,
esp. n. 72; cp. JM §132l). The relative clause is the syntactic and literary puzzle: what is the head of the relative? Is it the pronoun הוּא,
which refers to Boaz, or the noun יהוה within the PP? The choice is
significant, since if No'omi recognizes Yhwh's faithfulness here, the
ultimate resolution of the book begins here. Many commentators take
Boaz as the head of the relative and thus the null subject within the
relative as well as the antecedent of the pronoun in חסדו. This makes
discourse sense in that Boaz is the topic of the blessing and there is no
explicit switch of Topic. However, it is an overwhelming tendency in

the syntax of relative clauses that, unless explicitly identified (e.g., by the use בעז within the relative) or a clear result of syntactic movement (e.g., the relative head fronted and thus moved away from its relative clause), the nearest grammatically acceptable antecedent is the relative head. This strongly suggests that יהוה is the head as well as the verbal subject of עזב and the antecedent for the pronoun in חסדו. The syntactic ambiguity is probably intentional: the narrator uses this clause to signal that No'omi's redemption has begun.

Another, less theologically significant syntactic ambiguity within the relative is whether the subject of the verb עזב in the relative is null (and coindexed with the relative head) or the NP חסדו. If the former analysis is correct, then the conjoined phrases את החיים ואת המתים are PPs, "[he] has not forsaken his faithfulness with the living and the dead" (compare Gen 24:49). If the latter analysis is correct and חסדו is the subject (it is a syntactic subject elsewhere, e.g., Gen 24:27), then the conjoined phrases are accusative complements, "who his faithfulness has not forsaken the living or the dead." There is no good evidence for determining which option is intended.

וַתֹּאמֶר לָהּ נָעֳמִי קָרוֹב לָנוּ הָאִישׁ מִגֹּאֲלֵנוּ הוּא. Once again No'omi is named, keeping her on center stage. Her statement in these clauses consists of two null copula clauses, both of which exhibit Predicate-Subject order. Although this is often considered the normal order in "classifying" null copula clauses (WO §8.4.2), I questioned the usefulness of this description in my comment on v. 10. For the two clauses here I would instead see the predicates as fronted constituents for contrastive Focus: "the man is **near** to us, he is one of our **redeemers**."

מִגֹּאֲלֵנוּ. Consonantally the noun גאל within the PP looks singular "our redeemer," but the context of the partitive מן PP requires a plural "one of our redeemers." A number of Hebrew manuscripts provide the י between the ל and the suffix נו, although they almost certainly reflect textual corrections. But the י in the plural form is technically a *mater lectionis* and many other formally ambiguous cases

like this exist, some of which must be plural from the context (JM
§94j, esp. n. 19). (On the function of the גֹּאֵל, see Leviticus 25 and the
summaries in Hubbard 1988:188–89, and Bush 1996:136–37.)

וַתֹּאמֶר רוּת הַמּוֹאֲבִיָּה גַּם כִּי־אָמַר אֵלַי עִם־ 2:21
הַנְּעָרִים אֲשֶׁר־לִי תִּדְבָּקִין עַד אִם־כִּלּוּ אֵת כָּל־
הַקָּצִיר אֲשֶׁר־לִי:

Ruth, who is identified by name in this verse, now returns to
center stage with No'omi. She provides information that had not been
given in the exchange she had with Boaz: her special gleaning privileges are not limited to a single day but extend through the remainder
of the harvest season. By report the audience thus finds out that Boaz
is already fulfilling at least part of the redeemer's role by providing for
the women on a longer-term basis.

וַתֹּאמֶר רוּת הַמּוֹאֲבִיָּה גַּם כִּי־אָמַר אֵלַי. The narrator
not only returns to using Ruth's name in this clause, he also classifies
her as a מאביה, thereby reminding the audience of her foreign status
(the narrator also used this technique at the end of Act I, in 1:22). The
complement of the verb ותאמר is the reported speech beginning with
גם. Note that the reported speech itself contains reported speech.

גַּם | כִּי. The collocation of these two function words is unusual.
In the seven other cases in the Hebrew Bible, it means "moreover,
when . . ." (Josh 22:7; Prov 22:6) or "even though" (Isa 1:15; Hos 8:10;
9:16; Ps 23:4; Lam 3:8). Neither option makes sense in this context,
though. Interestingly, this is the only case in which the Masoretes
used a *paseq* | to signal their understanding that the two words are not
to be taken together (see Yeivin 1980:216–17). Taken separately, the
two items may be understood as "also (it is) that" (see JM §157a, esp.
n. 2; so Hubbard 1988:182, n. 6).

עִם־הַנְּעָרִים אֲשֶׁר־לִי תִּדְבָּקִין עַד אִם־כִּלּוּ אֵת כָּל־
הַקָּצִיר אֲשֶׁר־לִי. This complex clause is given as Boaz' words that

are quoted by Ruth in her conversation with No'omi. On the verb
תדבקין, see comment on v. 8. The main clause starts with a Focus-
fronted PP עִם הנערים אֲשֶׁר לִי, by which Boaz (or Ruth for Boaz)
highlights the unusual gleaning privileges accorded to Ruth. The relative clause אֲשֶׁר לִי is used to express a genitive relationship periphras-
tically (i.e., in place of the more common cliticization, or "construct
state," of the first noun), although determining a grammatical explanation for why Boaz (or Ruth for Boaz) used הנערים אֲשֶׁר לִי instead
of the simpler נְעָרַי (as he did with נַעֲרֹתַי in v. 8) remains elusive.

The temporal PP עַד אִם כִּלּוּ אֵת כָּל הקציר אֲשֶׁר לִי includes
a *qatal* (3cpl Piel √כלה) verb (a perfect used in the future), which
follows עַד only 44x compared to over 150x of עַד followed by an inf
constr (as in v. 23 below). The use of אִם in what contextually is a
temporal clause is also unusual but not unattested (WO §38.7a; JM
§166p), although combined with עַד it appears superfluous here (and
occurs only three other times: Gen 24:19, 33, and Isa 30:17). And the
second periphrastic genitive כָּל הקציר אֲשֶׁר לִי is used, perhaps to
maintain consistency with the matrix clause (for other periphrastic
genitive constructions in the book, see 2:3; 4:3).

2:22 וַתֹּאמֶר נָעֳמִי אֶל־רוּת כַּלָּתָהּ טוֹב בִּתִּי כִּי תֵצְאִי
עִם־נַעֲרוֹתָיו וְלֹא יִפְגְּעוּ־בָךְ בְּשָׂדֶה אַחֵר׃

Both women remain in the story-telling focus here and No'omi's
comment regarding the appropriateness of Ruth's activity in Boaz'
field provides a third-party confirmation both of Boaz' good intentions and of the real possibility of receiving ill-treatment as a gleaner.

טוֹב בִּתִּי כִּי תֵצְאִי עִם־נַעֲרוֹתָיו. The main clause within the
reported speech is a null-copula clause with a simple adjectival predicate, טוֹב, a vocative address בתי, and a complex clausal subject, the
noun clause כי תצאי עם נערותיו, literally, "that you go out with his
servant girls is good, my daughter" (English requires either an exple-

tive construction, "it is good . . ." or a switch in the constituent order.)
Since Hebrew lacks morphological distinctions for absolute, comparative, and superlative degrees, the adjective טוב could be any of the
three here, "it is good that," "it is better that," or "it is best that." Since
it makes less sense for No'omi to provide a simple ethical assessment
of the situation (the absolute degree), it stands to reason that the comparative or superlative are intended here. If it taken as a comparative,
No'omi can only be comparing working in Boaz' fields with working
in someone else's; if it is superlative, then gleaning in Boaz' field sur-
passes all other options facing Ruth (other fields, other non-gleaning
activities to provide food, etc.). Both options make equal sense, in my
opinion. See WO §14.4–5 on the three degrees of adjectives.

וְלֹא יִפְגְּעוּ־בָךְ בְּשָׂדֶה אַחֵר. This clause is syntactically
joined to the preceding clause but the juxtaposition with the preceding clause suggests a result or purpose clause interpretation, "so that"
or "in order that." The verb יפגעו, which I and many commentators take to have negative connotation, e.g., "abuse, assault, molest,"
takes an oblique complement, here בָךְ. The second ב PP is a locative
adjunct.

2:23 וַתִּדְבַּק בְּנַעֲרוֹת בֹּעַז לְלַקֵּט עַד־כְּלוֹת קְצִיר־
הַשְּׂעֹרִים וּקְצִיר הַחִטִּים וַתֵּשֶׁב אֶת־חֲמוֹתָהּ:

    Scene 3 and Act II as a whole end with a summary statement
indicating that Ruth took Boaz' proposal for gleaning and continued
to live with her mother-in-law. Whatever large-scale plot resolution
that the encounter with Boaz may have suggested to the audience is
deflated with this verse: the women have been provided for through
the harvest season, but what then? Both the audience and No'omi
apparently have the same "what now?" question in mind, which leads
to the actions of Act III.

וַתִּדְבַּק בְּנַעֲרוֹת בֹּעַז לְלַקֵּט עַד־כְּלוֹת קְצִיר־הַשְּׂעֹרִים
וּקְצִיר הַחִטִּים. Wayyiqtol 3fs Qal √דבק with a ב PP oblique

complement. The infinitive phrase (inf constr Piel √לקט) provides the purpose for the main clause and the עַד PP, with the inf constr (Qal √כלה), is a temporal adjunct.

וַתֵּשֶׁב אֶת־חֲמוֹתָהּ. *Wayyiqtol* 3fs Qal √ישׁב, with an oblique PP complement, אֶת חמותה, indicating accompaniment. This *wayyiqtol* clause does not carry the action or events of the narrative forward. Instead, it provides information in the form of a summary of Ruth's activities during the entire harvest season. Thus, the temporal domain of this *wayyiqtol* includes the temporal domain of the preceding *wayyiqtol* clause.

This scene starts to fulfill the expectations the audience has been given, with Ruth's delivery of the grain and No'omi's excited response regarding Boaz' role. The hints delivered at the beginning of the Act, in v. 1, seem to be working out exceedingly well. But then the Act ends abruptly, with no further interaction between Ruth and Boaz. Yes, the women are provided for through the harvest season. But what about their long-term care? Where has Boaz gone in this story? The Act as a whole ends anti-climactically, with the resolution of the primary plot problem—No'omi's emptiness—still unresolved.

ACT III

Act III presents a manufactured meeting between Ruth and Boaz. No'omi, whose concern parallels the lack of resolution the narrator wants the audience to feel at the end of Act II, devises a plan to have Ruth present herself to Boaz for marriage. The plan and its implementation do not quite match, though: whereas No'omi has Ruth's best interest in mind, Ruth takes advantage of her meeting with Boaz to address No'omi's welfare. All three characters in this Act exhibit the fulness of their honor and worth.

Act III, Scene 1: No'omi Hatches a Plan (vv. 1-6)

¹No'omi, her mother-in-law, said to her, "My daughter, should I not seek for you a resting-place where it will be better for you? ²So, now, isn't Boaz our relative whose servant-girls you were with? Look—he is winnowing at the threshing floor of barley tonight. ³So you should wash, perfume, and put on your clothes, and go down to the threshing floor. Don't let yourself be known to the man until he finishes eating and drinking. ⁴When he lies down, you shall note the place where he will lie and then enter, uncover the place of his feet, and lie down. He will tell you what you should do. ⁵And she said to her, "All that you say to me, I will do." ⁶So she went down to the treshing floor and acted according to all that her mother-in-law had commanded her.

וַתֹּאמֶר לָהּ נָעֳמִי חֲמוֹתָהּ בִּתִּי הֲלֹא אֲבַקֶּשׁ־לָךְ 3:1
מָנוֹחַ אֲשֶׁר יִיטַב־לָךְ:

The narrator gives no time indicators to situate this clause from the end of Act II (2:23). It is not long, though, before the the mention of threshing (v. 2) makes it clear that No'omi wasted little time in assessing the situation—presumably the lack of serious development in Ruth's relationship with Boaz—and devising a plan.

וַתֹּאמֶר לָהּ נָעֳמִי חֲמוֹתָהּ. No'omi is mentioned both by name and relationship to Ruth at the outset of Act III. The use of לה "to her" to refer to Ruth, however, indicates that she remains firmly as the story's focus; that is, only by assuming that Ruth is the primary character in the audience's mind could the narrator refer to her with a pronominal PP "to her" instead of "to Ruth." It is a subtle grammatical indicator that Act III will be mostly about Ruth just as Act II was.

בִּתִּי הֲלֹא אֲבַקֶּשׁ־לָךְ מָנוֹחַ אֲשֶׁר יִיטַב־לָךְ. This reported speech clause is the complement to the preceding verb תאמר. The vocative בתי is less likely a term of endearment, as it is often used nowadays, as it is a reminder to Ruth that she is in a socially subordinate position to No'omi. No'omi used it with both her daughters-in-law in 1:11, 12, 13 and with just Ruth in 2:2, 22, and Boaz used it with Ruth in 2:8. It may be that the narrator is attempting to project for No'omi the image of a mother-in-law who is taking control of a situation in a firm but benevolent manner (the firm-and-benevolent stance also fits Boaz' interactions with Ruth in chapters 2 and 3). No'omi's question is rhetorical, assumes the answer "Of course I should!," and thus requires assent. The verb אבקש (modal *yiqtol* 1cs Piel √בקש) is followed by the very light PP as an adjunct providing the goal and then by the accusative complement מנוח. The locative noun מנוח is modified by a relative clause in which מנוח has been raised out of the subject position. In the context the verb in the relative clause, ייטב, has an implicit comparative degree: "a place of rest that is good for you [versus here]" = "a place of rest that is better for you [than here]." Contrary to almost all commentators (e.g., Sasson 1979:63–64; Hubbard 1988:197; Bush 1996:144–45), the אשר clause is not a result or purpose clause in the vast majority of the Hebrew Bible, including Ruth (see Holmstedt 2006).

3:2 וְעַתָּ֗ה הֲלֹ֥א בֹ֙עַז֙ מֹֽדַעְתָּ֔נוּ אֲשֶׁ֥ר הָיִ֖ית אֶת־נַעֲרוֹתָ֑יו
הִנֵּה־ה֗וּא זֹרֶ֛ה אֶת־גֹּ֥רֶן הַשְּׂעֹרִ֖ים הַלָּֽיְלָה׃

No'omi follows her first rhetorical question with a second that
zeroes in Boaz as the object of her planning. No'omi exploits the circumstances of Ruth's gleaning experience—for Ruth, not herself.

וְעַתָּ֗ה הֲלֹ֥א בֹ֙עַז֙ מֹֽדַעְתָּ֔נוּ אֲשֶׁ֥ר הָיִ֖ית אֶת־נַעֲרוֹתָ֑יו.
No'omi's follow-up statement opens with ועתה. This is a temporal
adverb that also makes a logical connection between two assertions
(see WO §39.3.4f). In this case, No'omi uses it to make a logical connection between her desire to have Ruth settled well and her plans
for achieving it. The rhetorical question makes the object of No'omi's
incipient plan clear: Boaz. The null-copula clause בעז מדעתנו is Subject-Predicate and classifies Boaz as a relative (hence the rhetorical
nature of the question, since both women are already aware of the
truth-value of the assertion; see 2:20).

אֲשֶׁ֥ר הָיִ֖ית אֶת־נַעֲרוֹתָ֑יו. *Qatal* 2fs Qal √היה. The PP את
נערותיו is an adjunct of accompaniment. The most natural reading
of the relative clause is that its head is the closer NP מדעתנו not בעז
(see comment on 2:20). However, it is also possible to take the head
of the relative clause as בעז (so Sasson 1979:63; Hubbard 1988:199,
n. 16; Bush 1996:145). In this case, the head has not been raised;
instead, the relative clause has been "lowered" for two reasons: the
tendency for "heavy" constituents to be placed later in a clause (e.g.,
"heavy noun phrase shift") and the desire for the predicate to be in a
more salient position, right after the subject NP instead of following
the non-restrictive relative clause. It is difficult to determine which
option is the correct analysis, although I consider the former option
more likely by the principle of parsimony.

מֹֽדַעְתָּ֔נוּ. The use of a morphologically feminine form and the
/a/ linking vowel between the stem and the suffix are both unexpected. The noun itself appears to be a feminine version of the *Qere*
in 2:1 מודע. Why No'omi here uses *מֹדַעַת (on the morphology see

GKC §94h; also JM §88Le) here instead of מוֹדַע or מֵידָע that she
used in 2:1 is unclear, and speculation does nothing to add clarity.
More than the word itself, the suffix contains an oddity: instead of
the very regular וֹ‍ as the suffix on singular nouns, this form has נוּ,
which except for this one case appears only on prepositions and the
quantifier כֹּל (GKC 91f; JM §94h).

הִנֵּה־הוּא זֹרֶה אֶת־גֹּרֶן הַשְּׂעֹרִים הַלָּיְלָה. The verb in this
clause is a participle (ms Qal √זרה) with progressive aspect, "he is
winnowing." The initial הנה is presentative exclamation, "look!"
or "see here!" and orients the addressee (whether another character
within the narrative or the audience, or both) to an item, activity, or
event that the speakers considers important. (On והנה see comment
on 2:4.) The subject pronoun הוא does not carry Topic or Focus, as
it does with finite verbs, since it is syntactically required as a subject
for the predicative participle. The participle זרה is transitive and here
the accusative complement is assumed and thus covert; based on the
context שׂערים is surely intended. The phrase את גרן השׂערים is
a PP adjunct specifying the location; on the use of את for proximity, "near," see HALOT s.v.; WO §11.2.4; MNK §39.5. It is quite
possible that the threshing and winnowing were done concurrently,
which would necessitate that they happen in two close but separate
locations. Finally, the NP הלילה is used adverbially to situate the
event temporally, "tonight."

אֶת־גֹּרֶן הַשְּׂעֹרִים. Some commentators object to taking גרן
השׂערים as a clitic phrase (what is "the threshing-floor of barley"?)
and prefer to take השׂערים as the overt accusative complement of the
verb (Hubbard 1988:199; Sasson 1979:64–65; Bush 1996:149–50; cp.
Campbell 1975:117–19). Such a move leaves את גרן without its defin-
ing modifier, and an nonspecific גרן would be very awkward here.
Moreover, it may be that there were actually two different threshing-
floors, one for wheat and one for barley, or that at least No'omi thought
so (note that narrator uses simply גרן in v. 6).

3:3 וְרָחַצְתְּ | וָסַכְתְּ וְשַׂמְתְּ שִׂמְלֹתֵךְ [שִׂמְלֹתַיִךְ] עָלַיִךְ
וְיָרַדְתִּי [יָרַדְתְּ] הַגֹּרֶן אַל־תִּוָּדְעִי לָאִישׁ עַד כַּלֹּתוֹ
לֶאֱכֹל וְלִשְׁתּוֹת:

After setting the scene in the last verse, in this verse No'omi begins her direct instruction to Ruth. The bathing, perfuming, and dressing strongly suggest that No'omi intended for Ruth to present herself to Boaz as a potential bride. That Ruth was supposed to wait until Boaz had finished his meal reflects socially polite behavior or the ageless principle that a man with a full stomach is more easily persuaded.

וְרָחַצְתְּ | וָסַכְתְּ וְשַׂמְתְּ שִׂמְלֹתֵךְ [שִׂמְלֹתַיִךְ] עָלַיִךְ וְיָרַדְתִּי [יָרַדְתְּ] הַגֹּרֶן. The sequence of verbs are all modal *qatal* 2fs Qal (√רחץ, √סוך, and √ירד, respectively), indicating that No'omi considered these actions logically (not temporally) contingent upon her previous description statement הנה הוא זרה את גרן השערים. In other words, No'omi's purpose in making the הנה statement was not simply to provide Ruth with information, but to establish a situation as the motivation for the set of instructions. The syntax of the third clause in the sequence is straightforward: שמלתך is the accusative complement of the שמת and עליך is the oblique complement (the verb שים requires two complements, much like נתן). The syntax of the fourth clause is also clear: the NP הגרן is the complement of ירדתי, which normally takes oblique PP complements but may also have a bare NP as here (see also v. 6, below). The syntax of the first two clauses is more opaque. Quite often both Qal verbs are taken as veritable reflexives, "wash yourself" and "anoint yourself." However, since רחץ in particular occurs in the Hitpael and in the Qal takes external accusative complements (e.g., רגל in Gen 18:4), it might seem possible to take שמלתך as the object of all three verbs: "so wash, anoint, and put on your clothes." However, the verb רחץ is only attested with יד, רגל, or בשר as its complement whereas the verb כבס in the Piel is used for washing clothes. Thus, we should probably assume that רחצת (and probably also סכת) here has a covert complement, such as בשרך.

וְסַכְתְּ. On the vocalization of the *waw* conjunction with a *qamets* when the host word is monosyllabic or disyllabic with stress on the penultima, see GKC §104g; JM §104d.

שִׂמְלֹתֵךְ [שמלתיך]. The *Ketiv* is ambiguous consonantally: it could be a singular count noun "your garment," a singular non-count (collective) noun "your clothes," or a plural count noun written defectively (note that it also lacks a ו *mater lectionis* for the feminine plural ending) "your garments." The only significant difference among the three options concerns the semantics of the singular collective option: this would likely only be the correct interpretation if the collocation of שׂים and שׂמלה were an idiom for "putting on clothes," i.e., "getting dressed" (Hubbard 1988:197, n. 7). The *Qere* is unambiguously plural "garments" and as the more explicit of the two spelling possibilities it may reflect later scribal correction. However, since either spelling option makes good sense, it is in reality difficult, if not impossible, to identify which is the earlier reading.

וְיָרַדְתִּי [ירדת]. The *Ketiv* looks like a 1cs *qatal*, but a first-person verb is nonsensical in this verse (why would No'omi tell Ruth to get dressed up and then assert that she, No'omi, would go down to meet Boaz?). The *Qere* is almost certainly a correction to match the morphology of the surrounding verbs and to fit the context. But this does not solve the problem of the *Ketiv*'s morphology—is the 1cs agreement morph תי- on the verb a scribal error or might it be an archaism? Many commentators select the latter option and suggest that this ending is a real archaic element (e.g., Myers 1955:11; Sasson 1979:68–69; Hubbard 1988:197, n. 8). The ending תי- does fit the 2fs *qatal* morphology reconstructed for West Semitic (see Huehnergard 1995:2130).

It is also possible that it is an archaism used to color No'omi's speech, a literary strategy that I have noticed at other points in Boaz' and No'omi's speech (see Ruth 2:8-9 and §4). The primary obstacle to the archaism explanation is the use of regular 2fs forms in No'omi's speech in 2:19; 3:2, 4, and the first three verbs in this verse: if

No'omi's speech is archaic or if the narrator is attempting to make it sound so, then why not be consistent (cf. Irwin 2008)? But consistent archaisms, which depart from the audience's grammar (and in this case result in a confusion between the 1cs and 2fs verbs), would result in an undesirable degree of distraction from the story—it would create too much interference in the communicative process. Thus, it is used only on the last verb or a four-verb series, allowing the narrator to throw in a speech distinctive for No'omi without sacrificing clarity (in other words, the first three verbs establish beyond any doubt that all the verb are 2fs). Note a similar sequence of four modal *qatal* verbs with the last a similar תי- verb in v. 4. Note also that both of the תי- verbs in vv. 3 and 4 are at (or one word before) a major pausal break (both times an *atnah*). In fact, we need not assume that the narrator had access to knowledge of historical forms no longer in use; like תעבורי in 2:8, the תי- forms in 3:3, 4 could reflect the narrator's creative use of forms that were similar enough to "normal" forms for the audience to interpret but just a bit "odd." It might simply be coincidental that the forms resemble what we reconstruct as their histories. Indeed, I consider this interpretation of the data the likeliest.

אַל־תִּוָּדְעִי לָאִישׁ עַד כַּלֹּתוֹ לֶאֱכֹל וְלִשְׁתּוֹת. *Yiqtol* (modal) Niph 2fs √ידע. No'omi switches from the modal *qatal* verbs, which were expressing contingent future actions (see above), to a modal *yiqtol*. Such a verb switch is required for a negative instruction, since the modal *qatal* is never negated (WO §32.1.3c). The PP לָאִישׁ is an adjunct providing the external agent of the passive verb, and the PP עד כלתו לאכל ולשתות is a temporal adjunct.

עַד כַּלֹּתוֹ לֶאֱכֹל וְלִשְׁתּוֹת. This PP contains three infinitives. The first, כלתו (inf constr Piel √כלה with 3ms suffix), is the complement of the preposition עד. The second and third (Qal inf constr √אכל and √שתה, respectively) are conjoined complements of the first כלתו.

3:4 וִיהִי בְשָׁכְבֹוֹ וְיָדַעַתְּ אֶת־הַמָּקֹוֹם אֲשֶׁר יִשְׁכַּב־שָׁם
וּבָאת וְגִלִּית מַרְגְּלֹתָיו וְשָׁכָבְתִּי [ושכבת] וְהוּא יַגִּיד
לָךְ אֵת אֲשֶׁר תַּעֲשִׂין:

No'omi continues her instructions, leading Ruth to the feet of Boaz.

וִיהִי בְשָׁכְבֹוֹ. Following the preceding modal *yiqtol* clause, the jussive יְהִי (Qal 3ms √היה) is expected here. That is, since the modal *qatal* sequence had been interrupted, a main clause (i.e., a non-contingent modal verb) is used to establish the tense-aspect-mood foundation upon which the modal *qatal* forms following are built. The subject of the יהי could conceivably be the PP בשכבו, but it is more likely that the PP is the nominative predicate and the verb has a null expletive subject (see comment on 1:1, 19; 3:8, 13). The PP בשכבו is temporal and contains an inf constr (Qal √שכב) with a 3ms suffix referring back to Boaz.

וְיָדַעַתְּ אֶת־הַמָּקֹוֹם אֲשֶׁר יִשְׁכַּב־שָׁם. *Qatal* (modal) 2fs Qal √ידע. This modal *qatal* is contingent on the event identified in the preceding jussive clause: when he lies down, Ruth should take note of the place. The NP את המקום is the accusative complement. It is modified by a restrictive relative clause: it is not just any place that Ruth should notice, but the specific place where Boaz lies down. The choice of verb within the relative is interesting. Most relative clauses have *qatal* verbs and refer to an event as a whole (i.e., perfective aspect), whether the event describing the relative head was in the past or future. Both the participle and the *yiqtol* (indicative) are used when the event in the relative clause is in progress or durative, whether in the past, present, or future time frame (although the *yiqtol* is more common than the participle except in cases of performative actions, such as many in Deuteronomy that relate to "the land that I am [Yhwh is] giving you [Israel]"). Here, the imperfective aspect of the *yiqtol* (3ms Qal √שכב) indicates that Ruth is supposed to identify where Boaz is in the act of lying down and carry out her plan while he remains in this activity. The *qatal* would be ambiguous in a context like this since it would allow Boaz to have finished "lying" and then risen and left.

Note that within the relative clause the head מָקוֹם is resumed by the locative adverb שָׁם. Since the verb שׁכב does not seem to require a locative complement, the resumptive adverb (and thus also the head מָקוֹם) is an adjunct. Resumption in Hebrew relative clauses is required in the NP-internal position (e.g., "the king who ruled *his* country") or a complement (accusative, e.g., "the country that the king ruled *it*," or oblique, e.g., "the country that the king ruled over *it*"), but distinct trends in the comparative Semitic and non-biblical Hebrew data indicate that resumption at other positions within the relative clause is a later development in ancient Hebrew, viz. the second half of the first millennium B.C.E. (see Holmstedt 2008). This feature, then, may reflect the relative date of the book (see §3).

וּבָאת וְגִלִּית מַרְגְּלֹתָיו וְשָׁכָבְתִּי [וְשָׁכַבְתְּ]. *Qatal* (modal) 2fs Qal √בוא, Piel √גלה, and Qal √שכב. The complement of באת is gapped from the last clause, הַמָּקוֹם אֲשֶׁר יִשְׁכַּב שָׁם, and the accusative complement of גלית is the NP מרגלתיו, the precise meaning of which is an infamous interpretive crux in the book. Unfortunately grammar does not provide much help (see Sasson 1979:69–70 and Nielsen 1997:68–69 for overviews and different proposals). Morphologically, -מ prefix nouns are often locative in nature, and given the unambiguously locative use in 3:14, I take it as "the place of the feet." Grammatically, מרגלתיו is either the accusative complement of the verb גלית or it is an adjunct (and the complement of גלית is covert and thus somewhat ambiguous—what is Ruth supposed to uncover—Boaz, herself?) On the *Qere-Ketiv* variation with the last verb, see the comment on v. 3.

וְהוּא יַגִּיד לָךְ אֵת אֲשֶׁר תַּעֲשִׂין. *Yiqtol* (modal) 3ms Hiph √נגד. The initial subject pronoun is in the Topic position and marks a shift in the agent (see §2.4–5). It does not carry Focus-marking, since there is no alternative to set "he" [Boaz] against: who else could tell

Ruth what to do in that context since there are presumably only two people present (at least from the perspective of the narrative)? The PP לֹד is the oblique complement specifying the goal or recipient of the action of the verb יגיד, and the accusative complement is the null head of the restrictive relative clause, which is defined by the parameters that תעשׂין establishes. On the paragogic ן in תעשׂין, see the comment on 2:8.

3:5   וַתֹּאמֶר אֵלֶיהָ כֹּל אֲשֶׁר־תֹּאמְרִ֗י [אֵלַי] אֶעֱשֶׂה:

Ruth's response is short and to the point. She is a willing coconspirator in this plan.

כֹּל אֲשֶׁר־תֹּאמְרִ֗י [אֵלַי] אֶעֱשֶׂה. On כל as the head of a relative clause, see comment at 2:11; for other examples, see 3:11, 16; 4:9. The entire phrase כל אשר תאמרי is the accusative complement of the verb אעשׂה (*yiqtol* 1cs Qal √עשׂה), and the fronted position of the complement indicates that it has been raised for Focus (contra Bush 1996:154). The challenge when a complex phrase has been raised for Focus is identifying precisely where the Focus lies—is it the quantifier כל or the verb תאמרי? It cannot be on the subject of the verb since it is null. In this context, it is most likely that כל bears the Focus (resulting in fronting of the entire phrase): Ruth indicates that she will do anything and everything that No'omi says. Her response is no doubt another element of her characterization as a paragon of loyalty. It is often noted that the expected verb within the relative clause is אמרת, a *qatal* 2fs refering to what No'omi has just instructed Ruth to do. The *yiqtol* cannot function the same way: in the past time frame the *yiqtol* is used for durative, habitual, future-in-the-past, or past progressive events or actions. None of these options work in this clause. Here the *yiqtol* is best taken as a general future. Thus, Ruth's answer does not directly reference the plan that No'omi has just finished outlining; rather, Ruth provides No'omi with a sweeping statement of loyalty in line with her poetic utterance in 1:16-17—she "will do all that [No'omi] says."

[אֵלַי] ‎ ַ ‎ . The *Qere-Ketiv* appears to be a simple manuscript variant, likely reflecting parablepsis. That is, a scribe began with the א of אֵלַי, looked up and when he looked back down continued not with אֵלַי but with אֶעֱשֶׂה. Thus, the simpler and probably original text includes the PP.

3:6 וַתֵּ֖רֶד הַגֹּ֑רֶן וַתַּ֕עַשׂ כְּכֹ֥ל אֲשֶׁר־צִוַּ֖תָּה חֲמוֹתָֽהּ׃

This verse serves as a hinge between scenes. For Scene 1 it parallels Ruth's stated intent to carry out No'omi's plan in v. 5 with the report that she did so here in v. 6. For Scene 2 the verse moves Ruth (and the audience) to the new location at the threshing floor. Both clauses use the *wayyiqtol* to provide summaries and the two clauses are not in temporal sequence. The first clause indicates that Ruth went to the threshing, presumably preparing herself before she went, and the second verb relates Ruth's activity to the plan that No'omi presented. (On the use of the *wayyiqtol* for summaries, see comments on 1:18, 22).

וַתֵּ֖רֶד הַגֹּ֑רֶן. *Wayyiqtol* 3fs Qal √ירד. The verb ירד is a verb of motion that does not take accusative complements but oblique PP complements indicating the goal of the movement. In this case the NP הגרן lacks the expected ל or directional ה- (see also above, v. 3). Grammars often describe NPs that are clearly not the direct object but still fulfill the verb as "adverbial accusatives" (see WO §10.2.2; cf. JM §125n).

וַתַּ֕עַשׂ כְּכֹ֥ל אֲשֶׁר־צִוַּ֖תָּה חֲמוֹתָֽהּ. *Wayyiqtol* 3fs Qal √עשה. The כ PP is not the complement of the verb ותעש, since this verb in its meaning of "do, make, carry out" mostly takes accusative, not oblique, complements (HALOT, s.v. ##1–11). Instead, here the verb has the sense of "behaving" (HALOT, s.v. #12), and the כ PP is a manner adjunct indicating that Ruth acted in agreement with No'omi's instructions. As with the relative clause in v. 5, the relative head in this clause may be either כל as a substantive or a null head.

צִוַּ֖תָּה. *Qatal* 3fs Piel √צוה with 3fs suffix. The vowel in the

penultimate syllable is due to the changes that occur to the 3fs *qatal*
form when object suffixes are added. The base to which suffixes are
added for this verb is *צִוָּת. The addition of a 3ms הוּ or 3fs הָ suffix
results in the assimilation of the ה of the suffix to the ת of the base,
which explains the *dagesh* in the final ת: e.g., צִוָּת* + הָ > צִוַּתה* >
צִוַּתָּ. The ה that is written has nothing to do with the actual suffix but is a *mater lectionis* (GKC §59g); thus, contrary to most comments on this verse, we would not expect a *mappiq* in ה (see, e.g.,
Sasson 1979:72–73; Hubbard 1988:206 n. 2; cp. Myers 1955:18; Bush
1996:159).

Act III, Scene 2: The Plan is Mishandled and then Salvaged (vv. 7-15)

Scene 2 occurs at the threshing floor and reports how Ruth approached
Boaz, as No'omi had instructed, but let him fall asleep, which is not
mentioned by No'omi and was presumably not her intention. The
result is a situation equally tense and humorous, leaving the audience with two questions: What will Boaz do? and How could Ruth
have gotten herself into this scandalous situation? It is possible that
the narrator is taking advantage of Ruth's foreignness for dramatic
effect, e.g., she didn't quite understand No'omi or maybe they don't
look down on midnight shenanigans in Moab. The scene continues
through Boaz' impressive recovery and honorable solution to the both
of the requests put before him, as well as the sensitive situation that
Ruth has put herself in.

*⁷When Boaz ate and drank and his heart was happy, he went in to
lie down at the edge of the pile, then she secretly entered and uncovered
the place of his feet and lied down. ⁸It was in the middle of the night that
the man started and turned himself over - and behold, a woman was
lying at his legs. ⁹He said, "Who are you?!" She said, "I am Ruth, your
maid-servant; therefore you should spread your skirt over your maidser-
vant because you are a redeemer." ¹⁰He said, "Blessed are you to Yhwh,
my daughter. You have carried out your latter kindness better than your
first by not going after young men, whether poor or strong. ¹¹And now, my*

daughter, do not fear—all which you say, I will do for you, because the whole assembly of my people knows that you are a woman of virtue. *[12]And now, it is indeed true that I am a redeemer; however, there is a redeemer nearer than I.* *[13]Stay tonight and when morning comes, if he will redeem you, good!—let him redeem. But if he is not willing to redeem you, I shall redeem you—as Yhwh lives! Now lie down until morning."* *[14]So she laid down at the place of his feet until morning and rose before anyone could recognize someone else. He said, "Let it not be known that the woman entered the threshing floor."* *[15]And he said, "Take the cloak that is upon you and hold it." So she held it and he measured six barley, put them on it, and went to the city.*

3:7   וַיֹּ֨אכַל בֹּ֜עַז וַיֵּ֣שְׁתְּ וַיִּיטַ֣ב לִבּ֗וֹ וַיָּבֹא֙ לִשְׁכַּ֣ב בִּקְצֵ֣ה
הָעֲרֵמָ֔ה וַתָּבֹ֣א בַלָּ֔ט וַתְּגַ֥ל מַרְגְּלֹתָ֖יו וַתִּשְׁכָּֽב׃

This verse abruptly moves the story through the facts of the Boaz' meal and Ruth's adherence to No'omi's plan. The initial switch of agents, from Ruth in v. 6 to Boaz at the beginning of this verse, is made explicit with בעז. The switch back to Ruth is not made explicit and the burden of marking the shift is left to the verbal agreement features. There is a sense of extreme economy here, perhaps even impatience, as the narrator mentions only the actions and details necessary to set up the confrontation between Ruth and Boaz.

וַיֹּ֨אכַל בֹּ֜עַז וַיֵּ֣שְׁתְּ וַיִּיטַ֣ב לִבּ֗וֹ וַיָּבֹא֙ לִשְׁכַּ֣ב בִּקְצֵ֣ה הָעֲרֵמָ֔ה.
All four finite verbs are *wayyiqtol* 3ms Qal forms, from √אכל, √שתה, √יטב, and √בוא, respectively. The verbs ויאכל and וישת are transitive, but their complements, "food" and "drink," are often left covert. The clause וייטב לבו is an idiom for being in a good mood (see HALOT, s.v. יטב), and since it does not actually describe an action but a state of being, it is clearly an important narrative detail. So Boaz ate dinner, felt good, and presumably went straight to sleep—all of which makes abundant sense after a long day at the threshing floor. Why Boaz slept at this location, instead of going home, and why No'omi would know

this are never explained. Perhaps it was customary (or just good business sense) to stay on location until the threshing, winnowing, and sale or storage of the harvested grain was finished, or perhaps his presence was ceremonial (so Sasson 1979:65, 75–76). The use of ויבא here suggests that he "entered" some place or structure to sleep, although the oblique complement is left implied; given the context of the הערמה, it may be that Boaz slept inside a half-filled granary, similar in practice and function to a shepherd sleeping in the entrance to a sheepfold—to protect the goods. The infinitive phrase לשכב בקצה הערמה (inf constr Qal √שכב) is a purpose adjunct for ויבא.

וַתָּבֹא בַלָּט וַתְּגַל מַרְגְּלֹתָיו וַתִּשְׁכָּב. *Wayyiqtol* 3fs Qal √בוא, Piel √גלה, and Qal √שכב. Ruth, too, "entered" whatever structure in which Boaz was lying. The interesting detail here is the addition of the PP manner adjunct בלט: Ruth came in, uncovered some space at this feet, and lied down—all without his knowledge! This type of entrance was not mentioned by No'omi as part of her plan, nor was letting Boaz fall asleep, which led to an awkward and slightly scandalous situation.

3:8   וַיְהִי בַּחֲצִי הַלַּיְלָה וַיֶּחֱרַד הָאִישׁ וַיִּלָּפֵת וְהִנֵּה אִשָּׁה שֹׁכֶבֶת מַרְגְּלֹתָיו׃

The narrator finally provides an indication of time, which although vague does provide enough information to impress upon the audience the result of Ruth's execution of the plan. The narrator heightens the impact by shifting to Boaz' perspective for the climactic moment.

וַיְהִי בַּחֲצִי הַלַּיְלָה. On the use of היה with a null expletive subject, see comments on 1:1, 19, 3:4, 13. The temporal PP בחצי הלילה provides the oblique complement of the copular verb היה.

וַיֶּחֱרַד הָאִישׁ וַיִּלָּפֵת. *Wayyiqtol* 3ms Qal √חרד and Niph √לפת. Needless to say, Boaz was startled to find a woman lying with him in the middle of the night. The concise report of his reaction, which continues into the next verse, is dramatically effective. On the meaning of וַיִּלָּפֵת as "to turn/twist oneself around," see Sasson 1979:78–80.

וְהִנֵּה אִשָּׁה שֹׁכֶבֶת מַרְגְּלֹתָיו. The initial וְהִנֵּה signals Boaz' surprise (see comment on 2:4 for more on וְהִנֵּה). The use of the participle (fs Qal √שׁכב), which represents the action in progress, has the effect of giving the audience a glimpse of the situation through Boaz' eyes; we see him leaning up on his elbow and looking at the woman lying near him with shock and curiosity.

3:9   וַיֹּאמֶר מִי־אָתְּ וַתֹּאמֶר אָנֹכִי רוּת אֲמָתֶךָ וּפָרַשְׂתָּ
כְנָפֶךָ עַל־אֲמָתְךָ כִּי גֹאֵל אָתָּה:

Boaz' response is blunt. Ruth's answer is pregnant with meaning and seems to go well beyond No'omi's intent. A simple reading of No'omi's plan was that she was trying to arrange a marriage for Ruth, whereas Ruth combines the marriage request with an implicit request for Boaz to play the "redeemer," which can only refer to his relative No'omi's need for financial redemption. Ruth again demonstrates her concern for her mother-in-law by adding what is perhaps a risky condition to the offer of herself as a bride for Boaz.

וַיֹּאמֶר מִי־אָתְּ. The verb אמר typically takes a ל PP for the addressee of the speaking. The omission of the PP here likely reflects the narrator's interest in making Boaz' response as short and blunt as possible, thereby highlighting his surprise. The lack of a *sheva* under the final consonant of the pronoun אַתְּ is inexplicable; the simplest explanation (and only one that presents itself) is scribal error.

וַתֹּאמֶר אָנֹכִי רוּת אֲמָתֶךָ. Ruth uses deferential language in her answer: אנכי and אמה. On אנכי, see the comment at 2:10.

וּפָרַשְׂתָּ כְנָפֶךָ עַל־אֲמָתְךָ כִּי גֹאֵל אָתָּה. *Qatal* (modal) 2ms Qal √פרשׂ followed by a ms participle √גאל in the כִּי clause. Ruth uses a modal *qatal* to make her request logically contingent upon her

self-identification: "I am Ruth so you should do this." The NP כנפך
is the accusative complement of the verb, and the PP על אמתך is a
locative adjunct. With the כי clause Ruth provides a second motive
for Boaz to marry her: to play the redeemer (a role, by the way, that
Noʻomi conspicuously avoided assigning to Boaz in all of her planning in vv. 1-4). Grammatically this is clear, but this is the only occasion in the Hebrew Bible that marriage is linked to the role of the
redeemer (see further comment below on v. 13). Typically the custom
invoked for marriage that would apply to Noʻomi or Ruth is the levirate responsibility in which a man marries his deceased and childless
brother's widow in order to provide an heir for the dead man (see Deut
25:5-10; Gen 38). See 4:5 for further discussion on the use of the the
levirate law in the book of Ruth.

כְּנָפֶ֫ךָ. The Masoretes add vowels to this noun indicating it is a
defectively written dual. The consonants are ambiguous: it could be
singular or dual (written defectively). Boaz used the dual כנפיו in 2:12
in reference to Ruth's religious loyalties. It is likely that the occurrence
there influenced the Masoretes' reading of the example in this verse,
since the singular "bottom/edge (of a robe)" is used elsewhere in collocations referring to marriage, e.g., Deut 27:20; Ezek 16:8; Mal 2:16.

3:10 וַיֹּאמֶר בְּרוּכָ֨ה אַ֤תְּ לַֽיהוָה֙ בִּתִּ֔י הֵיטַ֛בְתְּ חַסְדֵּ֖ךְ
הָאַחֲר֔וֹן מִן־הָרִאשׁ֑וֹן לְבִלְתִּי־לֶ֗כֶת אַחֲרֵי֙ הַבַּ֣חוּרִ֔ים
אִם־דַּ֖ל וְאִם־עָשִֽׁיר׃

Boaz' response to Ruth's request, which continues through v. 13,
reveals that he has recognized both her good intentions and her confusion of two distinct customs in Israel: the duty of redemption and
the levirate obligation. In this verse he praises her actions.

בְּרוּכָ֨ה אַ֤תְּ לַֽיהוָה֙ בִּתִּ֔י. Participle pass Qal fs √ברך. While
Subject-Predicate word order is basic in participial clauses, the more
common order in statements of blessing or curse is participle-subject.

This is due to the Focus-fronting of the participle in order to contrast the state wished upon the addressee with alternatives. In other words, when you wish for someone to be blessed or cursed, that someone is assumed and not in Focus whereas the resultant state is the emphasized (to use a non-technical term). The PP ליהוה could be an adjunct indicating the source of the blessing (JM §132f), but it is more likely an oblique complement that specifies the goal, i.e., "may you be pronounced blessed to Yhwh" (WO §11.2.10d; JM §132g). The NP בתי is a vocative referring to Ruth and keeping the attention on Boaz' superior social status.

הֵיטַבְתְּ חַסְדֵּךְ הָאַחֲרוֹן מִן־הָרִאשׁוֹן. *Qatal* 2fs Hiph √יטב. The subject is null ("you") and the accusative complement is חסדך following by a manner (comparative) מן PP. The adjective האחרון modifies חסדך, which is gapped in the second phrase, leaving the adjective הראשון to fill the nominal role. The former case of loyalty refers to Ruth's return with and kindness toward No'omi; the latter case refers to Ruth's use of the threshing-floor situation to find a redeemer for No'omi.

לְבִלְתִּי־לֶכֶת אַחֲרֵי הַבַּחוּרִים אִם־דַּל וְאִם־עָשִׁיר. Inf constr Qal √הלך. The infinitive phrase, negated with לבלתי, is an adjunct to the preceding finite verb היטבת explaining how or by what Ruth accomplished חסד so well (WO §36.2.3e; JM §124o). The two adjectives, both modifying הבחורים, contrast with each other and the two אם work together as "whether . . . or . . ." (JM §175c). The conjoined phrases אם דל ואם עשיר serve as a merism: the two poles of a scale upon which young men fall thus includes all young men. Boaz' point was that Ruth had acted nobly in not choosing any young man but following her mother-in-law's plan to approach Boaz. Boaz' statement implies two features of the characters which the audience has not previously been told: Ruth must be a בחורה, since it is implied that she could have pursued young men and also Boaz must not be a בחור, since if he were he could not praise Ruth for not pursuing one.

3:11 וְעַתָּ֗ה בִּתִּי֙ אַל־תִּ֣ירְאִ֔י כֹּ֥ל אֲשֶׁר־תֹּאמְרִ֖י אֶֽעֱשֶׂה־לָּ֑ךְ
כִּ֤י יוֹדֵ֙עַ֙ כָּל־שַׁ֣עַר עַמִּ֔י כִּ֛י אֵ֥שֶׁת חַ֖יִל אָֽתְּ׃

Verses 11-13 describe Boaz' plan to address Ruth and No'omi's situation, now that he has been asked to do so.

וְעַתָּ֗ה בִּתִּי֙ אַל־תִּ֣ירְאִ֔י כֹּ֥ל אֲשֶׁר־תֹּאמְרִ֖י אֶֽעֱשֶׂה־לָּ֑ךְ. Jussive 2fs Qal √ירא. Boaz begins this clause and the first clause of the next verse with ועתה. This temporal adverb, which No'omi also used in 3:2, makes a logical connection between two assertions (see WO §39.3.4f). In all these cases the adverb makes a temporal and logical connection between the clause it introduces and the preceding clause. In this case Boaz connects his positive response to Ruth's request with the statement he just made about her admirable behavior: Boaz recognizes her quality and will act because of it. His first step is to assuage any trepidation she may have with אל תיראי. He then indicates that he will do anything she says. Note that כל אשר תאמרי, the accusative complement of the verb אעשה, is Focus fronted and the verb inside the relative is a *yiqtol*—the verb indicates that this is not an assertion that Boaz will take care of what Ruth has already requested (a perfective *qatal*) but of anything that she is requesting or will request (a imperfective *yiqtol*). Thus, the narrator gives Boaz a statement nearly identical to Ruth's in 3:5, no doubt to affirm the fundamental loyalty and good will of both characters. (On כל as the head of a relative clause, see comment at 2:11; for other examples, see 3:5, 16; 4:9).

כִּ֤י יוֹדֵ֙עַ֙ כָּל־שַׁ֣עַר עַמִּ֔י כִּ֛י אֵ֥שֶׁת חַ֖יִל אָֽתְּ. Participle ms Qal √ידע. With this כי clause Boaz clarifies his motivation to act on Ruth's and No'omi's behalf—it is not because either woman was in need but because of the exemplary character Ruth has demonstrated. The normal order for participial clauses, even when they are imbedded as here, is subject-participle. The fronted participle has been raised for Focus, to indicate the breadth (all) and strength (without a doubt) of the community's knowledge concerning Ruth's character.

The second כִּי clause is the complement of the verb יודע. Within the
כִּי clause is a null-copula clause with the predicate fronted for Focus:
they all **know** that Ruth is a **woman of virtue**. The narrator has Boaz
use two significant innertextual links in this clause. First, שַׁעַר עַמִּי
may be a metonymy for the whole people instead of the specific legal
council that we see in chapter 4, but nonetheless foreshadows the climactic scene in chapter 4. Second, the assessment of Ruth as an אֵשֶׁת
חַיִל matches the narrator's assessment of Boaz as an אִישׁ גִּבּוֹר חַיִל
in 2:1.

3:12 וְעַתָּה כִּי אָמְנָם כִּי אם גֹאֵל אָנֹכִי וְגַם יֵשׁ גֹּאֵל
קָרוֹב מִמֶּנִּי׃

This verse continues Boaz' plan, but introduces a significant
complication: Boaz does not have the first right to redemption in this
case.

וְעַתָּה כִּי אָמְנָם כִּי אם גֹאֵל אָנֹכִי. As with the last verse,
Boaz begins with the temporal-logical adverb וְעַתָּה, orienting Ruth
to information highly relevant to his commitment to do whatever
Ruth requests. He affirms that he is one who could fulfill the role
of redeemer for Noʻomi. While the gist of this clause appears clear,
the syntax is tricky. After וְעַתָּה, the sequence of כִּי אמנם כִּי אם is
complicated: how do the two instances of כִּי work and what effect
does the inclusion or omission of the unpointed אם have? (The אם is
unpointed as one of the eight examples of the *Ketiv welo Qere* "written
but not read"; Yeivin 1980:§102). Of the words, אמנם is the easiest
to classify: it is one of the few morphological adverbs in BH; more
precisely, it is a "disjunct adverb" that conveys "the speaker's attitude
toward the form of the utterance ('truly, truthfully, roughly')" (WO
§39.3.4; cf. MNK §41.3.8; JM §164). On the adverb ם- ending, see
comment on 1:21.

The function word כִּי is the thorny issue. The essential challenge,
since the word is multivalent, is identifying how each occurrence here

is used. כִּי may introduce conditional, temporal, causal, complement/
noun, adversative (often with אִם), and concessive clauses as well as
introduce an emphatic declaration ("surely/certainly/indeed") (see
WO §§38–39; MNK §40.9, and the relevant clause sections in JM).
In this clause Boaz does not seem to be setting out a condition (e.g.,
"and now, if it were true . . ."), time orientation (e.g., "and now, when it
is true . . ."), cause (e.g., "and now, because it is true . . ."), noun clause
(e.g., "and now, that it is true . . ."), or adversative (e.g., "and not, but
it is true . . ."). That leaves either a concessive use (e.g., "although it
is true . . .") or emphatic use (e.g., "it is indeed true . . ."). The choice
between the two depends on the second כִּי as well as the content of the
following coordinated clause, which as a concessive clause (see below),
suggests that this כִּי is emphatic.

The second כִּי is more easily identified: since there is no proposition before the adverb אָמְנָם for it to modify, it must be that the כִּי
clause is the proposition that Boaz asserts is אָמְנָם, thus, "and now,
although/indeed it is true that I am a redeemer, . . ." Of the fourteen
biblical occurrences of this rare adverb (Gen 18:13; Num 22:37; 1 Kgs
8:27; 2 Kgs 19:17; Isa 37:18; Ps 58:2; Job 9:2; 12:2; 19:4-5; 34:12;
36:4; Ruth 3:12; 2 Chr 6:18), only one other verse has a כִּי noun clause
following אָמְנָם (Job 12:2). Yet even in the twelve cases without כִּי
following אָמְנָם, the adverb is best taken as an adverbial predicate
followed by a nominalized clause, "it is truly/true (that). . . ." The אִם
seems to have been taken by the Masoretes as a disruptive element,
thereby motivating the *Ketiv welo Qere*. When אִם follows כִּי, the collocation is overwhelmingly a strong adversative, "but . . . !" Here such
a meaning does not fit the context, since Boaz is not contrasting his
self-classification as a גֹּאֵל with a contrary opinion. Nor do the other
meanings of אִם fit: the conditional (e.g., "and now, it is true that if I
am a redeemer, . . .")—there is no good "then"-apodosis for this condition—or the affirmation that developed out of the oath formula (e.g.,
"and now, it is true surely I am a redeemer"), which is redundant with
the אָמְנָם. Instead, it is likely that the אִם is a case of dittography:
some scribe wrote the first כִּי אָמְנָם and followed with the second

כִּי clause by accidently starting the same initial sequence of letters, כִּי אִם, before continuing correctly.

גֹּאֵל אָנֹכִי. Although גֹּאֵל can be parsed as a participle ms Qal √גאל, the same *qotel* pattern is used for an agentive noun (see comment at 2:3). That is the case here: גֹּאֵל is not a participial predicate indicating progressive action, "redeeming," but an agentive role, "redeemer." The word order of this null-copula clause is Predicate-Subject, which reflects the Focus-fronting of the predicative גֹּאֵל to assert that Boaz is a redeemer over against the alternative (e.g., not a redeemer). Boaz' use of the 1cs pronoun אנכי is noteworthy. As I noted at 2:10, אני is the default pronoun used by individuals with a perceived social status when speaking to someone of the same or lower status, whereas אנכי is the default pronoun for those of lower status when speaking to someone of higher status. Here, Boaz could rightfully use אני, but places himself on the same social level as Ruth by using אנכי.

וְגַם יֵשׁ גֹּאֵל קָרוֹב מִמֶּנִּי. This clause adds Boaz' significant caveat, which is unfortunate for Ruth (and for readers or listeners interested in a quick resolution): there is someone else who has the right of redemption. The initial adverb גַם modifies the entire clause and may be additive or concessive. If it is additive ("moreover"), it indicates that the following information qualifies the information in the previous clause. In such a concessive capacity, it may be translated as a "though, although, however." See comments at 1:5, 12; 2:8 and WO §39.3.1; MNK §41.4.5. The adjective קָרוֹב followed by the comparative מִן PP result in an adjective phrase modifying the noun גֹּאֵל.

3:13 לִינִי| הַלַּיְלָה וְהָיָה בַבֹּקֶר אִם־יִגְאָלֵךְ טוֹב יִגְאָל וְאִם־לֹא יַחְפֹּץ לְגָאֳלֵךְ וּגְאַלְתִּיךְ אָנֹכִי חַי־יְהוָה שִׁכְבִי עַד־הַבֹּקֶר:

Boaz concludes with a directive for Ruth to remain there for the rest of the night as well as a promise that he will inquire into the redemption issue.

לִינִי ׀ הַלַּיְלָה. Impv 2fs Qal √לין. The primary vowel in II-י
verbs, particularly the prefix pattern forms (imperfect, jussive, imperative, infinitives), can be misleading since it looks like the theme vowel
of the Hiphil. But the semantics of this verb (and, e.g., שִׁית, שִׂים)
and the lack of a ה prefix on the perfect forms (e.g., לָן) indicate that
the correct *binyan* is Qal. The imperative is followed by the definite
NP הלילה, which here is used as a temporal adverb, "tonight" (see
comment on 1:12).

וְהָיָה בַבֹּקֶר. *Qatal* (modal) 3ms Qal √היה. The modal *qatal*
indicates that this clause is contingent—in this case temporally and
logically—on the preceding event (Ruth's spending the night). On
the use of היה in scene-setting temporal clauses, see the comment on
1:1, 19; 3:4, 8.

אִם־יִגְאָלֵךְ טוֹב יִגְאָל. Both verbs are modal *yiqtol* or jussive
3ms Qal √גאל, with a 2fs accusative suffix on the first verb. The
initial conditional אם establishes the basic modal semantics of both
the protasis and the apodosis. Some commentators take טוב as an
adverb, e.g., "if he redeems well," and other take it as a finite verb
with null expletive subject, "(it) is good" (on null expletive subjects,
see comment in 1:1; on טוב inflected as a *qatal* verb, see HALOT, s.v.;
JM §80q). Alternately, טוב may simply be an adjectival predicate of
a one-part null copula clause, "(it is) good," which has in this context
an exclamatory value, "good!"

וְאִם־לֹא יַחְפֹּץ לְגָאֳלֵךְ וּגְאַלְתִּיךְ אָנֹכִי חַי־יהוה. This clause
presents a second conditional statement that expresses the antithesis
of the first. Though the אם establishes the essential modality of the
clause, the verb יחפץ is formally ambiguous: morphologically it could
be a modal *yiqtol* or jussive. The collocation with לא clarifies that
יחפץ is a modal *yiqtol*. On the use of לא in a modal *yiqtol* clause, see
comment on 2:8. The infinitive phrase (inf constr Qal √גאל with 2fs
accusative suffix) is the complement of the verb יחפץ.

וּגְאַלְתִּיךְ אָנֹכִי חַי־יהוה. *Qatal* (modal) 1cs Qal √גאל with
2fs accusative suffix. It is fitting (and common) in a conditional apo-

dosis to find a modal *qatal*, given its semantic contingency. Since a subject pronoun is not required with finite verbs in Hebrew, an overt pronoun typically marks Topic or Focus. In this case, the pronoun marks Focus: Boaz is contrasting himself with the alternative made explicit in the last verse, the other redeemer. As a Focus-marked constituent, the pronoun is in a very high position in the clause and is thus typically the first constituent. Here the modal *qatal* has been raised over the subject, resulting in V-S order. The חַי יהוה at the end of the clause is an interjection in the form of an oath exclamation (WO §40.2.2; JM §165e); as an interjection, the phrase חַי-X most often sits on the margins of clauses, mostly in front. Here Boaz leaves his exclamation in the final position, which may have been syntactically required by the raising of the modal *qatal*.

יִגְאָלֵךְ ... לְגָאֳלֵךְ ... וּגְאַלְתִּיךְ. The use of 2fs suffixes on all three verbs is noteworthy. Boaz identifies Ruth as the object of the redemption, but according to the description in Leviticus (25:25; cf. 25:47–49), the גֹּאֵל is הַקָּרֹב אֵלָיו "the near(est) to him," that is, the closest relative to the one who has come upon hard times and has had to sell his land. Thus, the גֹּאֵל is of the same family or clan, but is Ruth considered family by virtue of her marriage? Whose land is being redeemed here? Is it No'omi's husband's, as chapter 4 indicates? If so, then why does Boaz direct the גֹּאֵל activity at Ruth? For readers who expect the story to fall right in line with the Pentateuchal descriptions of the "redeemer" as well as the "levirate" responsibility, the book of Ruth is a puzzle. It has, among other ideas, been suggested that the origins of the story antedate the Pentateuchal legislation. But it is more likely that the traditions are being manipulated for the sake of the plot. By keeping the question "Who is being redeemed here?" front and center in the audience's mind, the story-teller is masterfully weaving together two stories of redemption: No'omi's spiritual redemption and Ruth's "romantic" (for lack of a better term) redemption.

שִׁכְבִי עַד־הַבֹּקֶר. Impv 2fs Qal √שׁכב. Boaz' last words for the night are blunt. The verb שִׁכְבִי is intransitive, although it often takes a temporal adjunct (here הבקר עד), or locative adjunct, or both. In this instance the location is implied: "here" or "with me."

3:14 וַתִּשְׁכַּב מַרְגְּלָתָו [מרגלותיו] עַד־הַבֹּקֶר וַתָּקָם
בְּטֶרֶום [בטרם] יַכִּיר אִישׁ אֶת־רֵעֵהוּ וַיֹּאמֶר אַל־
יִוָּדַע כִּי־בָאָה הָאִשָּׁה הַגֹּרֶן:

With this verse the narrator moves quickly from the midnight conversation to the morning. It is clear that avoiding any public suspicion of inappropriate behavior on Ruth's part is Boaz' primary concern; two of the three clauses in the verse are given to the topic of Ruth not being seen at the threshing-floor.

וַתִּשְׁכַּב מַרְגְּלָתָו [מרגלותיו] עַד־הַבֹּקֶר. *Wayyiqtol* 3fs Qal √שכב. The narrator has Ruth follow Boaz' last instruction exactly, with the addition only of the NP מרגלתו, which is unambiguously a locative adjunct "(at) the place of his feet," regardless how one takes this noun with the verb גלה in vv. 4, 7 (see comment on v. 4). The *Qere* מרגלותיו makes the fpl morphology clear whereas the *Ketiv* looks like a fs NP "the place of his foot," which makes little sense.

וַתָּקָם בְּטֶרֶום [בטרם] יַכִּיר אִישׁ אֶת־רֵעֵהוּ. *Wayyiqtol* 3fs Qal √קום, *yiqtol* 3ms Hiph √נכר. The verb קום in the Qal is intransitive and thus the ב PP is a temporal adjunct. Within the PP טרם is a temporal adverb "not yet," which with ב becomes "before." The *yiqtol* verb within the subordinate clause is modal in that it signifies capability, "before a man could recognize another." Note the V-S order, which was triggered by either the initial adverb or the raising of the modal *yiqtol*. The *Qere* presents the spelling of the word טרם everywhere else (Hebrew Bible, DSS, Ben Sira) and, as with many *Qere-Ketiv* cases, is likely a manuscript variant (as also noted in the BHS textual note) rather than a Masoretic correction. There is no good explanation for the ו in the *Ketiv*.

וַיֹּאמֶר אַל־יִוָּדַע כִּי־בָאָה הָאִשָּׁה הַגֹּרֶן. *Wayyiqtol* 3ms Qal

√אמר, jussive 3ms Niph √ידע, and *qatal* 3fs Qal √בוא. The person shift from the 3fs verb (which can only refer to Ruth) to the 3ms verb (which can only refer to Boaz) is unmarked, although the agents are clear. The verb אמר can denote "internal speech," particularly with the PP בלב "in [his/her] mind"; here the PP is missing but אמר by itself does occur elsewhere (e.g., Gen 20:11; 42:4; Exod 3:3; 1 Sam 20:26; Sasson 94; Hubbard 220, n. 3) in contexts suggesting internal speech. If Boaz is not speaking to himself, then his comments are addressed obliquely to Ruth (directly addressing Ruth but referring to her as האשה would be referentially awkward). Note the V-S order of the jussive clause, with the כי clause as the subject. Note also the V-S order within the כי clause: the verb באה has been raised from its basic position after the subject האשה due to the presence of the כי. Though he NP הגרן lacks a preposition, it is still best taken as the oblique complement of the verb באה, which does not take accusative complements (see comment on ותרד הגרן in 3:6).

The implied relationship between the two syntactically coordinated clauses is that this second clause explains the motivation for the first: Ruth rose early so that no one would know she had spent the night with Boaz. Although this could be taken as a bit of sneaking around, and thus an implicit admission of guilt, the audience has been given no clear reason in the preceding scene to suspect socially inappropriate behavior by Ruth and Boaz (the arguments of those who infer sexual connotations from the collocation of שכב and מרגלות notwithstanding). Thus, it seems much more likely that Boaz' concern is to protect Ruth from even the hint of impropriety, which may have adversely affected her already tenuous social standing (contra Sasson 1979:94ff).

3:15 וַיֹּ֗אמֶר הָ֠בִי הַמִּטְפַּ֧חַת אֲשֶׁר־עָלַ֛יִךְ וְאֶֽחֳזִי־בָ֖הּ
וַתֹּ֣אחֶז בָּ֑הּ וַיָּ֤מָד שֵׁשׁ־שְׂעֹרִים֙ וַיָּ֣שֶׁת עָלֶ֔יהָ וַיָּבֹ֖א
הָעִֽיר׃

Befitting Boaz' proven good character, he loads Ruth up with grain before she returns home. He provides for both women at every opportunity. After Boaz' instruction to Ruth, the narrative report uses a quick succession of verbs, almost staccato-like, to move the action along quickly to the next scene.

הָבִי הַמִּטְפַּ֫חַת אֲשֶׁר־עָלַ֫יִךְ. Impv fs Qal √יהב. The expected form of the fs imperative is הֲבִי, with a reduced first vowel (compare דְּעִי); the form here, with the full vowel, is anomalous (GKC §69o; JM §75k). The verb יהב "to give" only occurs in the Hebrew Bible in the imperative but is well-known from other West Semitic languages. In some cases, it seems to have become an exhortation similar to English "come," as in "come on!" or "come, now" (it is not an interjection, contra HALOT, s.v. and JM §105e). Here it has its lexical meaning, "give," although in English "take" or "get" makes a smoother translation.

אֲשֶׁר־עָלַ֫יִךְ. The relative clause contains a one-constituent null-copula clause. The PP עליך is the predicate while the subject is המטפחת, which has been raised out of the relative to be its head.

וְאֶחֳזִי־בָהּ. Impv fs Qal √אחז. The verb אחז may take an accusative complement but just as often takes an oblique complement with a ב PP, as here. The morphological shape of verb אחז suggests that either of the two prefix patterns was available: that of dynamic I-Guttural with the /u/-theme vowel (וַתֶּאֱחֹז or here with אֶחֳזִי) or, as in the next clause, a I-Alef (וַתֹּאחֶז) (see GKC §63, 68; JM §68, 73).

וַתֹּ֫אחֶז בָּהּ. Wayyiqtol 3fs Qal √אחז.

וַיָּ֫מָד שֵׁשׁ־שְׂעֹרִים. Wayyiqtol 3ms Qal √מדד. Boaz is the covert subject and the שֵׁשׁ שְׂעֹרִים is the accusative complement. The NP שֵׁשׁ שְׂעֹרִים must be elliptical for something like שֵׁשׁ קָמְצֵי שְׂעֹרִים "six handfuls of barley" (what she could carry in her cloak), since שְׂעֹרִים "barley" is not a count noun and thus cannot be enumerated with שֵׁשׁ.

וַיָּ֫שֶׁת עָלֶ֫יהָ. Wayyiqtol 3ms Qal √שׁית. The accusative complement of the verb is covert, gapped from שֵׁשׁ שְׂעֹרִים in the last clause.

The 3fs suffix in the oblique PP complement עֶלֶיהָ could refer to Ruth but more likely it refers to her מִטְפַּחַת since that is her means of transporting the grain.

וַיָּבֹא הָעִיר. *Wayyiqtol* 3ms Qal √בוא. On בוא taking an NP complement without the expected preposition, see comment on 1:2. With this short clause Boaz exits the stage until the beginning of chapter 4.

Act III, Scene 3: Waiting for a Resolution (vv. 16-18)

Scene 3 narrates the last direct interaction between No'omi and Ruth. Whereas Boaz exited the narrative abruptly at the end of v. 15, Ruth returns to No'omi to report about her night.

¹⁶*When she came to her mother-in-law, she said, "'Who' are you, my daughter?" Then she related to her all which the man had done for her.* ¹⁷*She said, "These six (measures of) barley he gave to me, because he said, 'Do not go to your mother-in-law empty-handed.'"* ¹⁸*And she said, "Sit down, my daughter, until you know how the the matter falls out, because the man will not rest but will finish the matter today."*

3:16 וַתָּבוֹא אֶל־חֲמוֹתָהּ וַתֹּאמֶר מִי־אַתְּ בִּתִּי וַתַּגֶּד־לָהּ
אֵת כָּל־אֲשֶׁר עָשָׂה־לָהּ הָאִישׁ:

No'omi's first question betrays the purpose of her plan, if the audience was not already clear about it.

וַתָּבוֹא אֶל־חֲמוֹתָהּ וַתֹּאמֶר מִי־אַתְּ בִּתִּי. *Wayyiqtol* 3fs Qal √בוא and √אמר. No'omi's question is blunt and to the point: "Who are you?" But the question is not one of identification, since No'omi knew that it was Ruth and called her בִּתִּי, but one of classification, i.e., are you still Ruth as I know you, or are you Ruth as Boaz' betrothed? The use of מִי instead of the expected genitive לְמִי, "whose are you?" is explained as a use of מִי to inquire about one's condition (WO §18.2d; similarly Sasson 1979:100–101; Hubbard 1988:224, n. 5; Bush 1996:184–85).

וַתַּגֶּד־לָהּ אֵת כָּל־אֲשֶׁר עָשָׂה־לָהּ הָאִישׁ. *Wayyiqtol* 3fs
Hiph √נגד and *qatal* 3ms Qal √עשׂה. The accent on the first syllable
of both ותגד and עשׂה is due to the following monosyllabic word—
biblical Hebrew (at least as it was heard by the Masoretes) preferred
not to have two primary stressed syllables in adjacent position. When
this situation occurs, as it does twice here, the stress on the first word
moves back a syllable; this is called נָסֹג אָחוֹר or נְסִיגָה "falling back"
(GKC §29e; JM §31c). The first PP לה is the oblique complement
indicating the goal and the following phrase is the accusative complement. (On כל as the head of a relative clause, see comment at 2:11; for
other examples, see 3:5, 11; 4:9). Note the V-S order inside the relative
due to the initial אשר. Also note that the very "light" adjunct PP לה
raised with the verb; it is very common in Hebrew and cross-linguistically to see "light" phrases attach and raise with a verb.

3:17 וַתֹּאמֶר שֵׁשׁ־הַשְּׂעֹרִים הָאֵלֶּה נָתַן לִי כִּי אָמַר ()
[אֵלַי] אַל־תָּבוֹאִי רֵיקָם אֶל־חֲמוֹתֵךְ:

    Although v. 16 indicated that Ruth told No'omi "everything" that
Boaz did for her, the report in Ruth's own words that the narrator gives
us jumps to the gift of the barley at the very end of the episode (even
though No'omi's response in v .18 takes for granted that Ruth gave
her the whole story). By the choice of what was reported the narrator
keeps the audience focused on the plot problem: No'omi's redemption, whether from her anger toward God, her extreme bereavement,
or her daily needs.

    שֵׁשׁ־הַשְּׂעֹרִים הָאֵלֶּה נָתַן לִי. *Qatal* 3ms Qal √נתן. The
O-V order is not basic under any circumstances (cp. MacDonald
1975:164–65) and thus the order here reflects the raising of the accusative complement of the verb, שׁשׁ השׁערים האלה, to the front of
the clause for pragmatic reasons. The question is why? The entity שׁשׁ
שׁערים is known within the narrative from v. 15, but it is not known
to No'omi within the world of the narrative. Thus Topic-fronting (see

§2.5) would not make any sense unless the narrator is violating the narrative world to drive a point home for the audience. But the fact that Boaz gave Ruth שֵׁשׁ שְׂעֹרִים is hardly a transformative event in the narrative, which leaves us with Focus-fronting. Focus requires a membership set that is contextually or logically established and of which the Focus constituent is a member. The simplest membership set is {six handfuls of barley, not six handfuls of barley, nothing at all, . . .} and there is little else that makes sense for this context. It would thus seem that Ruth is asserting that, of all that happened that night, the most tangible outcome is that Boaz gave her at least something—the barley—rather than nothing.

כִּי אָמַר () [אֵלַי] אַל־תָּבוֹאִי רֵיקָם אֶל־חֲמוֹתֵךְ **.** *Qatal* 3ms Qal √אמר and jussive 2fs Qal √בוא. The כִּי clause provides the motivation of Boaz' gift, which was not provided when the gift was given in v. 15 (see Campbell 1975:129; Sasson 1979:101–2; Hubbard 1988:225). The PP אל חמותך indicates that, according to Ruth, Boaz sent her home with the barley to provide for No'omi. On the manner adverb רֵיקָם, see comment on 1:21 and note the explicit inner-textual link between this scene and the end of Act I. The primary text does not have the PP אלי, but it is indicated in the margin and represents a case of the rare *Ketiv welo Qere* "read though it is not written." Syntactically the verb אמר often takes an adjunct specifying the addressee, but in many cases this PP is absent (see, e.g., 1:11, 12; 4:8) and the addressee is assumed because its identity is contextually clear. Thus, there is no good way to determine whether the presence or absence of the PP is textually better in this clause. If the PP were original, it could have been accidentally omitted by parablepsis (i.e., the scribe's eye skipped to the negative אל due to the resemblance of אלי to אל). However, it is equally plausible that the PP was not in the original text, but was added by some scribe due to how common the collocation אמר אל is.

3:18 וַתֹּאמֶר שְׁבִי בִתִּי עַד אֲשֶׁר תֵּדְעִין אֵיךְ יִפֹּל דָּבָר כִּי לֹא יִשְׁקֹט הָאִישׁ כִּי־אִם־כִּלָּה הַדָּבָר הַיּוֹם׃

Scene 3 and Act III as a whole end with No'omi's advice for
Ruth to wait patiently for Boaz to take care of the redemption business. No'omi seems sure that it will unfold before a single day is up,
although the audience is not privy to the reason for her confidence.

שְׁבִי בִתִּי עַד אֲשֶׁר תֵּדְעִין אֵיךְ יִפֹּל דָּבָר. Impv 2fs Qal
ישׁב√, *yiqtol* 2fs Qal ידע√ (on the paragogic נ, see comment on 2:8),
and *yiqtol* 3ms Qal נפל√. The verb ישׁב often takes a locative adjunct;
here the location is covert and presumably פֹה "here" or עִמִּי "with
me" is to be understood. The overt adjunct, indicating the information that No'omi (and thus the narrator) considered important, is the
temporal עַד PP. The preposition עַד is followed by a null-head relative
clause, for which the null-head can be reconstructed as a generic time-
related NP, e.g., "until (the time) that . . ." or "until (the day) that. . . ."
This is common for temporal and locative clauses with a generic head
that is specified by the information within the relative (e.g., בַּאֲשֶׁר,
כַּאֲשֶׁר, לַאֲשֶׁר). Within the relative clause the verb תֵּדְעִין takes a
complement clause that is an embedded interrogative אֵיךְ יִפֹּל דָּבָר.
Note that the initial manner interrogative אֵיךְ triggers the raising of
the verb יִפֹּל over the subject דָּבָר, resulting in V-S order.

שְׁבִי. What Ruth would have done other than "sitting" is unclear:
the narrator provides no hint that Ruth and No'omi have a back-up
plan, and since the harvest is over it is even unclear what work Ruth
could have gone out to do. Therefore it is likely that שְׁבִי should be
taken literally, "sit down!" with the understood alternative "spend the
time pacing." Note the inner-textual link with the end of Act II—just
as the Ruth ended the harvest season by "staying" with her mother-
in-law, so too the threshing-floor plan ends with Ruth "staying." The
narrator has once again left the plot unresolved, although this time
there is some defined hope for a resolution.

דָּבָר. The subject of the embedded interrogative, דָּבָר, is curi-
ously indefinite whereas English would require a definite NP, "the
matter." Definiteness is both a morphological and semantic issue.
Morphologically definiteness refers to the presence or absence of a

definite article, but semantically it reflects a noun's identifiability and specificity (see WO §13.2 for brief introduction; on indefinite NPs in questions see JM §137p). While English and Hebrew are often quite similar in how the three issues (definiteness, identifiability, and specificity) converge, differences do exist. In this case, the Hebrew NP is identifiable (it refers to how Boaz will handle Ruth's redemption request) but non-specific, since neither Ruth nor No'omi know what shape the process will take.

כִּי לֹא יִשְׁקֹט הָאִישׁ כִּי־אִם־כִּלָּה הַדָּבָר הַיּוֹם. *Yiqtol* 3ms Qal √שקט and *qatal* (modal) Piel 3ms √כלה. The first כי clause explains No'omi's advice for Ruth to sit: Boaz will finish it today. Within the כי clause are one negative and one positive statement that complement each other. The negative statement (note the V-S order produced by the כי) indicates that Boaz will not rest; the adversative positive statement (again note the V-S order due to the initial כי אם as well as to the modality of the *qatal* verb) explains what it means that Boaz won't rest—he'll sort the matter out that very day.

כִּי־אִם־כִּלָּה. The collocation of כי and אם produce a strong adversative to contrast the following information with the preceding (GKC §163a; JM §172c; cf. WO §39.3.5d). With adversatives the challenge is identifying precisely what is being contrasted. In this case, it is not the entire negative assertion of the first statement that provides the base for the antithesis but the verbal action alone (without the negative): "the man won't rest but [rather than resting] he will finish the matter today." It is also possible that the כי אם clause is exceptive in that it presents the precise conditions in which the polarity of the preceding statement would be changed: "the man won't rest unless [the following condition is fulfilled:] he finishes the matter today" (see GKC §163c; WO §38.6b; JM §173b).

הַדָּבָר. Whereas דבר in the preceding clause is identifiable but non-specific, the second mention is definite due to the referentiality created by the first mention. That is, no further light has been shed on the precise nature of the matter that Boaz will sort out (it remains

non-specific). The two instances of דבר in this one verse highlight
that definiteness is not only tied to the semantic features of the lexical item as they are perceived by the speaker and addressee (whether
characters within the narrative world or the narrator and audience)
but also to the developing discourse world of the unfolding text.

Scene 3 returns to the primary plot problem: No'omi's "emptiness." There are two explicit inner-textual links with the preceding
Acts. The adverb ריקם (see 1:21 and 3:17) brings No'omi's situation
back into center stage and the verb ישב (see 2:23 and 3:18) keeps
Ruth's situation also in center stage. Thus the narrator sets up the last
Act (chapter 4) to resolve both issues. Boaz passing from view at the
end of Scene 2 (v. 15) serves to increase the drama and tension as the
audience waits to see how Boaz will deal both the redemption rights
and marriage request.

ACT IV

Act IV (chapter 4) is structured in three scenes: Boaz with the nearer redeemer and elders, Boaz marrying Ruth and "redeeming" No'omi, and the ending genealogy. Act IV thus delivers the resolution that the audience has been waiting for, but not without some tension with the nearer redeemer and shrewd maneuvering by Boaz. Structurally, this final act of the story unfolds in the reverse order that the plot has unfolded. Whereas No'omi's problem was introduced first and remained the primary issue throughout, first Ruth and then Boaz became the focus of the action. In Act IV it is Boaz who is the focal point first, followed by Ruth, who is married but otherwise strikingly absent from the rest of the story, and finally No'omi, whose emptiness is refilled.

Act IV, Scene 1: Boaz Deals at the City Gate (vv. 1-8)

At the end of the last Act No'omi reassures Ruth that Boaz will not hesitate to finish the matter. Such a statement inherently establishes a question: will he do it and how? This scene answers the question in dramatic fashion. The setting shifts almost jarringly from Ruth and No'omi to Boaz at the city gate, the nearer redeemer is quickly brought on stage, the city elders are gathered (as if they had all been standing around waiting for something interesting to happen!), and Boaz dictates everyone actions in an almost comical fashion.

¹And Boaz went up to the gate and sat down there. And look—the redeemer is passing by about whom Boaz had spoken. And he said, "Turn aside, sit here, friend." So he turned aside and sat down. ²Then he took ten men of the city elders and said, "Sit here," so they sat down. ³He said to the redeemer, "The portion of the field that belongs to our brother, Elimelek—No'omi who has returned from the territory of Moab now sells it. ⁴So I thought that I would uncover your ear by saying, 'Acquire it in front of those sitting here, before the elders of my people. If you will redeem, then redeem. If you will not redeem it, tell me so I may know, because you alone have the right of redemption, and I after you.'" And he said, "I will redeem." ⁵Then Boaz said, "On the day you acquire the field from the hand of No'omi and from Ruth the Moabite, the wife of the dead man I shall acquire in order to establish the name of the dead man over his inheritance." ⁶And the redeemer said, "I'm not able redeem it for myself so that I don't ruin my own inheritance. Take for yourself—you—my redemption right, because I'm unable to redeem." ⁷(Now this was how to confirm any transaction—formerly in Israel, concerning the redemption procedure and the exchange: a man drew off his sandal and he gave it to his companion. This was the witnessing act in Israel.) ⁸And the redeemer said to Boaz, "Acquire it for yourself," and he drew off his sandal.

4:1 וּבֹ֨עַז עָלָ֣ה הַשַּׁ֩עַר֩ וַיֵּ֨שֶׁב שָׁ֜ם וְהִנֵּ֣ה הַגֹּאֵ֣ל עֹבֵ֗ר אֲשֶׁ֧ר דִּבֶּר־בֹּ֛עַז וַיֹּ֥אמֶר ס֥וּרָה שְׁבָה־פֹּ֖ה פְּלֹנִ֣י אַלְמֹנִ֑י וַיָּ֖סַר וַיֵּשֵֽׁב׃

This clause moves the audience from being home with Ruth and No'omi to sitting at the city gates with Boaz. No temporal clues are provided, suggesting that the narrator wants the audience to take Boaz' actions and the entire event as unfolding at the same time or immediately after the just-finished conversation between the two women. The sequence of events in this verse as well as in v. 2 are quick, with Boaz directing action and the redeemer and elders (v. 2) responding without delay. Little time is spent getting to the dialogue of vv. 3-8.

וּבֹ֨עַז עָלָ֣ה הַשַּׁ֩עַר֩. *Qatal* 3ms Qal √עלה. The S-V order reflects two phenomena, one pragmatic and one literary. Pragmatically, the subject בעז is Topic-fronted: in the previous pericope (Act III, Scene 3, 3:16-18) Ruth and No'omi were the agents and thus the available Topics. Boaz had left for the city in 3:15 and was not at all present in the ensuing three verses. In 4:1, there is a shift to Boaz as the agent, which is signaled by the Topic-fronting. Literarily, the shift in Topic also signals a shift in scene and, in this case, setting (from home with Ruth and No'omi to the city with Boaz). But there is no explicit shift in time and the avoidance of a past narrative *wayyiqtol* clause, which often implies temporal succession, allows for the event in this clause to be perceived as contemporaneous with the preceding scene (or even temporally anterior, since it is conceivable that Boaz reached the city before Ruth reached No'omi). It is in contexts like this that the word order serves multiple purposes; yet from a linguistic perspective it is important to keep the levels distinct. The formal pragmatics (Topic-fronting) of the word order produces the S(Topic)-V word order (which is only superficially identical to basic S-V order), whereas the use of the resulting word order for a literary purpose is a matter of convention.

וַיֵּשֶׁב שָׁם. *Wayyiqtol* 3ms Qal √יֹשׁב. The narrator switches back to a *wayyiqtol* clause and the economy of the narrative—"Boaz came and sat down"—is likely meant to reflect Boaz' business-like attitude.

וְהִנֵּה הַגֹּאֵל עֹבֵר אֲשֶׁר דִּבֶּר־בֹּעַז. Participle ms Qal √עבר. According to Berlin (1983:92–95), הנה expresses surprise or suddenness of an event and is often used to orient the audience to the point-of-view of a particular character. In this verse, הנה indicates "that Boaz suddenly saw the *goel*, . . . not that the *goel* arrived immediately" (93). The participle contributes to the perspective orientation: the progressive semantics of the participle indicate that, from Boaz' viewpoint, the nearer redeemer was in the process of passing by when Boaz noticed him. The tense-less nature of the participle means that the progressive aspect of the redeemer's passing could be set in the past, present, or even future. Most translations take their cue from the general past setting of the story as well as the *wayyiqtol* clauses that are on either side and translate the clause similar to this: "and look—the redeemer *was* passing by." But if it is correct to take the combination of the הִנֵּה and the participle as a signal that the event is depicted from Boaz' perspective, the use of the present tense in translation would better reflect the literary goals of the narrator: "and look—the redeemer *is passing* by."

הַגֹּאֵל ... אֲשֶׁר דִּבֶּר־בֹּעַז. *Qatal* 3ms Piel √דבר. In main clauses, the verb within the relative clause דבר often takes a PP specifying the goal (i.e., a אל PP for "to speak *to someone*") or content (i.e., a על PP for "to speak *about something/someone*"), although the oblique PP may be covert (Miller 1996:§6.3.3.6, esp. n. 97). Within relative clauses, if a verb requires an oblique PP complement (not adjunct), resumption using the required preposition and an anaphoric suffix matching the relative head is obligatory, e.g., הַמָּקוֹם אֲשֶׁר אַתָּה עוֹמֵד עָלָיו Exod 3:5 (Holmstedt 2002:§2.5; 2008). However, as JM notes, PP resumption with verbs of saying is often omitted (§158i), as we see here. Given both the requirement for the resumption when the relative head has been raised from within an oblique complement and the omission of such resumption with verbs of saying, the logical conclusion is that the oblique PPs with, e.g., דבר and אמר, are not complements but rather adjuncts, allowing the adjunct PP to be omitted within a relative (note the absence of PPs with אמר in, e.g., 1:11, 12, and many more). Thus, the semantics of the verbs of speech in Hebrew are different than the similar verbs in English, which require the preposition (e.g., "the redeemer who Boaz had spoken *about*").

The relative clause אשר דבר בעז is extraposed: the participle עבר intervenes between the relative head גאל and the relative clause itself. This is not common in the Hebrew Bible, but it does exist elsewhere (see Holmstedt 2001) and often appears when the relative clause is a larger constituent than the predicate, as in this case. Given that constituent size and complexity seem to be the common denominator in cases of relative clause extraposition, the placement of the relative clause down the clause away from its head is likely a language processing issue—the clause as a whole is easier to process with the predicate closer to the head than the relative clause would otherwise allow.

סּוּרָה שְׁבָה־פֹּה פְּלֹנִי אַלְמֹנִי. Impv ms Qal √סור and √ישׁב. Both imperatives have the additional suffix -ה (as does הגידה in v. 4), which is used "when the action of the verb is directed toward the speaker" (Fassberg 1999:13). The locative adverb פה is an oblique complement for the verb √ישׁב; that is, it seems that in Hebrew one cannot just "sit," but must sit "somewhere," whether the "somewhere" is syntactically overt (as here), gapped from a previous clause, or covert but reconstructable from the context.

פְּלֹנִי אַלְמֹנִי. This is not a personal name, but a common NP. The etymology of either element is unknown. It is commonly understoodd as a reference to a person or place that is not known, not remembered, or not important enough to name, e.g., "such-and-such" or "so-and-so." It is illogical for Boaz not to have actually known the character's name, since within the world of the narrative Boaz had told Ruth of him at the threshing-floor and identified him without any reported problem at the city gate. Thus, the use of פלני אלמני reflects the narrator's direct intrusion into the story. But the narrator could have used a name, since from a story-telling perspective the characters exist for the sake of the story, whether they correspond to historical figures or not. So why the abstraction? Berlin is probably the closest in her assessment that the narrator deliberately avoided the concreteness of the character's name in order to assert control over the narrative and to keep the story "more story-like" (1983:101; see also Bush 1996:196–97).

וַיָּסַר וַיֵּשֵׁב. *Wayyiqtol* 3ms Qal √סור and √ישׁב. The subject of the two verbs is not overt, although contextually it is clear that the nearer redeemer is intended (see v. 2 for further comment). Neither verb is modified with PPs, such as "from his path" or "there," whether the verbal semantics require the PPs as complements or not. For both verbs the PPs are implied from the context, satisfying the semantic requirements of the verbs. The lack of overt PPs is likely connected to the desired literary affect of the staccato-like verb sequence: the nearer redeemer does what Boaz has commanded without qualification, a clear signal that Boaz is in complete control of this situation from the outset.

4:2   וַיִּקַּח עֲשָׂרָה אֲנָשִׁים מִזִּקְנֵי הָעִיר וַיֹּאמֶר שְׁבוּ־פֹה
וַיֵּשֵׁבוּ׃

As with v. 1, Boaz directs (note the imperative) and the elders do as he says.

וַיִּקַּח עֲשָׂרָה אֲנָשִׁים מִזִּקְנֵי הָעִיר. *Wayyiqtol* 3ms Qal √לקח. The agentive subject of the verb is not made explicit. The last subject, of וַיָּסַר וַיֵּשֵׁב in v. 1, was the nearer redeemer, but the primary agent in this scene is unquestionably Boaz. The NP עֲשָׂרָה אֲנָשִׁים is the accusative complement of וַיִּקַּח and the partitive מִן PP מִזִּקְנֵי הָעִיר is an adjunct indicating the source of the עֲשָׂרָה אֲנָשִׁים.

שְׁבוּ־פֹה וַיֵּשֵׁבוּ. Impv mpl and *wayyiqtol* 3mpl Qal √ישב. As in v. 1, the locative adverb פֹה is an oblique complement. Boaz' interaction with the city elders is as blunt as it was with the nearer redeemer. Similarly, as the redeemer responded immediately and did what Boaz commanded, so do the men here.

4:3   וַיֹּאמֶר לַגֹּאֵל חֶלְקַת הַשָּׂדֶה אֲשֶׁר לְאָחִינוּ לֶאֱלִימֶלֶךְ
מָכְרָה נָעֳמִי הַשָּׁבָה מִשְּׂדֵה מוֹאָב׃

The property of Elimelek is presented as the primary topic of the meeting. Thus Boaz initiates what the audience must take as the formal redemption procedure. As with the concept of redemption presented in the Pentateuch, the issue is the land and the financial security of the owner. The purpose of buying Elimelek's land, which would not be a permanent transaction since it would presumably revert back to Elimelek's clan in a Jubilee year, would be to provide support for the Elimelek's bereaved family. The buyer and his heirs would benefit from the annual produce until the next Jubilee.

חֶלְקַת הַשָּׂדֶה אֲשֶׁר לְאָחִינוּ לֶאֱלִימֶלֶךְ מָכְרָה נָעֳמִי
הַשָּׁבָה מִשְּׂדֵה מוֹאָב. *Qatal* 3fs Qal √מכר. The use of the *qatal*
here can only be performative—the land has not yet been sold, but
is now at this very meeting being sold. The performative use of the
qatal is semantically indicative; though a speech act, it is set apart
by its speech-time instantaneousness (perfective aspect plus present
time). The raising of the verb to created the V-S order of the clause
is triggered by the Focus-fronted accusative complement. As with the
previous verses, the subject of the verb is not overt but can be easily
reconstructed from the agreement features of the verb (3ms) and the
context (Boaz is the primary agent and thus initiates the conversation).
In keeping with the use of פלני אלמני in v. 2, the nearer redeemer
remains unnamed and henceforth is simply referred to as הגאל.

חֶלְקַת הַשָּׂדֶה. With the Focus-fronted NP חלקת השדה אשר
לאחינו לאלימלך Boaz immediately establishes what the meeting is
about. It is possible that the Focus works on two levels. Within the
world of the narrative, it sets Elimelek's property over against other
property issues that might have been active between Boaz and the
nearer redeemer and thus needing the witness of the city elders. Within
the narrated world, the contrast is not between Elimelek's property
and other properties, but between No'omi's sale of Elimelek's field
and the marriage of Ruth. In other words, for the audience a different
membership set is active than what is likely for the characters within
the scene. The contrast involving No'omi's sale versus Ruth's marriage leaves the audience with this question: when will Boaz address
Ruth's status? For the men within the narrative, especially the nearer
redeemer, Ruth's status is well off the radar, making Boaz' insertion
of this issue in v. 5 all the more startling.

אֲשֶׁר לְאָחִינוּ לֶאֱלִימֶלֶךְ. The relative clause includes a null-
copula clause with one constituent, the genitive ל PP predicate. The
covert subject has been raised out of the relative clause as its head,
and resumption at the subject position within a relative is extremely
rare in Hebrew (see Holmstedt 2008). The second ל PP לאלימלך is

in apposition with the first PP. It would also have been grammatical to have had just the NP אֱלִימֶלֶךְ in apposition to אָחִינוּ, both within the scope of the PP. There appears to be no advantage or greater clarity in the use of the so-called periphrastic genitive אֲשֶׁר ל instead of chain of cliticized nouns, *חֶלְקַת שְׂדֵה אָחִינוּ (see also 2:3, 21), so the narrator's motivation for this syntactic choice remains opaque.

נָעֳמִי הַשָּׁבָה מִשְּׂדֵה מוֹאָב. *Qatal* 3fs Qal √שוב with prefixed relative הַ. See also 1:22; 2:6; and comment at 1:8. Contrary to arguments that the verb should be taken as a participle, the context—referencing an event that as a whole exists in the past—suggests that the semantics of the *qatal* are appropriate where the progressive semantics of the participle are not. The PP מִשְּׂדֵה מוֹאָב is an ablative PP adjunct (see WO §11.2.11). Since no special legal arrangement is mentioned, the narrator assumes that the audience would have accepted a widow owning the property of her deceased husband. This seems a bit unusual in light of the highly patriarchal society described in the Bible, although general inheritance issues are not addressed in the Pentateuch and women are never forbidden as heirs (see Sasson 1979:111–12; Bush 1996:202–4).

4:4　וַאֲנִי אָמַרְתִּי אֶגְלֶה אָזְנְךָ לֵאמֹר קְנֵה נֶגֶד הַיֹּשְׁבִים
וְנֶגֶד זִקְנֵי עַמִּי אִם־תִּגְאַל גְּאָל וְאִם־לֹא יִגְאַל הַגִּידָה
לִּי וְאֵדְעָ [ואדעה] כִּי אֵין זוּלָתְךָ לִגְאוֹל וְאָנֹכִי
אַחֲרֶיךָ וַיֹּאמֶר אָנֹכִי אֶגְאָל:

There is yet no hint that the issue under discussion concerns anything other than the land the belonged to their relative Elimelek. Boaz seems to be waiting until it is completely necessary to reveal that No'omi and Ruth are somehow involved in the deal.

וַאֲנִי אָמַרְתִּי. *Qatal* 1cs Qal √אמר. The use of אמרתי is very likely an abbreviated form of the idiom for internal speech or thought, אמר בלב (see comment on 3:14; Campbell 1975:144; Bush 1996:204–

5; cp. Sasson 1979:115–16). The rest of the verse except for the last three words (the nearer redeemer's initial response) is the reported speech complement of אמרתי. With the overt subject pronoun, Boaz inserts himself into the property issue. Since subject pronouns are syntactically non-obligatory with finite verbs, they carry Topic or Focus when they are overt. In this case, the pronoun is more likely a Topic. Boaz had activated Noʻomi as an agent in the last verse, but here shifts the attention to himself and his idea to present Noʻomi's property issue at the city gate. In contrast to later in the verse, Boaz uses אני and thus asserts his equal social standing at the outset of the conversation (although just a few clauses later he tones down his approach and uses אנכי as a sign of deference). On the use of אני and אנכי, see comments at 2:10 and 3:12; also see Revell 1995:203, 206–7.

אֶגְלֶה אָזְנְךָ לֵאמֹר. *Yiqtol* (modal imperfect or jussive) 1cs Qal √גלה. The לֵאמֹר phrase is an adjunct PP and appears to be one of the rare uses of לֵאמֹר as a (gerundive) infinitive, "by saying," rather than as a complementizer introducing reported speech (Miller 1996:§4.3.2.2). The form is ambiguous since the morphology of III-ה verbs obscures the typically marker of the first person jussive (or "cohortative"), the ־ה suffix. The context suggests that Boaz is relaying an intention by means of reported speech (to himself) situated at the time that he first had the idea; the jussive is the conjugation used for expressing intention. Alternatively, this could be a complement clause without reported speech and without an overt complementizer, in which case the verb would be a modal *yiqtol*: "I thought (that) I would uncover your ear. . . ."

The use of אמר for internal speech is often followed by the content of the thinking as indirect speech, e.g., with a כי complement clause, rather than direct speech, as we may have here. If this is direct reported speech, the use of the jussive is not out of place (contra Sasson 1979:115): this is what Boaz told himself in the past. The 2ms suffix, however, is an intrusion and fits only the context of the current setting at the city gate, not Boaz' past thoughts. That is, the proper deixis for Boaz' previous thought would have included a 3ms suffix "I shall uncover *his* ear," whereas the 2ms suffix "I shall uncover *your* ear" is the deixis of the conversation with the nearer redeemer and the elders. The deictic tension may reflect the narrator's language economy and desire to keep the audience focused on the current situation; or the 2ms suffix is precisely what we would expect if this is not reported speech and is a complement clause.

קְנֵה נֶגֶד הַיֹּשְׁבִים וְנֶגֶד זִקְנֵי עַמִּי. Impv ms Qal √קנה and participle mpl Qal √ישׁב. The complement of the transitive verb קנה is covert and is easily recoverable from the preceding information as the property of Elimelek. The appositional PPs נגד הישׁבים and נגד זקני עמי are locative adjuncts. The NP זקני עמי inside the second PP further defines the first NP הישׁבים. The ו between the appositional phrases is what WO call the "epexegetical" use (§39.2.4; cf. JM §177a), which highlights that the basic function of the ו is simply to mark phrasal and clausal boundaries.

אִם־תִּגְאַל גְּאָל. *Yiqtol* (modal) 2ms and impv ms Qal √גאל. The conditional אם establishes the basic modality of the clause. Note that Boaz addresses the nearer redeemer with the imperative (as he did in v. 2), rather than with the more polite 2ms jussive. As with קנה in the preceding clause, the complement of the verbs here as well as in the rest of the verse is assumed: Elimelek's property. The alternative is to take גאל as an intransitive form of the verb, "to serve as redeemer"; this has been suggested in order to skirt the fact that the narrator nowhere suggests that Elimelek's land has been alienated from the clan (as in Lev 25:25) and thus the "redemption" process would not technically apply (so Hubbard 1988:237, n. 5; cp. Bush 1996:207–9).

וְאִם־לֹא יִגְאַל הַגִּידָה לִּי. *Yiqtol* (modal) 3ms Qal √גאל and impv ms Hiph √נגד, with ה- suffix (see comment on v. 1). This conditional statement is the antithesis to the first, and the protasis in this conditional allows Boaz to insert his own interest. On the verb יגאל, the Versions and multiple Hebrew manuscripts have a 2ms verb תגאל. This parallels the verb in the previous conditional and makes good sense in the context. Thus, most commentators emend with the

Versions (see, e.g., Hubbard 1988:237, n. 6; Bush 1996:190, 209–10),
although the supposed textual error in the MT continues to defy satis-
factory explanation. Sasson argues that the 3ms verb reflects Boaz' brief
shift to address the elders rather than the nearer redeemer (1979:118),
but such a dynamic use of language better fits an acted play in which
the visual cues are available rather than a narrated story.

וְאֵדְעָ [ואדעה] כִּי אֵין זוּלָתְךָ לִגְאוֹל. Modal *yiqtol* or jussive
1cs Qal √ידע and inf constr Qal √גאל. The *Ketiv* lacks the ה suffix
that marks the first-person form as a jussive, whereas the *Qere* has the
longer form. It matters little for the sense of the verse, though. Syntactically this clause is coordinated with the previous clause, but contextually it provides the purpose, and both the jussive and the modal
yiqtol are used in such constructions. Within the clause, the כי clause
is the complement of the verb אדע. Within the כי clause, זולתך is the
subject, אין is the negative copula, and לגאל is the predicate.

וְאָנֹכִי אַחֲרֶיךָ. This is null-copula clause that continues the כי
clause above. On the use of אנכי versus אני, see comments on 2:10
and 3:12. Here both Boaz and the nearer redeemer (in the next clause)
appear to use אנכי in deference to each other. Thus the conversation
as a whole appears to be quite cordial.

וַיֹּאמֶר אָנֹכִי אֶגְאָל. *Wayyiqtol* 3ms Qal √אמר and *yiqtol* 1cs
Qal √גאל. The subject of ויאמר is not specified, but contextually
the subject is clearly the nearer redeemer (note especially that Boaz
is explicitly identified as the subject in the next clause). The reported
speech is the complement of the verb ויאמר. Within the reported
speech, the subject pronoun is overt (see comments above on the use
of אנכי versus אני). Here the overt pronoun is a Focus: the nearer
redeemer asserts that *he* will do it, as opposed to Boaz, the other member of the contextually established set of possible redeemers. The complement of the verb is left covert, as with the other instances of גאל in
this verse. The understood complement is Elimelek's property, which
No'omi is selling. That nearer redeemer's acceptance of the redemption responsibility palpably heightens the tension of the scene: Boaz is
supposed to get the land and the girl, but how can that happen now?

4:5 וַיֹּ֣אמֶר בֹּ֔עַז בְּיוֹם־קְנוֹתְךָ֥ הַשָּׂדֶ֖ה מִיַּ֣ד נָעֳמִ֑י וּ֠מֵאֵת
רֹ֣ות הַמּוֹאֲבִיָּ֤ה אֵֽשֶׁת־הַמֵּת֙ קָנִ֔יתִי [קניתה] לְהָקִ֧ים
שֵׁם־הַמֵּ֖ת עַל־נַחֲלָתֽוֹ׃

This verse is the interpretive crux of the Act IV. What precisely are
Boaz' conditions for the sale? Which woman comes with the land?

בְּיוֹם־קְנוֹתְךָ֥ הַשָּׂדֶ֖ה מִיַּ֣ד נָעֳמִ֑י וּ֠מֵאֵת רֹ֣ות הַמּוֹאֲבִיָּ֤ה
אֵֽשֶׁת־הַמֵּת֙ קָנִ֔יתִי [קניתה] לְהָקִ֧ים שֵׁם־הַמֵּ֖ת עַל־נַחֲלָתֽוֹ.
Inf constr Qal √קנה with 2ms suffix, participle ms Qal √מות (twice),
qatal (modal) 1cs (or 2ms; see comment below) Qal √קנה, and inf
constr Hiph √קום.

בְּיוֹם־קְנוֹתְךָ. An infinitive phrase as the complement to בְ, כְ,
or some other temporal preposition is a common construction to
establish a temporal setting; see 1:1, 19 (2x); 3:3, 4. In this verse, the
בְ PP with the infinitive phrase is a temporal adjunct for the following
main clause (see next comment).

וּמֵאֵת רֹות הַמּוֹאֲבִיָּה. The interpretive challenge in this phrase
is also a textual issue: how do we take מֵאֵת רֹות? The complex word
מֵאֵת may either be the preposition מִן attached to the preposition אֵת
"from with" or the preposition מִן attached to the object marker אֵת.
The latter interpretation of אֵת is by far more common and Ruth is
thus taken as the complement of the following verb קניתה. But the
role of the prefixed מ is obscure and many also follow the Vulgate in
emending מאֵת to גַם אֵת, assuming that the ג had been mistakenly
written as a ו. More recently it has been suggested that the מ in וּמֵאֵת
is an "enclitic" מ attached to the conjunction. The result is the same:
Ruth is the complement of קניתה.

A simpler explanation than scribal error or resorting to phenomena unattested elsewhere in BH is to take מאֵת as a compound preposition, "from with," indicating that Ruth is presented as the co-heir of
the land. The verb קנה is frequently used with both מִיד (e.g., below
at v. 9 and Gen 33:19; 39:1; Lev 25:14) and מאֵת (e.g., Gen 25:10,;

49:30; 50:13; Lev 25:15; 27:24; Josh 24:32; 2 Sam 24:24; 1 Kgs 16:24)
to signify the current/previous owner of the material involved in the
transaction. Admittedly, Ruth was not mentioned in v. 3 as a property seller and she is not mentioned in v. 9, and taking וּמֵאֵת רוּת
הַמּוֹאֲבִיָּה with the previous material and not with the following אֵשֶׁת
הַמֵּת runs counter to the Masoretic understanding as reflected in the
טְעָמִים. But it is possible that the narrator (and hence Boaz) was mas-
saging the flow of information to create a deliberate—and delight-
ful—ambiguity. If the nearer redeemer (and the audience) took וּמֵאֵת
רוּת הַמּוֹאֲבִיָּה with בְּיַד נָעֳמִי as the sellers, then the referent of the
phrase אֵשֶׁת הַמֵּת becomes ambiguous—does it refer to Ruth or to
No'omi? In fact, the phrase אֵשֶׁת הַמֵּת is ambiguous as it is: after all,
who is "the dead man" most likely to come to mind if not Elimelek?
And who was Elimelek's wife? Not Ruth.

קָנִ֫יתִי [קניתה] לְהָקִים שֵׁם־הַמֵּת עַל־נַחֲלָת֑וֹ. The *Ketiv*
is clearly a 1cs *qatal* with modal semantics "I shall acquire" or past in
the future semantics "I will have acquired," but the *Qere* may be taken
in three ways: 1) as a 2ms form with the final /a/ vowel written with a
mater lectionis ה "you shall acquire"; 2) as a 2ms form with a 3fs suffix
"you shall acquire her"; or 3) as a 1cs form (written without the final
י) with a 3fs suffix "I shall acquire her." Even if the *Qere* is taken to
have a 3fs suffix, which would provide a syntactic complement for the
verb קָנִיתִי, it remains unclear what the anaphoric pronominal suffix
points back to. The question of the verb's object brings us back to the
discussion of וּמֵאֵת רוּת הַמּוֹאֲבִיָּה אֵשֶׁת הַמֵּת. Is it Ruth that will be
acquired with the property or is it the ambiguous אֵשֶׁת הַמֵּת, which
could describe Ruth but more likely describes No'omi (see previous
comment)?

לְהָקִים שֵׁם־הַמֵּת עַל־נַחֲלָת֑וֹ. The infinitive phrase is an
adjunct of the verb indicating the purpose of the action. Within the
infinitive phrase the NP שֵׁם הַמֵּת is the accusative complement and
the PP עַל נַחֲלָתוֹ is a locative adjunct. Note again that the referent of
הַמֵּת "the dead one" is not specified. This phrase describes the levir

responsibility (see Deut 25:5-10, esp. v. 6), even though neither the nearer redeemer nor Boaz technically qualify as a levir. Boaz thus asserts that, regardless which woman is acquired with the property and who acquires her, part of the deal is to provide an heir for this family.

There are many choices to make in this difficult verse, and my synthesis departs from most treatments (Zevit [2005:595–99] reached similar conclusions to those I have). I take the entire verse to be a carefully crafted release of information intended to paint the nearer redeemer into a corner and to reverse the deflating end of the last verse. The momentum of the story up to this point indicates that Boaz should be the redeemer and with this verse Boaz betrays his own desire to be the redeemer. Without maligning Boaz' character, this verse is an example of עָרְמָה worthy of the sages (see Prov 1:4, 8:12). The verse as a whole adds a condition to the purchase that Boaz mentions only *after* the nearer redeemer indicates his willingness to redeem Elimelek's property. This sequence suggests that while Boaz wanted to play the part of the redeemer, he had to wait to see what the other fellow would choose before upping the ante. The condition represents the higher stakes, however we taken them. My analysis runs counter to the Masoretic טַעֲמִים and the vast majority of commentators, although it sticks to the text of B19a. Boaz indicates that on the day the nearer redeemer purchases the property from No'omi <u>and</u> Ruth, Boaz himself (reading קָנִיתִי [the *Ketiv*]) will acquire the wife of the deceased in order to play the role of the levir and produce an heir. The ambiguity of the phrase אֵשֶׁת הַמֵּת is intentional and, while it could (and later does) describe Ruth, it could also (and is likely taken as such by the nearer redeemer) describe No'omi. Boaz' stated intention to produce an heir for Elimelek is a bluff crafted to produce exactly what happens, a change of mind by the nearer redeemer, conceding the right of redemption to Boaz. Thus Boaz intertwines two distinct Israelite customs, the redeemer and the levir. The rhetorical force of this move, whether or not it is legally accurate, was to intimidate the nearer redeemer by suggesting that the advantage of the purchased property would be fleeting.

Other options for the verse are clearly available, but however we put the pieces together, the result should make sense in light of the effect achieved and described in the next verse.

4:6 וַיֹּאמֶר הַגֹּאֵל לֹא אוּכַל לִגְאוֹל [לִגְאָל] ־לִי פֶּן־
אַשְׁחִית אֶת־נַחֲלָתִי גְּאַל־לְךָ אַתָּה אֶת־גְּאֻלָּתִי כִּי
לֹא־אוּכַל לִגְאֹל:

However one understands v. 5, the nearer redeemer interprets Boaz' conditions to be disadvantageous for him and thus passes the right of redemption to Boaz.

וַיֹּאמֶר הַגֹּאֵל. The shift in verbal agent is explicit—the nearer redeemer responds with an immediate reversal. The complement of the verb of speaking is the reported speech in the remainder of the verse. The addressee, often specified by a PP adjunct, is assumed from the context (e.g., לְבֹעַז).

לֹא אוּכַל לִגְאוֹל [לִגְאָל] ־לִי. *Yiqtol* 1cs Qal √יכל and inf constr Qal √גאל. The infinitive phrase is the complement of the verb אוּכַל, and the adjunct PP לִי within the infinitive phrase is a "dative of advantage" (WO §11.2.10d; see also GKC §119s; JM §133d). The complement of the infinitive לִגְאוֹל is covert, but presumably remains the same as all the previous cases: the property of Elimelek. The plene spelling of the *Ketiv* reflects the infinitive with the Masoretic [o] vowel whereas the *Qere* reflects the prosodic cliticization of the infinitive to the following PP, resulting in vowel lowering and the Masoretic *qamets-hatuf* [כ].

פֶּן־אַשְׁחִית אֶת־נַחֲלָתִי. *Yiqtol* 1cs Hiph √שחת. This negative purpose clause provides the motivation for the reversal. Whatever Boaz intended to communicate in v. 5, the nearer redeemer decided that the added condition made the deal personally toxic. It could be that the nearer redeemer was only willing to purchase the land because Elimelek's line had come to an end with the death of his three sons. Thus the redemption purchase would not have reverted back to anyone in a Jubilee year but would have been permanent. Boaz' stated intention to provide an heir for Elimelek would have removed the long-term advantage to the nearer redeemer's property. Even if one reads the *Qere* in v. 5 as a 2ms verb, the result is the same: in a levirate situation (which Boaz has made this, regardless if it is technically correct), it matters not at all who provides the seed for the heir; the child legally belongs to the other family line.

גְּאַל־לְךָ֤ אַתָּה֙ אֶת־גְּאֻלָּתִ֔י. Impv ms Qal √גאל. The PP לְךָ is the so-called dative of advantage (see comment on 1:4, 11) and follows the imperative to indicate that the speaker (the nearer redeemer) considers the result of carrying-out the imperative to be in Boaz' interest. The NP אֶת גאלתי is the accusative complement of the verb—this is the first time an overt complement has been provided for גאל and suggests that while the land is the concrete object of redemption (i.e., what is actually redeemed), grammatically the verb takes this derivationally related NP (i.e., the "cognate accusative," similar to וַיַּחֲלֹם חֲלוֹם in Gen 37:5; see WO §10.2.1g; MNK §33.3.5; JM §125q). The 2ms subject pronoun אתה following the imperative and PP should not be taken as a syntactic subject but as a post-verbal adjunct (see also comment on the phrase הוא ואשתו ושני בניו in 1:1). When overt pronouns are inserted into the syntactic subject position, they typically precede the verb (unless the verb is a *wayyiqtol*). And yet the pragmatic function is similar: here the pronoun is a Focus constituent and serves to highlight the contrast between the speaker (the nearer redeemer) and the addressee (Boaz), i.e., "**you** do it (not me)."

כִּי לֹא־אוּכַל לִגְאֹל. The nearer redeemer repeats his initial statement in this verse. It is not a redundant phrase, though, since it serves to make explicit the contrast that is implicit in the use of the pronoun אתה for Focus in the last clause. Perhaps the need for an explicit contrast, instead of a contextually discernible implicit one, reflects the nearer redeemer's near panic at the situation he almost stumbled into.

וְזֹאת לְפָנִים בְּיִשְׂרָאֵל עַל־הַגְּאוּלָּה וְעַל־הַתְּמוּרָה֩ 4:7
לְקַיֵּם כָּל־דָּבָר שָׁלַף אִישׁ נַעֲלוֹ וְנָתַן לְרֵעֵהוּ וְזֹאת
הַתְּעוּדָה בְּיִשְׂרָאֵל:

This verse is an aside addressed to the audience. It does not carry
the action of the story forward but is a narratorial intrusion to give
the audience cultural information deemed to be important for understanding the events of the transaction, particularly the drawing off of
a sandal reported in the next verse. That the narrator thought it necessary that his audience might not know the procedure implies that the
narrator and audience lived at some temporal distance from the world
created within the narrative. It is impossible to know whether the procedure actually existed at a time before the audience's or whether the
procedure was manufactured by the narrator to give the world within
the story a sense of age.

Note how the conjunction וֹ indicates the initial clause boundary, separating the entire verse, with its introductory explanation, the
description of the custom itself, and the concluding identification,
from the preceding material. However, we should not read any further
function into the וֹ beyond marking a clause boundary; rather, it is the
lack of a past narrative *wayyiqtol* that signals that this information is
not part of the narrative sequence.

וְזֹאת לְפָנִים בְּיִשְׂרָאֵל עַל־הַגְּאוּלָּה וְעַל־הַתְּמוּרָה לְקַיֵּם
כָּל־דָּבָר. A null-copula clause, with the demonstrative pronoun זֹאת
as the subject. Note that the demonstrative, as a deictic item, "points"
to something in the discourse. In this case the information to which
זֹאת points (the sandal ceremony) is yet to come, since the predicate
of this clause is rather long. Four adjunct PPs precede the complement of the null copula: the temporal adjunct לפנים, the locative
adjunct בישראל, and the two PPs על התמורה and על הגאולה that
specify the circumstances "about" which this statement applies (WO
§11.2.13). The feminine demonstrative is often used when what is

pointed at is abstract (WO §6.4.2, 6.6d), in this case, a description of a custom. The infinitive phrase, לְקַיֵּם כָּל דָּבָר, is the complement of the null copula, i.e., "this (procedure) was to confirm something."

לְקַיֵּם. Inf constr Piel √קום.

שָׁלַף אִישׁ נַעֲלוֹ וְנָתַן לְרֵעֵהוּ. Modal *qatal* 3ms Qal √שלף and *qatal* 3ms Qal √נתן. The V-S word order of the first clause reflects the modality of the verb; that is, the modality has triggered the raising of the verb over the subject. BH uses the modal *qatal* to express habitual activity in the past (e.g., Gen 29:3; 1 Sam 1:3, 9:9; see Cook 2002:230–31), which is clearly the setting for the statement in this clause: the modal verbs שָׁלַף and נָתַן indicate that this was (but no longer is) the typical procedure for sealing transactions.

וְזֹאת הַתְּעוּדָה בְּיִשְׂרָאֵל. A null-copula clause, with the demonstrative זֹאת as the subject (this time pointing to what has just been described) and the NP הַתְּעוּדָה as the predicate. The PP בְּיִשְׂרָאֵל does not modify the null-copula but is contained within the NP הַתְּעוּדָה as an adjunct specifying what kind of witnessing act, in much the same way that adjectives modify nouns, i.e., it was an Israelite witnessing act.

4:8   וַיֹּאמֶר הַגֹּאֵל לְבֹעַז קְנֵה־לָךְ וַיִּשְׁלֹף נַעֲלוֹ׃

The conclusion to the conversation between Boaz and the nearer redeemer is brief and ends with what was, as the audience has just been informed, the method for sealing the deal at that time. With this conclusion the plot resolution has begun but is not yet complete.

וַיֹּאמֶר הַגֹּאֵל לְבֹעַז קְנֵה־לָךְ. *Wayyiqtol* 3ms Qal √אמר and impvms Qal √קנה. Presumably the subject is overtly specified here, even though the nearer redeemer was the last character to speak, in case the intervening narratorial comment distracted the audience from the flow of the plot. The PP לְבֹעַז provides the adjunct specifying the goal of the speech, i.e., the addressee. When the addressee is contextually obvious, it is often omitted, raising the question of why it is specified here. The simplest reason is that, just as with the overt subject, the addressee is specified after the intervening v. 7 in order to avoid any ambiguity. It is also possible the mention of both in the same verse, which happens only here in the chapter, may be in preparation for the scene's climax (so Hubbard 1988:252). The quote itself is the complement of וַיֹּאמֶר. Within the reported speech the PP לְךָ is an adjunct providing the "dative of advantage" (see comment on 1:4, 11), but the complement of the transitive verb קנה is left unspecified and thus must be reconstructed from the context (the verb קנה is also used without an overt complement in v. 4, as are most occurrences of the verb גאל in this chapter).

וַיִּשְׁלֹף נַעֲלוֹ. *Wayyiqtol* 3ms Qal √שׁלף. The subject is covert, which is because there is no switch in the agent—the nearer redeemer was the one just speaking and now is the one who takes his sandal off. The complement of the verb is נעלו. This action presumably motivated the narrator's intrusion in v. 7 to explain the transaction custom. Without that explanation (assuming the audience knew nothing of such practices), the nearer redeemer's behavior here would have seemed random and perhaps downright odd. Moreover, only part of the custom is narrated here; the audience is left to fill in the remainder for themselves, which they are able to do based on the information in v. 7.

Act IV, Scene 2: Ruth is Married, No'omi is Redeemed (vv. 9-17)

Scene 2 completes the plot resolution. Boaz marries Ruth; Ruth gives birth to a son; No'omi is thus "refilled."

⁹*Then Boaz said to the elders and all the people, "You are witnesses today that I now acquire all that belonged to Elimelek and all that belonged to Kilyon and Mahlon from the hand of No'omi.* ¹⁰*Also Ruth, the Moabitess, the wife of Mahlon, I now acquire for myself as a wife to establish the name of the dead man upon his inheritance, that is, so that the name of the dead man will not be cut off from his kinsmen or from the gate of his place. You are witnesses today!"* ¹¹*And all the people who were at the gate*

and the elders said, "We are witnesses. May Yhwh make the wife who is
about to come to your house like Rachel and Leah, who built the house of
Israel, the two of them. Therefore make sons of character in Ephratha and
proclaim a name in Bethlehem, ¹²and may your house be like the house of
Perez whom Tamar bore for Judah, from the seed which the Yhwh gave to
you from this young girl." ¹³Then Boaz took Ruth and she became his wife.
Then he went in to her and Yhwh gave her a pregnancy and she bore a son.
¹⁴Then the women said to No'omi, "Blessed be Yhwh who has not left you
without a redeemer today! Let his name be proclaimed in Israel! ¹⁵And he
shall become your life-restorer and shall sustain your old age, because your
daughter-in-law, whom you love, has bore him—she who has been better
for you than seven sons." ¹⁶Then No'omi took the child and set him on her
lap and became his foster-mother. ¹⁷The neighbors named him, saying, "A
son has been born for No'omi!" and they named him "'Obed." He was the
father of Jesse, the father of David.

4:9   וַיֹּ֨אמֶר בֹּ֜עַז לַזְּקֵנִ֣ים וְכָל־הָעָ֮ם עֵדִ֣ים אַתֶּם֮ הַיּוֹם֒ כִּ֣י
קָנִ֜יתִי אֶת־כָּל־אֲשֶׁ֣ר לֶאֱלִימֶ֗לֶךְ וְאֵ֛ת כָּל־אֲשֶׁ֥ר לְכִלְי֖וֹן
וּמַחְל֑וֹן מִיַּ֖ד נָעֳמִֽי׃

Done dealing with the nearer redeemer, Boaz turns to the community—immediately, within the narrative sequence—and declares
his intention to redeem No'omi. As with his initial declaration of the
issue in vv. 3-5, Boaz first addresses No'omi's situation. Ruth's waits
until the next verse.

וַיֹּאמֶר בֹּעַז לַזְּקֵנִים וְכָל־הָעָם עֵדִים אַתֶּם הַיּוֹם. The
syntactic subject בעז is overt and signals a switch in agent; it thus
functions as a Topic even though it cannot be raised over the *wayyiqtol*
verb (see §2.5). The reported speech is the complement of the verb
ויאמר, and the adjunct PP לזקנים וכל העם is the goal (addressee).
Note that the preposition ל is not repeated before כל העם; instead the
ל prefixed to זקנים "takes scope over" (includes within its domain)
both of the following NPs. It is possible that this choice, rather than

repeating the preposition, signals that the coordinated NPs are viewed as a single, complex entity rather than two distinct groups. The quote itself is a null-copula clause with Predicate-Subject order and the NP הַיּוֹם is used as a time adverbial. The Predicate-Subject order reflects the Focus-fronting of עֵדִים in order to contrast the addressee's relevant "classification" as witnesses with any other potential role (see also comment on 2:10).

כִּי קָנִיתִי אֶת־כָּל־אֲשֶׁר לֶאֱלִימֶלֶךְ וְאֵת כָּל־אֲשֶׁר לְכִלְיוֹן וּמַחְלוֹן מִיַּד נָעֳמִי. *Qatal* 1cs Qal √קנה. The verb is likely a performative, "I hereby acquire" (see comment above on מכר in v. 3). This כִּי clause is a noun complement clause; that is, it is a complement to the noun עֵדִים in the preceding null-copula clause. Many nouns, like עֵדִים, are derived from or at least closely related to verbs that take accusative complements; as such, the nominalized action may still take a complement, as we have here (English examples are the nouns "solution" and "destruction"). The complement may take the form of a bound construction, e.g., "witnesses of an event" (see WO §9.5.2) or, as here, be a nominalized clause, with either כִּי or אשׁר (see WO §38.8; JM §157). Within the כִּי clause, the accusative complement of the verb קנה is explicit, a rarity in this chapter. If there was any doubt previous to this, it is now clear that what was being discussed was the acquisition of what Elimelek, Mahlon, and Kilyon left behind. Note that all three "dead men" are listed here, providing no disambiguation for the referent of the NP המת in v. 5. On כל as the head of a relative clause, see comment at 2:11; for other examples, see 3:5, 11, 16. Finally, note that only No'omi is listed as the previous owner, מִיַּד נעמי.

4:10 וְגַם אֶת־רוּת הַמֹּאֲבִיָּה אֵשֶׁת מַחְלוֹן קָנִיתִי לִי
לְאִשָּׁה לְהָקִים שֵׁם־הַמֵּת עַל־נַחֲלָתוֹ וְלֹא־יִכָּרֵת
שֵׁם־הַמֵּת מֵעִם אֶחָיו וּמִשַּׁעַר מְקוֹמוֹ עֵדִים אַתֶּם
הַיּוֹם׃

Here Boaz adds his intention to take Ruth as his wife and indicates that, just as he indicated to the nearer redeemer, he will fulfill the levirate role for the brother-less Mahlon and thus ensure that Mahlon's line continues. With vv. 9-10 Boaz has fulfilled his promise to Ruth on the threshing-floor that we would address both her requests—the implicit marriage request and the explicit redemption request.

‫וְגַ֣ם אֶת־ר֣וּת הַמֹּאֲבִיָּה֩ אֵ֨שֶׁת מַחְל֜וֹן קָנִ֧יתִי לִ֣י לְאִשָּׁ֗ה‬. In contrast to the ambiguity in v. 5, where Boaz used ‫מֵאֵת רוּת‬, here the ‫גם אֶת רות‬ indicates that Ruth is a second object of the deal (the clarity here suggests to me that the ambiguity in v. 5 is intentional). The ‫ו‬ is simply a coordinator or clause boundary marker and the initial ‫גם‬ is additive (MNK §41.4.5.2; see also ‫גם‬ in 1:5, 12; 2:8, 15, 16, 21; 3:12) and perhaps also marks the accusative complement NP ‫את רות המאביה אשת מחלון‬ with Focus. Even if ‫גם‬ does not contribute to the Focus on the complement, the fronted position of the long NP makes it clear: whereas the statement of intention in the preceding verse was general and covered whatever may have belonged to the dead men, here Boaz zeroes in on what he considers the most salient part of the transaction. The adjunct PP ‫לי‬ specifies the "dative of advantage" (see comments above on 1:4, 11 and also 4:6, 8). The oblique complement PP ‫לאשה‬ indicates both the goal of the verb as well as the new function of the accusative complement: Ruth is taken "to be a wife" (compare the similar construction in 1:11; GKC §119t; WO §11.2.10; MNK §39.11.1.1.c).

‫לְהָקִ֤ים שֵׁם־הַמֵּת֙ עַל־נַחֲלָת֔וֹ‬. Inf constr Hiph √‫קום‬. This infinitive phrase is an adjunct to the preceding verb, ‫קניתי‬, and provides the purpose, as the same phrase did in v. 5. The exact repetition in Boaz' mouth, first to the nearer redeemer and then to the community of witnesses, is used to reinforce the characterization of Boaz as a man who does what he says. The NP ‫שם המת‬ is the accusative complement, and the PP ‫על נחלתו‬ is a locative adjunct.

‫וְלֹא־יִכָּרֵ֧ת שֵׁם־הַמֵּ֛ת מֵעִ֥ם אֶחָ֖יו וּמִשַּׁ֣עַר מְקוֹמ֑וֹ‬. Yiqtol 3ms Niph √‫כרת‬. This negative purpose clause further explains the preceding purpose infinitive phrase. The initial ‫ו‬ may be understood as a case of the "epexegetical" use (WO §39.2.4), although I suggest that the וֹ simply marks the clause boundary and the "epexegetical" (i.e., clarifying) relationship with the preceding information is simply implied. The NP שֵׁם הַמֵּת is the subject of the passive verb and the coordinate PPs מֵעִם אֶחָיו and מִשַּׁעַר מְקוֹמוֹ are ablative adjuncts of the verb (WO §11.2.11d).

עֵדִים אַתֶּם הַיּוֹם. The final clause of this verse is a null-copula clause. It is repeated exactly from v. 9, at the beginning of Boaz' long statement. It serves to remind the audiences—the audience within the narrative and the audience of the narrative—of Boaz' primary goal, which is to have his actions witnessed and thus legitimized. The repetition also serves as an inclusio, marking the beginning and ending of the speech.

וַיֹּאמְרוּ כָּל־הָעָם אֲשֶׁר־בַּשַּׁעַר וְהַזְּקֵנִים עֵדִים יִתֵּן 4:11
יְהוָה אֶת־הָאִשָּׁה הַבָּאָה אֶל־בֵּיתֶךָ כְּרָחֵל| וּכְלֵאָה
אֲשֶׁר בָּנוּ שְׁתֵּיהֶם אֶת־בֵּית יִשְׂרָאֵל וַעֲשֵׂה־חַיִל
בְּאֶפְרָתָה וּקְרָא־שֵׁם בְּבֵית לָחֶם:

The community responds with a one-word affirmation of their role as witnesses followed by an extended blessing. The blessing, like the genealogy at the end of the chapter, connects Boaz and Ruth with the patriarchal age. The community's wish is for the new relationship to be fecund, just as the wives of Jacob produced the twelve eponymous tribal ancestors. Thus, Boaz will be rewarded for his benevolence and Ruth will receive the children she never had with Mahlon.

וַיֹּאמְרוּ כָּל־הָעָם אֲשֶׁר־בַּשַּׁעַר וְהַזְּקֵנִים עֵדִים. *Wayyiqtol* 3mpl Qal √אמר. Both groups that Boaz has addressed, the more general כל העם אשר בשער and the more specific הזקנים, respond with a one-word affirmative answer: עדים. The one-word response is the minimal requirement for an affirmative answer, since BH reflects an "echoing" question-answer system and there is no word for "yes" (as כֵּן is in Modern Hebrew) (see comment on 1:13).

יִתֵּן֩ יְהֹוָ֨ה אֶת־הָאִשָּׁ֜ה הַבָּאָ֣ה אֶל־בֵּיתֶ֗ךָ. *Yiqtol* (jussive) 3ms Qal √נתן and participle fs Qal √בוא (note that the Masoretic טעם marks the stress on the final syllable). The V-S word order of this clause as well as the general context reflects the modality of verb יתן. The subject is יהוה and the accusative complement is את האשה הבאה אל ביתך. The nuance of נתן here is not "give" but "make" (see HALOT, s.v., qal #13; BDB, s.v. Qal #3), and the following כ PP (see next comment) provides the oblique second complement for the verb, specifying the goal, which in this case is agreement in kind between the accusative complement, "the woman," and the content of the PP.

כְּרָחֵ֤ל ׀ וּכְלֵאָה֙ אֲשֶׁ֨ר בָּנ֤וּ שְׁתֵּיהֶם֙ אֶת־בֵּ֣ית יִשְׂרָאֵ֔ל. *Qatal* 3cpl Qal √בנה. The two כ PPs are coordinated and then modified as a single item by the אשר relative clause. The two heads of the relative clause provide the point of comparison that serves as the oblique second complement of the verb יתן in the main clause. The relative clause provides the third element of the comparison, the specific terms of the wished for agreement between Ruth and the two women of tradition: the wish is for Ruth to be like them, not in any random way but specifically in the way that they were the mothers of many important sons. (See WO §11.2.9 on the semantics of comparisons with כ.) Note that שתיהם is not the syntactic subject of בנו, the verb within the relative clause. The syntactic subjects are רחל and לאה, both of which have been raised out of the relative clause in its formation. שתיהם serves as an adjunct to the raised heads and is used to clarify that both women are in view within the relative—such a resumptive element is nearly demanded by the coordinate nature of the relative heads. If there were no resumption by שתיהם or a similar constituent, the relative clause could be taken to modify just the nearest possible antecedent, לאה.

שְׁתֵּיהֶם֙. On the apparent masculine pronominal suffix referring to feminine antecedents, see comment on 1:8.

וַעֲשֵׂה־חַ֣יִל בְּאֶפְרָ֔תָה. Impv ms Qal √עשה. The ms morphology of the imperative indicates that it is directed at Boaz, not Ruth.

Syntactically, the imperative in this clause as well as the imperative in the next clause are coordinated and not formally subordinate, to each other or to the jussive in the preceding clause. The sequence of jussive-imperative-imperative is not common, yet since it also not common to direct an imperative at יהוה, we should refrain from reading any special pragmatics or rhetorical nuances in the sequence. In other words, all three clauses reflect the audience's desire, with the initial jussive used in deference to יהוה and the second and third imperatives used more directly with Boaz. On the difficulty regarding the meaning of עֲשֵׂה חַיִל, see Hubbard 1988:253–54, n. 12; Bush 1996:240–43. I think that the best sense in the context of this book is that it is an abbreviation for עֲשֵׂה גִבּוֹרֵי חַיִל "make mighty men of character," i.e., have sons that turn out like yourself. As such, it is both a wish for Boaz and Ruth and a comment on Boaz' character that the community desires a whole clan of men who act like him. Note that אֶפְרָתָה is another second name for Bethlehem and stands in parallelism with בֵית לֶחֶם in the next clause.

וּקְרָא־שֵׁם בְּבֵית לָחֶם. Impv ms Qal √קרא. The accusative complement is שֵׁם and the locative PP בבית לחם may be an oblique complement, although it is not always clear if this verb requires one; thus, the PP may also be an adjunct. The nuance of קרא and שֵׁם is not easy to determine here (for the various options, see Hubbard 1988:260; Bush 1996:240–43). The verb קרא combined with the noun שֵׁם is often idiomatic for "naming" someone, and so it would seem most natural to understand קרא שֵׁם as "name them" (i.e., the sons you will produce). But the PP בבית לחם complicates the meaning, since it is unclear why the offspring would be "named in Bethlehem." Moreover, קרא can also mean "to proclaim" or "announce" something (e.g., Lev 25:10), and שֵׁם can refer to a reputation (e.g., Prov 22:1) or even the continuation of one's name by means of descendants (e.g., 1 Chr 5:24). Thus, it may be that, if the previous instruction refers to progeny, then this instruction also refers to the resulting perpetuation of a Boaz' name though his sons, his legacy.

4:12 וִיהִי בֵיתְךָ כְּבֵית פֶּרֶץ אֲשֶׁר־יָלְדָה תָמָר לִיהוּדָה
מִן־הַזֶּרַע אֲשֶׁר יִתֵּן יְהוָה לְךָ מִן־הַנַּעֲרָה הַזֹּאת:

The blessing continues from v. 11 with a connection to one generation after the tribal ancestors. Perez was a son of Judah and, notably, the head of the lineage in the genealogy in vv. 18-22.

וִיהִי בֵיתְךָ כְּבֵית פֶּרֶץ אֲשֶׁר־יָלְדָה תָמָר לִיהוּדָה. Jussive 3ms Qal √היה. Not only does the form of the verb (יְהִי instead of the imperfect יִהְיֶה) signal that it is a jussive, the V-S word order does as well. The PP כבית פרץ is the complement of the verb יהי (see comment on וַיְהִי in 1:2). The NP פרץ is modified by an appositive relative clause. The אשׁר has triggered the raising of the V to produce the V-S order. The PP ליהודה is an adjunct PP specifying the person for whom the action is directed (the "dative of advantage"). The complement of the verb ילדה has been raised as the relative head and is not overt in the relative clause itself (i.e., the raising has left a "gap").

מִן־הַזֶּרַע אֲשֶׁר יִתֵּן יְהוָה לְךָ מִן־הַנַּעֲרָה הַזֹּאת. Yiqtol 3ms Qal √נתן. This PP is a second adjunct of the verb ילדה and provides the material out of which the thing is made (or "born" in this case) (WO §11.2.11d; JM §133e). The NP הזרע, which is the complement of the preposition, is also modified by a relative clause, and this relative is restrictive since it specifies precisely which זרע this is. The head of the relative has been raised from the accusative complement position within the relative. Note the V-S order within the relative, reflecting the triggered raising of the verb over the subject. The verb of the relative clause is an indicative (imperfective) yiqtol and reflects the community's assumption that יהוה will provide the couple with children. The PP לך is an oblique complement of נתן and provides the goal. And the מן PP provides the material or source of the item given.

4:13 וַיִּקַּח בֹּעַז אֶת־רוּת וַתְּהִי־לוֹ לְאִשָּׁה וַיָּבֹא אֵלֶיהָ וַיִּתֵּן
יְהוָה לָהּ הֵרָיוֹן וַתֵּלֶד בֵּן:

With concision the narrator reports that Boaz took Ruth as her wife and all that the community wished upon them came to fruition.

וַיִּקַּח בֹּעַז אֶת־רוּת וַתְּהִי־לוֹ לְאִשָּׁה וַיָּבֹא אֵלֶיהָ. *Wayyiqtol* 3ms Qal √לקח, √בוא, with intervening 3fs √היה. On the sequence ל ... היה ל ..., see comment on 1:11. Since in some ways the second clause, ותהי לו לאשה is redundant with the first, it is likely an explicit inner-textual link with 1:11—whereas there No'omi expressed extreme doubt that she could provide husbands for her bereaved daughters-in-law, that is precisely what God has done for Ruth. Thus Ruth's loyalty is rewarded yet again. In the last clause, the PP אליה is the oblique complement of the verb ויבא, which requires a directional goal. Here and in many other cases, the collocation of בוא and אל are often idiomatic for "entering in" sexually (cf. Gen 6:4; Deut 22:13; Ezek.23:44; Prov 6:29).

וַיִּתֵּן יְהוָה לָהּ הֵרָיוֹן וַתֵּלֶד בֵּן. *Wayyiqtol* 3ms Qal √נתן and 3fs Qal √ילד. The NP הריון is from the root הרה and exhibits the -*ān* Semitic suffix, which becomes -*ōn* in Hebrew (JM §88Mb). In the narrative world, God's response is immediate, and this is signaled in dramatic fashion by the quick succession of verbs in this and the preceding clause: Boaz took her, she became his wife, they consummated it, and God allowed her to become pregnant.

4:14 וַתֹּאמַרְנָה הַנָּשִׁים אֶל־נָעֳמִי בָּרוּךְ יְהוָה אֲשֶׁר לֹא הִשְׁבִּית לָךְ גֹּאֵל הַיּוֹם וְיִקָּרֵא שְׁמוֹ בְּיִשְׂרָאֵל:

This verse is intriguing as much for what it does not say as for what it does. It does not mention the birth of a son to Ruth and Boaz. It does not mention Ruth or Boaz by name, nor is it directed at either of them. And yet coming on the heals of the birth announcement in v. 13, the audience expects a first response, either to the birth itself or perhaps to all the joyful events of vv. 9-13 (redemption, marriage, birth). The speaker is a group of women (presumably of Bethlehem), similar to those who interacted with No'omi at the end of chapter 1.

And also like the end of chapter 1, they address No'omi, not Ruth or Boaz, and their topic is not explicitly the birth of a son, but Yhwh's redemption of No'omi. The narrator's use of a third party gives the response a slightly greater sense of objectivity, and the point here is to associate the birth of a son to Ruth with Yhwh's redemption of No'omi, thereby bringing the plot full circle to No'omi's original complaint that Yhwh had emptied her.

וַתֹּאמַרְנָה הַנָּשִׁים אֶל־נָעֳמִי בָּרוּךְ יְהוָֹה אֲשֶׁר לֹא הִשְׁבִּית לָךְ גֹּאֵל הַיֹּום. *Wayyiqtol* 3fpl Qal √אמר. The adjunct PP אל נעמי provides the goal of the verb, i.e., in this case, the addressee of the speaking (on the adjunct status of אל PP with verbs of speaking, see the comment on דִּבֶּר in v.1).

בָּרוּךְ יְהוָֹה אֲשֶׁר לֹא הִשְׁבִּית לָךְ גֹּאֵל הַיֹּום. This reported speech is the complement of ותאמרנה. It is itself a null-copula clause with the predicate ברוך preceding the subject יהוה for Focus (contrasting how the women view יהוה with alternative opinions of his treatment of No'omi). The appositive relative clause that modifies the subject contains the information motivating the women's declaration of God's blessedness: he has provided a redeemer.

לֹא הִשְׁבִּית לָךְ גֹּאֵל הַיֹּום. *Qatal* 3ms Hiph √שבת. The clause is formulated as a negative, "he has not left you without a redeemer" to provide an implicit contrast with No'omi's attitude the last time the women interacted with her, in chapter 1. There she blamed יהוה for her problems and, although it is not stated in the narrative, we can infer from this clause that she doubted יהוה would provide her with a redeemer. The PP לך is an adjunct for the verb השבית and provides the person whom the action benefits. The NP גאל is the accusative complement, and the NP היום functions as an adverbial (time) adjunct.

וְיִקָּרֵא שְׁמֹו בְּיִשְׂרָאֵל. Jussive 3ms Niph √קרא. Note the V-S order in the modal clause. The subject of the verb is שמו and the PP בישראל is a locative adjunct. The ambiguity in this clause is twofold. First, to what does the 3ms suffix on שמו refer, the agent of the

preceding clause, Yhwh, or the nearer NP, גֹּאֵל, which is the object
in the preceding clause? Second, as I indicated in v. 11, the verb קרא
combined with the noun שֵׁם is often idiomatic for "naming" someone, but קרא can also mean "to proclaim" or "announce" something.
Again, as in v. 11, it would seem most natural to understand יקרא
שְׁמֹו here as "naming," were it not for the PP בְּיִשְׂרָאֵל. Why would
the newborn child be "named in Israel"? It thus makes better sense to
"proclaim Yhwh's name in Israel" in thankful response to his deeds
on behalf of No'omi. The ambiguity continues in the next verse.

4:15   וְהָיָה לָךְ לְמֵשִׁיב נֶפֶשׁ וּלְכַלְכֵּל אֶת־שֵׂיבָתֵךְ כִּי כַלָּתֵךְ
אֲשֶׁר־אֲהֵבַתֶךְ יְלָדַתּוּ אֲשֶׁר־הִיא טֹובָה לָךְ מִשִּׁבְעָה
בָּנִים:

This verse is a continuation of the women's response in v. 14 and
affirms the completeness of Yhwh's care for No'omi. The second half
identifies Ruth, how she loved No'omi and gave birth to a her grandson, as a significant, if not the most significant, means of Yhwh's care
for No'omi.

וְהָיָה לָךְ לְמֵשִׁיב נֶפֶשׁ וּלְכַלְכֵּל אֶת־שֵׂיבָתֵךְ. *Qatal* 3ms
Qal √היה, followed by participle ms Hiph √שיב and inf constr Pil-
pel √כול. Either the verb היה governs both PPs, לְמֵשִׁיב נפשand
לכלכל את שיבתך, or a second occurrence of היה is gapped in the
second half. One feature that suggests that second option is the different syntax of היה in each half. In the first half היה combines with
the ל PP complement לְמֵשִׁיב נפש to produce the idiom "to serve as
X" or "to become X" (HALOT, s.v. #7), i.e., "he has/shall become
your soul-restorer." But since the second half has an infinitive phrase,
the syntax differs; that is, "to become *sustaining* your old age" is not
grammatical and the infinitive is not used as a substantive, e.g., "to
become your old age *sustainer*." Instead, the covert, gapped verb היה
in the second half functions as an auxiliary verb, providing the tense-
aspect-mood for infinitive לכלכל, which as the complement of the

null copula provides the semantic content, i.e., "he shall sustain your old age" (see WO §36.2.3g).

Now for the agent and modality of היה: If this clause continues the jussive יקרא from v. 14, then היה is a modal *qatal* and the subject must be the גאל (understood as the newborn grandson; i.e., he shall be your life-restorer). Thus the grandson will play the role of the redeemer for Noʻomi's future well-being just as Boaz has for her current financial security. If the clause does not continue the preceding jussive (which could be taken as an interrupting exclamation) but rather the indicative *qatal* השבית before that, the subject must be יהוה, i.e., he has been your life-restorer. Either option is grammatical, but the clear reference to the grandson in the next clause ("she bore *him*") make the contextual choice clear: it is a modal verb with the גאל grandson as the subject.

מֵשִׁיב נֶפֶשׁ. The participle is not in the construct form (which would be מְשִׁיב), making the NP נפש the accusative complement. Note the use of the verb שׁוּב that was thematic in chapter 1, in what Noʻomi told her two daugthers-in-law to do (1:8, 11, 12), what ʻOrpah did but Ruth did not do (1:15-16), and what Noʻomi asserted that Yhwh had done to her (1:21). In this verse as in Noʻomi's accusation in 1:21 the verb is in the Hiphil. The implications of Noʻomi's redemption by Boaz and by her new grandson here in chapter 4 are thus made explicit: her life has been "returned.".

כִּי כַלָּתֵךְ אֲשֶׁר־אֲהֵבַתֶךְ יְלָדַתּוּ אֲשֶׁר־הִיא טוֹבָה לָךְ מִשִּׁבְעָה בָּנִים. The כי clause as a whole provides the motive for the preceding assertion: the child will become Noʻomi's soul-restorer precisely because of his source: Noʻomi's loyal and loving daughter-in-law. The syntax of the clause is complicated because the first relative clause intervenes between the subject כלתך and the verb ילדתו. Moreover, a second relative clause modifying כלתך is extraposed (that is, at a distance from its head). Finally, the word order with the כי clause reflects the Focus-fronting of the subject NP—whereas normally כי triggers the verb to raise over the subject, here the subject has in turn itself raised over the verb to signal its Focus-marking ("because **your daughter-in-law** [and not the sons who died] . . . "). That כלתך is a Focus constituent is reinforced by the two relative clauses that make further comment on the NP. The effect of the whole, somewhat convoluted clause is a subtle reproach aimed at No'omi: whereas her perspective was that God had emptied her completely by taking her husband and sons, the women here make the point brutally clear that God had been providing for her the entire time, and continues to do so, by means of her daughter-in-law.

אֲהֵבָ֫תֶךְ‎. *Qatal* 3fs Qal √אהב with 2fs accusative suffix. On the 3fs *qatal* with object suffixes, see JM §62d and Paradigm 3; on אהב with suffixes, see also GKC §59c, i.

יְלָדַ֫תּוּ‎. *Qatal* 3fs Qal √ילד with 3ms accusative suffix. On the assimilation of the 3ms suffix וה- back into the ת- of the 3fs *qatal* in its suffix-taking form, see GKC §59g, JM §62d. Note that the relative clause following this verb has a null copula, which copies the semantics of the preceding overt verb, ילדתו; thus, both the main clause "(she) has bore him" and the relative clause with the null copula "(she) has been better than seven sons" are translated as past events. For the relative clause this makes particularly good sense within the narrative, since it refers back to Ruth's actions in the story rather than some general quality.

4:16 וַתִּקַּ֨ח נָעֳמִ֤י אֶת־הַיֶּ֙לֶד֙ וַתְּשִׁתֵ֣הוּ בְחֵיקָ֔הּ וַתְּהִי־ל֖וֹ לְאֹמֶֽנֶת:

The narrator moves the audience out of the reported speech of vv. 14-15 and back to the description of events. This verse is the climax of the entire story since with No'omi's embracement of the Ruth's son her bereavement is nullified and she is "refilled."

וַתִּקַּ֨ח נָעֳמִ֤י אֶת־הַיֶּ֙לֶד֙ וַתְּשִׁתֵ֣הוּ בְחֵיקָ֔הּ וַתְּהִי־ל֖וֹ לְאֹמֶֽנֶת‎. *Wayyiqtol* 3fs Qal √לקח, √שית with 3ms accusative suffix, and √היה. In the first clause, נעמי is the subject and also a Topic since the previous agents were the women who spoke in vv. 14-15 and Ruth, "your daughter-in-law" in the subordinate clause in v. 15. In the second clause, the verb שית takes two complements, one accusative (the suffix הו-) and one oblique, the PP בחיקה, providing the locative goal. On the construction היה ... ל ... ל in the third clause, see above v. 13 and comment on 1:11.

וַתִּקְרֶאנָה לוֹ הַשְּׁכֵנוֹת שֵׁם לֵאמֹר יֻלַּד־בֵּן לְנָעֳמִי 4:17
וַתִּקְרֶאנָה שְׁמוֹ עוֹבֵד הוּא אֲבִי־יִשַׁי אֲבִי דָוִד: פ

The women respond again, this time to name the child, who is referred to as Noʿomi's son and as the grandfather of King David. This verse thus ties up a loose end (the boy's name is finally revealed) and weaves the story into the larger narrative of Israel's past. (On the neighbor women as a plot device rather than those who actually would have named an infant, the features of the naming formula used here, and the connection of the name "ʿObed" to the previous narrative, see Bush 1996:259–62.)

וַתִּקְרֶאנָה לוֹ הַשְּׁכֵנוֹת שֵׁם לֵאמֹר יֻלַּד־בֵּן לְנָעֳמִי. *Wayy-iqtol* 3fpl Qal √קרא and *qatal* 3ms Pual √ילד. Note that the oblique complement PP לו precedes the subject השכנות (which is also a Topic, due to the shift in agents); it is common for "light" PPs to raise with the verb. The accusative complement שם, though, follows the subject, which (barring Topic or Focus marking) is normal for full NP complements, regardless whether they are "light" or "heavy." The לאמר clause is the accusative complement of ותקראנה.

יֻלַּד־בֵּן לְנָעֳמִי. Within the reported speech, the V-S order is not triggered by any syntactic constituent, such as כי or אשר. In fact, this is the only such example of non-triggered V-S order in the book. I see two options. The V-S order could be an affectation, a feature to set the women's speech at a distance from the audience's natural syntax (see §4). Or the V-S order reflects a rare case of a verb fronted for Focus. From the context we already know that the boy has been born, and that No'omi has taken for herself some sort of caretaker role. Moreover, the specific context—a exclamation by the women of Bethlehem—suggests that this is no simple clause; rather, it is a statement of surprise, and what could be more surprising than old No'omi having a "son." So the Focus-fronting of the verb may serve to present a counter-expectation statement: No'omi, a widow who is presumably beyond the age of child-bearing (at least according to her impassioned assertion in 1:12), has—amazingly!—"given birth." Once again the narrator gives the community women a statement that turns an assertion of No'omi's from chapter 1 on its head.

Note that if there were any Focus-marking for No'omi, which is tempting to read, then we should have the active verb with No'omi as an explicit subject. Instead, the use of the passive clause in Ruth 4:17 makes it clear that the Focus is on the event, not the participants.

וַתִּקְרֶאנָה שְׁמוֹ עוֹבֵד הוּא אֲבִי־יִשַׁי אֲבִי דָוִד. The second naming formula finally gives the boy a name, "'Obed." The following null-copula has Subject-Predicate order, with the subject a personal pronoun. Since the narrator chose the null-copula strategy (rather than, e.g., a relative clause), the pronoun is syntactically obligatory and does not signal Topic or Focus.

Act IV, Scene 3: A Royal Genealogy (vv. 18–22)

The final scene of Act IV as well as the entire book describes no narrative action but rather an abbreviated genealogy connecting David—through Boaz and Perez, a son of Judah (Gen 46:12; 1 Chr 4:1)—to the Patriarchal narrative. Since the plot problem has been resolved, with a coda in v. 17 that connects No'omi, Boaz, Ruth, and 'Obed to a time and figures well-known to the audience (Berlin 1983:109), the genealogy has often been taken as a later editorial addition. Indeed, the genealogy here cannot function as genealogies typically do, either to provide literary structure to a larger narrative or "to ground a claim to power, status, rank, office, or inheritance in an earlier ancestor. Such genealogies are often used by rulers to justify their right to rule and by office-holders of all types to support their claims" (Wilson 1992:930). The story of Ruth does not legitimize David, though, so it has been suggested that the opposite might be the case: that the story is connected to David to elevate the status of the relative unknown characters in the story (Berlin 1983:110). Such a goal would have been better served, however, by placing the characters in genealogical context at the beginning of the story, not waiting until the very end. In fact, besides Genesis 2:4, this is the only other case in which the genealogy comes after the narrative instead of before it. Thus, it seems more likely that the genealogy in Ruth serves a different purpose than elsewhere—to "portray the significance of the resolution of [the] story," which has a value in and of itself but also because because "it provided an integral link in the family line that led two generations later to David" (Bush 1996:268).

Sasson makes a convincing argument concerning the form and function of the genealogy (1979:178–84). Based on a study of biblical genealogies in which the seventh person listed was worthy of attention, he argues that the genealogy in Ruth was arranged so that the story's protagonist was the seventh in line. Moreover, he notes another biblical pattern of organizing genealogies into (often historically artificial) blocks of ten generations; this fits the genealogy at the end of Ruth, which has David in the tenth and final spot. Finally, Sasson suggests that the genealogy begins with Perez as the founder of David's line and not his more famous father, Judah, or grandfather, Jacob, because the author "wished to retroject the beginnings of David's line into the Eisodus [move into Egypt; RDH]" (184).

[18]Now these are the generations of Perez:
Perez begat Hezron,
[19]Hezron begat Ram,
Ram begat Amminadab,
[20]Amminadab begat Nahshon,
Nahshon begat Salmah,

²¹*Salmah begat Boaz,*
Boaz begat 'Obed,
²²*'Obed begat Jesse,*
Jesse begat David.

4:18 וְאֵ֙לֶּה֙ תּוֹלְד֣וֹת פָּ֔רֶץ פֶּ֖רֶץ הוֹלִ֥יד אֶת־חֶצְרֽוֹן׃
19 וְחֶצְרוֹן֙ הוֹלִ֣יד אֶת־רָ֔ם וְרָ֖ם הוֹלִ֥יד אֶת־עַמִּֽינָדָֽב׃
20 וְעַמִּֽינָדָב֙ הוֹלִ֣יד אֶת־נַחְשׁ֔וֹן וְנַחְשׁ֖וֹן הוֹלִ֥יד אֶת־
שַׂלְמָֽה׃ 21 וְשַׂלְמוֹן֙ הוֹלִ֣יד אֶת־בֹּ֔עַז וּבֹ֖עַז הוֹלִ֥יד
אֶת־עוֹבֵֽד׃ 22 וְעֹבֵד֙ הוֹלִ֣יד אֶת־יִשָׁ֔י וְיִשַׁ֖י הוֹלִ֥יד
אֶת־דָּוִֽד׃

וְאֵ֙לֶּה֙ תּוֹלְד֣וֹת פָּ֔רֶץ. This is a Subject-Predicate null-copula clause with a demonstrative pronoun as the subject. The demonstrative is here cataphoric ("forward looking") and points to the coming genealogy itself. Besides here this phrase occurs only in the Pentateuch: Gen 2:4; 6:9; 10:1; 11:10, 27; 25:12, 19; 36:1, 9; 37:2; Num 3:1. Those included in this genealogy are the same as the list in 1 Chr 2:5-15.

פֶּ֖רֶץ הוֹלִ֥יד אֶת־חֶצְרֽוֹן. Like the genealogies of, for example, Terah (Gen 11:27) and Isaac (Gen 25:19), this genealogy at the end of Ruth uses the הוליד-X-Y structure (compared to the ויולד-X-Y structure, e.g,. Gen 6:10, 1 Chr 1:34). The S-V order of this first clause, פרץ הוליד את חצרון, reflects basic Hebrew word order. Perez has already been introduced and, as the only available agent, is not a Topic or Focus. After this first clause, though, multiple possible agents are available for each verb, and thus the S-V order of the subsequent clauses reflects Topic-fronting.

The names of the ancestors in the genealogy due to not figure into plot development as the names in chapter 1 did. Thus, their meanings are not important literarily. The only oddity in the genealogy is the use of both שלמה (v. 20) and שלמון (v. 21) for the same person. However, a comparison of all the names here with the same list in 1 Chr 2:5-15 suggests that many names simply had alternate spellings: 1 Chr 2:11 has שלמא, and 1 Chr 2:12-13 alternates between ישי and אישי for David's father.

BIBLIOGRAPHY

Abegg, Martin G., Jr. 1998. "The Hebrew of the Dead Sea Scrolls." Pp. 325–58 in *The Dead Sea Scrolls After Fifty Years: A Comprehensive Assessment*. Vol 1., edited by P. W. Flint and J. C. VanderKam. Leiden: Brill.

Andersen, Francis I. 1970. *The Hebrew Verbless Clause in the Pentateuch*, JBLMono 14. Nashville: Abingdon.

———. 1974. *The Sentence in Biblical Hebrew*. The Hague, The Netherlands: Mouton Publishers.

The Assyrian Dictionary of the Oriental Institute of the University of Chicago. 1956–. Chicago: The University of Chicago. [= CAD]

Bar-Asher, Elitzur Avraham. 2009. "Dual Pronouns in Semitics and an Evaluation of the Evidence for their Existence in Biblical Hebrew." *Ancient Near Eastern Studies* 46:32–49.

Bar-Efrat, Shimon. 1989. *Narrative Art in the Bible*. Sheffield: Sheffield Academic Press.

Barr, James. 1989a. "'Determination' and the Definite Article in Biblical Hebrew." *Journal of Semitic Studies* 34 (2):307–35.

———. 1989b. *The Variable Spellings of the Hebrew Bible. The Schweich Lectures of the British Academy 1986*. Oxford: Oxford University Press.

Bergey, Ronald L. 1983. "The Book of Esther—Its Place in the Linguistic Milieu of Post-Exilic Biblical Hebrew Prose: A Study of Late Biblical Hebrew." Ph.D. diss., Dropsie College, Philadelphia.

Berlin, Adele. 1983. *Poetics and Interpretation of biblical Narrative*. Sheffield: Almond Press. [Repr. 1994, Eisenbrauns]

Brown, Francis, S. R. Driver, and C. A. Briggs. [1906] 1979. *The New

Brown–Driver–Briggs Hebrew–English Lexicon. Peabody, Mass.: Hendrickson. [= BDB]

Bush, Frederic W. 1996. *Ruth, Esther.* Word Biblical Commentary 9. Dallas: Word Books.

Buth, Randall. 1999. "Word Order in the Verbless Clause: A Generative-Functional Approach." Pp. 79–108 in *The Verbless Clause in Biblical Hebrew: Linguistic Approaches,* edited by Cynthia L. Miller. Linguistic Studies in Ancient West Semitic 1. Winona Lake, Ind.: Eisenbrauns.

Campbell, Edward F. 1975. *Ruth: A New Translation with Introduction, Notes, and Commentary.* Anchor Bible 7. Garden City, N.Y.: Doubleday.

Campbell, Lyle. 2004. *Historical Linguistics: An Introduction.* 2nd ed. Edinburgh: Edinburgh University Press.

Cook, John A. 2002. "The Biblical Hebrew Verbal System: A Grammaticalization Approach." Ph.D. diss., University of Wisconsin.

———. 2008a. "The Hebrew Participle and Stative in Typological Perspective." *Journal of Northwest Semitic Languages* 34 (1):1–19.

———. 2008b. "The Vav-Prefixed Verb Forms in Elementary Hebrew Grammar." *The Journal of Hebrew Scriptures* 8 (3):1–16.

Cook, John A., and Robert D. Holmstedt. 2009. "Biblical Hebrew: A Student Grammar." Unpublished ms. (http://individual.utoronto.ca/holmstedt/Textbook.html.)

Dobbs-Allsopp, F. W. 2004–7. "(More) On Performatives in Semitic." *Zeitschrift für Althebräistik* 17–20:36–81.

Dresher, Bezalel E. 1994. "The Prosodic Basis of the Tiberian Hebrew System of Accents." *Language* 70 (1):1–52.

Easterly, Ellis. 1997. "A Case of Mistaken Identity: The Judges in Judges Don't Judge." *Bible Review* 13 (2):41–43, 47.

Fassberg, Steven E. 1999. "The Lengthened Imperative קָטְלָה in Biblical Hebrew." *Hebrew Studies* 40:7–13.

Fowler, Jeaneane D. 1988. *Theophoric Personal Names in Ancient Hebrew: A Comparative Study.* JSOTSupp 49. Sheffield: Sheffield Academic Press.

Gordon, Elizabeth, and Mark Williams. 1998. "Raids on the Articulate: Code-Switching, Style-Shifting and Post-Colonial Writing." *The Journal of Commonwealth Literature* 33 (2):75–96.

Greenstein, Edward L. 2003. "The Language of Job and Its Poetic Function." *Journal of Biblical Literature* 122 (4):651–66.

Guenther, Allen R. 2005. "A Typology of Israelite Marriage: Kinship, Socio–Economic, and Religious Factors." *Journal for the Study of the Old Testament* 29 (4): 387–407.

Herman, David. 2001. "Style-Shifting in Edith Wharton's The House of Mirth." *Language and Literature* 10 (1):61–77.

Hoftijzer, Jacob. 1985. *The Function and Use of the Imperfect Forms with Nun Paragogicum in Classical Hebrew.* Studia Semitica Neerlandica. Assen: Van Gorcum.

Holmstedt, Robert D. 2001. "Headlessness and Extraposition: Another Look at the Syntax of אשר." *Journal of Northwest Semitic Languages* 27 (1):1–16.

———. 2002. "The Relative Clause in Biblical Hebrew: A Linguistic Analysis." Ph.D. diss., University of Wisconsin.

———. 2005. "Word Order in the Book of Proverbs." Pp. 135–54 in *Seeking Out the Wisdom of the Ancients: Essays Offered to Honor Michael V. Fox on the Occasion of His Sixty-fifth Birthday*, edited by R. L. Troxel, K. G. Friebel, and D. R. Magary. Winona Lake, Ind.: Eisenbrauns.

———. 2006. "The Story of Ancient Hebrew ʾăšer." *Ancient Near Eastern Studies* 43:7–26.

———. 2008. "The Relative Clause in Canaanite Epigraphic Texts." *Journal of Northwest Semitic Languages* 34 (2):1–34.

———. 2009a. "Word Order and Information Structure in Ruth and Jonah: A Generative-Typological Analysis." *Journal of Semitic Studies* 54 (1):111–39.

———. 2009b. "So-Called 'First-Conjunct Agreement' in Biblical Hebrew." Pp. 105–29 in *Afroasiatic Studies in Memory of Robert Hetzron: Proceedings of the 35th Annual Meeting of the North American Conference on Afroasiatic Linguistics* (NACAL 35), edited by C. Häberl. Newcastle on Tyne, UK: Cambridge Scholars.

Hubbard, Robert L. 1988. *The Book of Ruth.* New International Commentary on the Old Testament. Grand Rapids: Eerdmans.

Huehnergard, John. 1995. "Semitic Languages." Pp. 2117–34 in *Civilizations of the Ancient Near East,* edited by J. M. Sasson. New York: Charles Scribner's Sons.

Hurvitz, Avi. 1982. "Ruth 2:7—'A Midrashic Gloss'?" *Zeitschrift für die alttestamentliche Wissenschaft* 95:121–23.

———. 2000. "Can Biblical Texts be Dated Linguistically? Chronological Perspectives in the Historical Study of Biblical Hebrew." Pp. 143–60 in *Congress Volume: Oslo 1998.* VTSupp 80, edited by A. LeMaire and M. Sæbø. Leiden: Brill.

———. 2006. "The Recent Debate on Late Biblical Hebrew: Solid Data, Experts' Opinions, and Inconclusive Arguments." *Hebrew Studies* 47:191–210.

Irwin, Brian P. 2008. "Removing Ruth: *Tiqqune Sopherim* in Ruth 3.3-4?" *Journal for the Study of the Old Testament* 32 (3):331–38.

Jastrow, Marcus. 1950. *A Dictionary of the Targumim, the Talmud Babli and Yerushalmi, and the Midrashic Literature.* New York: Pardes.

Joüon, Paul, and Takamitsu Muraoka. 2006. *A Grammar of Biblical Hebrew.* 2nd ed. Rome: Editrice Pontificio Istituto Biblico. [= JM]

Kautzsch, Emil. 1910. *Gesenius' Hebrew Grammar.* Translated by A. E. Cowley. 2nd English ed. Oxford: Clarendon. [= GKC]

Koehler, Ludwig, Walter Baumgartner, and Johann Jakob Stamm, eds. 1994–2000. *The Hebrew and Aramaic Lexicon of the Old Testament.* Translated and edited under the supervision of M. E. J. Richardson. Leiden: Brill. [= HALOT]

Kroch, Anthony. 1989. "Reflexes of Grammar in Patterns of Language Change." *Language Variation and Change* 1:199–244.

Lipiński, Edward. 2001. *Semitic Languages: Outline of a Comparative Grammar.* 2nd ed. OLA 80. Leuven: Peeters Publishers.

Longacre, Robert E., and Shin Ja J. Hwang. 1994. "A Textlinguistic Approach to the Biblical Hebrew Narrative of Jonah." Pp. 336–58 in *Biblical Hebrew and Discourse Linguistics,* edited by R. D. Bergen. Winona Lake, Ind.: Eisenbrauns.

MacDonald, J. 1975. "Some Distinctive Characteristics of Israelite Spoken Hebrew." *Bibliotheca Orientalis* 23 (3/4):162–75.

van der Merwe, Christo H. J., Jackie A. Naudé, and Jan H. Kroeze. 1999. *A Biblical Hebrew Reference Grammar.* Sheffield: Sheffield Academic Press. [= MNK]

Miller, Cynthia L. 1994. "Introducing Direct Discourse in Biblical Hebrew Narrative." Pp. 199–241 in *Biblical Hebrew and Discourse Linguistics,* edited by R. D. Bergen. Winona Lake, Ind.: Eisenbrauns.

———. 1996. *The Representation of Speech in Biblical Hebrew Narrative.* Atlanta: Scholars Press.

———. 2005. "Linguistics." Pp. 657–69 in *Dictionary of the Old Testament: Historical Books,* edited by B. T. Arnold and H. G. M. Williamson. Downers Grove, Ill.: InterVarsity.

Moore, Michael S. 1997. "Two Textual Anomalies in Ruth." *Catholic Biblical Quarterly* 59 (2):234–43.

Muraoka, Takamitsu. 1985. *Emphatic Words and Structures in Biblical Hebrew.* Jerusalem: Magnes.

———. 2000. "Hebrew." Pp. 340–45 in *Encyclopedia of the Dead Sea Scrolls,* edited by L. H. Schiffman and J. C. VanderKam. New York: Oxford University Press.

Myers, Jacob M. 1955. *The Linguistic and Literary Form of the Book of Ruth.* Leiden: Brill.

Naudé, Jacobus A. 1999. "Syntactic Aspects of Co-ordinate Subjects with Independent Personal Pronouns." *Journal of Northwest Semitic Languages* 25 (2):75–99.

Nielsen, Kirsten. 1997. *Ruth: A Commentary.* Old Testament Library. Louisville, Ky.: Westminster John Knox.

Pat–El, Na'ama. 2009. "The Development of the Semitic Definite Article: A Syntactic Approach." *Journal of Semitic Studies* 54/1: 19–50.

Qimron, Elisha. 1986. *The Hebrew of the Dead Sea Scrolls.* HSS 29. Atlanta: Scholars Press.

Rainey, Anson F. 1990. "The Prefix Conjugation Patterns of Early Northwest Semitic." Pp. 407–20 in *Lingering Over Words: Studies in Ancient Near Eastern Literature in Honor of William L. Moran*, edited by T. Abusch, J. Huehnergard, and P. Steinkeller. Atlanta: Scholars Press.

de Regt, Lénart J. 1996. "The Order of Participants in Compound Clausal Elements in the Pentateuch and Earlier Prophets: Syntax, Convention or Rhetoric?" Pp. 79–100 in *Literary Structure and Rhetorical Strategies in the Hebrew Bible*, edited by L. J. de Regt, J. de Waard, and J. P. Fokkelman. Winona Lake, Ind.: Eisenbrauns.

Rendsburg, Gary A. 1980. "Late Biblical Hebrew and the Date of 'P'." *Journal of the Ancient Near Eastern Society* 12:65–80.

———. 1996. "Linguistic Variation and the 'Foreign' Factor in the Hebrew Bible." *Israel Oriental Studies* 15:177–90.

———. 1999. "Confused Language as a Deliberate Literary Device in Biblical Hebrew Narrative." *The Journal of Hebrew Scriptures* 2 (6):1–20.

———. 2001. "Once More the Dual: With Replies to J. Blau and J. Blenkinsopp." *Ancient Near Eastern Studies* 38:28–41.

Revell, E. J. 1993. "Concord with Compound Subjects and Related Uses of Pronouns." *Vetus Testamentum* 43 (1):69–87.

———. 1995. "The Two Forms of First Person Singular Pronoun in Biblical Hebrew: Redundancy or Expressive Contrast?" *Journal of Semitic Studies* 40 (2):199–217.

Rooker, Mark F. 1994. "Diachronic Analysis and the Features of Late Biblical Hebrew." *Bulletin for Biblical Research* 4:135–44.

Sáenz–Badillos, Angel. 1993. *A History of the Hebrew Language*. Translated by J. Elwolde. Cambridge: Cambridge University Press.

Sakenfeld, Katharine D. 1999. *Ruth*. Interpretation. Louisville, Ky.: Westminster John Knox.

Sasson, Jack M. 1979. *Ruth: A New Translation with a Philological Commentary and a Formalist-Folkorist Interpretation*. Baltimore: Johns Hopkins University Press.

Shulman, Ahouva. 1996. "The Use of Modal Verb Forms in Biblical Hebrew Prose." Ph.D. diss., University of Toronto.

———. 2000. "The Function of the 'Jussive' and 'Indicative' Imperfect Forms in Biblical Hebrew Prose." *Zeitschrift für Althebraistik* 13 (2):168–80.

Smith, Mark S. 1991. "Converted and Unconverted Perfect and Imperfect Forms in the Literature of Qumran." *Bulletin of the American Schools of Oriental Research* 284:1–16.

Sternberg, Meir. 1987. *The Poetics of Biblical Narrative: Ideological Literature and the Drama of Reading.* Bloomington: Indiana University Press.

Waltke, Bruce K., and Michael O'Connor. 1990. *An Introduction to Biblical Hebrew Syntax.* Winona Lake, Ind.: Eisenbrauns. [= WO]

Wilson, Robert R. 1992. "Genealogy, Genealogies." Pp. 929–32 in *The Anchor Bible Dictionary.* Vol. 2: *D–G,* edited by D. N. Freedman. New York: Doubleday.

Wise, Michael O. 1990. "A Calque from Aramaic in Qoheleth 6:12; 7:12; and 8:13." *Journal of Biblical Literature* 109 (2):249–57.

Wolfenson, Louis B. 1911. "The Character, Contents, and Date of Ruth." *The American Journal of Semitic Languages and Literatures* 27 (4): 285–300.

Yeivin, Israel. 1980. *Introduction to the Tiberian Masorah.* Translated by E. J. Revell. Atlanta: Scholars Press.

Young, Ian, Robert Rezetko, and Martin Ehrensvärd. 2008. *Linguistic Dating of Biblical Texts.* 2 vols. London: Equinox.

Younger, K. Lawson. 2002. *Judges and Ruth.* The NIV Application Commentary. Grand Rapids: Zondervan.

Zevit, Ziony. 2005. "Dating Ruth: Legal, Linguistic, and Historical Observations." *Zeitschrift für die alttestamentliche Wissenschaft* 117:574–600.

AUTHOR INDEX

223

SUBJECT INDEX